POSTCOLONIAL CONFIGURATIONS

POSTCOLONIAL CONFIGURATIONS

Dictatorship, the Racial Cold War, and Filipino America

JOSEN MASANGKAY DIAZ

DUKE UNIVERSITY PRESS   *Durham and London*   2023

© 2023 DUKE UNIVERSITY PRESS
All rights reserved

Designed by Matthew Tauch
Project editor: Ihsan Taylor
Typeset in Garamond Premier Pro by Westchester Publishing Services

Library of Congress Cataloging-in-Publication Data
Names: Diaz, Josen Masangkay, [date] author.
Title: Postcolonial configurations : dictatorship, the racial Cold War, and Filipino America / Josen Masangkay Diaz.
Description: Durham : Duke University Press, 2022. | Includes bibliographical references and index.
Identifiers: LCCN 2022028091 (print)
LCCN 2022028092 (ebook)
ISBN 9781478019350 (paperback)
ISBN 9781478016694 (hardcover)
ISBN 9781478023968 (ebook)
Subjects: LCSH: Filipino Americans—History—20th century. | Filipino Americans—Social conditions—History—20th century. | Philippines—Foreign relations—United States—History—20th century. | United States—Foreign relations—Philippines—History—20th century. | Philippines—Politics and government—1946– | Philippines—Economic conditions—1946– | BISAC: SOCIAL SCIENCE / Ethnic Studies / American / Asian American & Pacific Islander Studies | HISTORY / Asia / Southeast Asia
Classification: LCC E184.F4 D539 2023 (print) | LCC E184.F4 (ebook) | DDC 305.899/2110973—dc23/eng/20220815
LC record available at https://lccn.loc.gov/2022028091
LC ebook record available at https://lccn.loc.gov/2022028092

Cover art: Carlo Ricafort, *The Baroque Precinct*, 2016. Oil on canvas. 36 × 48 in. Courtesy of the artist.

For my parents

CONTENTS

ix   *Acknowledgments*

1   Introduction: Unmaking Configurations

27   **ONE.** The Fictions of National Culture

58   **TWO.** Balikbayan Movements

85   **THREE.** The New Filipina Melodrama

113   **FOUR.** The Filipino Humanitarian

138   Conclusion: Reckoning with the Body

153   *Notes*
187   *Bibliography*
209   *Index*

ACKNOWLEDGMENTS

At the heart of this book is a fascination with and appreciation for all the tremendous and banal ways that the "I" gives way to other forms of collectivity and sociality, of friendship and kinship; the ways that we are formed by one another, moved by one another, undone by one another. I offer my gratitude to the many people who have helped form, move, and undo my thinking over the past several years. Any good that comes from these pages belongs to them, too.

Against much advice to move on from a place, I hardheadedly attended graduate school where I finished college. As it turns out, the reasons to stay kept coming. I learned from a stellar group of teachers there: Patrick Anderson, Fatima El-Tayeb, Yến Lê Espiritu, Rosemary George, Shelley Streeby, Nicole Tonkovich, and K. Wayne Yang. I still refer back to a course that I took with Lisa Yoneyama during my first quarter of graduate school, where I learned that theory is only as useful as its political commitments. Jody Blanco insisted on slow and careful scholarship and asked difficult questions that I often find myself repeating when I sit down to write. From Introduction to Asian American Literature to McNair thesis to dissertation, Lisa Lowe has been an unfailing model of incisive and principled study and deeply generous mentorship.

My gratitude to a cohort of classmates that turned into a group of dear friends: Amanda Solomon Amorao, Christina Carney, Zulema Diaz, Kyung Hee Ha, Ren Heintz, Anita Huizar-Hernández, Eunsong Kim, Joo Ok Kim, Ashvin Kini, Rebecca Kinney, Angela Kong, Salar Mameni, Jacqueline Munguia, Marilisa Navarro, Linh Nguyen, Yumi Pak, Jason Magabo

Perez, Christopher Perreira, Reema Rajbanshi, Violeta Sanchez, Lila Sharif, Vineeta Singh, Davorn Sisavath, Thea Quiray Tagle, Sarika Talve-Goodman, and Salvador Zárate. Chien-ting Lin has been an astute interlocutor, tempered cheerleader, and steady travel partner. I cannot imagine making it through graduate school without him. Elsewhere on campus, Victor Betts, Nancy Magpusao, Agustin Orozco, Joseph Ruanto-Ramirez, Patrick Velasquez, and Edwina Welch kept the doors open.

I moved to Oakland for a short time to think away from San Diego. Between writing days, donut breaks at the lake, and nights out, Nick Mitchell, Yumi Pak, Molly Porzig, Dorothy Santos, Hyejin Shim, and Thea Quiray Tagle helped make that year an important one.

So many have offered insight, support, and encouragement at various stages of research and writing: Paul Michael Leonardo Atienza, Elizabeth Ault, Christine Bacareza Balance, Nerissa Balce, Sony Corañez Bolton, Rick Bonus, Long Bui, Lucy Burns, Genevieve Clutario, Sara Jo Cohen, Kathleen De Guzman, Adrian De Leon, Karlynne Ejercito, J. C. Fermin, Valerie Francisco, Vernadette Gonzalez, Karen Hanna, Emily Hue, Allan Isaac, Jenny Kelly, Marisol LeBron, Zack Linmark, Allan Lumba, Simeon Man, Martin Manalansan, Alden Sajor Marte-Wood, Najwa Mayer, Victor Mendoza, Paul Nadal, Edward Nadurata, Mike Hoa Nguyen, Jan Padios, Robyn Rodriguez, Joy Sales, Mark John Sanchez, Stephanie Santos, Thomas Sarmiento, Cathy Schlund-Vials, Sarita See, Mejdulene Shomali, Harrod Suarez, Neferti Tadiar, June Yuen Ting, Tony Tiongson, and M. T. Vallarta.

At the University of San Diego, my colleagues in the Department of Ethnic Studies have cleared out space for me to grow into the job: Esther Aguilar, May Fu, Angel Hinzo, Perse Lewis, Jesse Mills, Gail Perez, and Alberto Pulido. Kate Boersma, Christopher Carter, Evelyn Cruz, Colin Fisher, Evelyn Kirkley, Judith Liu, Marcelle Maese, Amanda Makula, Julia Medina Antonieta Mercado, Channon Miller, Amanda Petersen, Atreyee Phukan, T. J. Tallie, Karen Teel, and Jillian Tullis have offered mentorship and camaraderie. Support from Noelle Norton, Kristin Moran, Pauline Powell, and the rest of the dean's office has advanced my research. My students—past, present, and future—make it all make sense.

Since 2012, travel to Manila has been instrumental to my work. Oscar Campomanes, Carlos Celdran, Adam Crayne, Jomar Cuartero, J. Neil Garcia, Wendell Jose, Rolando Tolentino, and Brian Ziadie helped make the city feel less overwhelming. At National Central University in Taiwan, the Center for the Study of Sexualities provided an intellectually rich and warm place to present early iterations of this book. I thank Naifei Ding, Chien-ting Lin, and Amie Parry for their hospitality.

My visiting fellowship with the Asian American Studies Center at UCLA provided invaluable time and resources to complete significant sections of the book. I thank Victor Bascara, Melany De La Cruz, Barbra Ramos, Irene Suico Soriano, Karen Umemoto, and David Yoo for their support. At the University of Hawaiʻi, Belinda Aquino, Pia Arboleda, Brian Chung, Elena Clariza, Vernadette Gonzalez, Joyce Mariano, and Clemen Montero offered space for me to workshop my ideas at a critical time in my writing. They made my visit especially generative. I spent a summer with the Southeast Asian Studies Summer Institute at UW-Madison, learning about the intricacies and joy of language from Clemen Montero. It has proven invaluable.

Earlier versions of chapter 2 and chapter 3 were published in the *Journal of Asian American Studies* and *ALON: Journal for Filipinx American and Diasporic Studies*, respectively. Rick Bonus, José Capino, Martin Manalansan, and Anita Mannur along with the anonymous reviewers provided invaluable feedback that helped me develop the current chapters.

Ken Wissoker has been an advocate from the beginning, helping me rethink how I share ideas with others. My thanks to Ryan Kendall, Ihsan Taylor, the talented team at Duke University Press, and Cathy Hannabach at Ideas on Fire for making the publication process much easier than it could be. The careful engagement that the two manuscript reviewers offered to this book is one that I hope to repay.

My gratitude to friends in San Diego and elsewhere for offering healthy respite from the work: Andrew Amorao, Carmela Capinpin, Dennis Chin, Ray Elkins, Jayzee Francisco, Rena Fried-Chung, Vivian Fried-Chung, Kenny Gong, Hazel Hamann, Taica Hsu, Harper Keenan, Trinh Le, Emma Lierley, A. J. Kim, Ana Laura Martinez, Roy Perez, Kimmy Wong; the Kaus and the Vasilezes; and Candice Kandi Custodio-Tan, Grace Shinhae Jun, Suparna Kudesia, Kristina Piggy Mananquil, and the rest of the Asian Solidarity Collective crew.

J Alexander Diaz and Erin Diaz (and Cole and Sloane) and the whole lot of the Masangkays and the Diazes here, in Manila, Taal, Lipa, Imus, and everywhere along the way guided and trusted me. My grandmother Norma Masangkay is my favorite historian and the best storyteller I know. My parents, Arsenia Masangkay Diaz and Jose Alejandro Diaz, are on every page of this book, migrants of the martial law period whose experience of movement and becoming might not otherwise materialize into any form of historical monumentalism but whose lives have become the embodiment of care and worldmaking. I write most things with them in mind.

Julia Rhee has listened to every facet of this book, the good and the bad, even when it existed as a set of hopes, anxieties, and a hundred pages of iPhone notes. My love to her (and to our Mona and Mory) for carving out the sweetest corner of the world for us, the place I rush to return at the end of every day.

INTRODUCTION

Unmaking Configurations

FILIPINO AMERICA AS NATIONAL HISTORY

In 2011, the names of activists Silme Domingo and Gene Viernes were etched onto the Bantayog ng mga Bayani (the Wall of Martyrs Memorial) in Quezon City, Manila. The wall is part of a larger memorial that remembers those who "lived and died in defiance" of Ferdinand Marcos's dictatorship in the Philippines.[1] In 1982, gunmen murdered the men outside the meeting hall of the International Longshoremen's and Warehousemen's Union (Local 37) at Pioneer Square in Seattle, Washington. The investigation and trial that followed the assassination linked the killings to union leaders in the United States, cronies of Philippine president Ferdinand Marcos, and the Marcos regime itself. As of 2011, Domingo and Viernes were the only Filipino Americans whose names were listed on the wall.[2]

On the Bantayog, Domingo and Viernes join hundreds of other heroes of the anti–martial law movement, individuals vetted by a Research and Documentation Committee to ensure "that the name of obscure, unknown martyrs in remote places may be brought to light."[3] Every year, the committee charged with the maintenance of the memorial adds more names to the wall.[4] The quest to identify, name, and honor those who might otherwise be "unknown martyrs" has become a key feature of the struggle to "never again, never forget" martial law and the Marcos dictatorship, which lasted

FIGURE I.1 Bantayog ng mga Bayani memorial sculpture.
Photo: Rhea Claire Madarang/Rappler.

from 1965 to 1986.[5] This vetting seeks to uncover the individual stories of the heroes to reveal the extent of the regime's violence.

In addition to the wall, the memorial includes a sculpture that represents the "self-sacrifice of a fallen figure of man, held in one hand by the rising figure of a woman who symbolizes the Motherland, while her other hand reaches for the glorious son of freedom" (figure I.1).[6] Following the arc of homogeneous, empty time, the memorial underwrites the dictatorship as an aberrant yet significant moment within an otherwise progressive national history that gestures toward liberation.[7] Not reflective of the country's colonial inheritances or its cacique politics, the memorial positions the dictatorship as an unprecedented abuse of governmental power. The "glorious son of freedom" is the abstract and universal telos of a national sovereignty guided by the liberal promise of republicanism. Characterized by a "political anxiety" about the state of the Philippine republic, the memorial confirms the nation as the primordial location of freedom, where freedom exists in contradistinction to an exceptional dictatorship and in accordance with post-1986 state discourses about the return to democracy.[8]

Memorializing marks no beginning or end; rather, it operates as an ongoing task of historical revision, wherein grappling with and making sense of martial law and the Marcos regime offer an avenue for contending with and legitimizing present political conditions. Within this framework, the memorial overdetermines the lives of the martyrs, who are called into recognition by the memorial itself, and transforms them into a singular entity made to personify the romance of the "Motherland." This memory work constructs "monuments of a historical consciousness" that arrest Domingo and Viernes as figures of a national history about the fall of dictatorship and the rise of democracy.[9] As heroes of an anti–martial law movement and defenders of the republic, they come into visibility within the boundaries of this national story.

In several US-based studies of the Marcos dictatorship, however, the assassination of Domingo and Viernes is a catalyst for memorializing a distinct Filipino American social movement.[10] Domingo and Viernes's political work with the Katipunan ng mga Demokratikong Pilipino (KDP, or the Union of Democratic Filipinos) reveals the ways that Filipinos in the United States cultivated a transnational anti–martial law movement that threaded the violence of the dictatorship both to US imperialism in the Philippines and to the racialized and classed discrimination of Filipinos in the United States.[11] Their struggle against the labor exploitation of Filipino cannery workers and the displacement of low-wage and poor communities by urban development in Seattle reflects a political consciousness that formed alongside Black, Indigenous, Third World, and other resistance movements in the United States in the late 1960s and throughout the 1970s. Within these narratives, Domingo and Viernes personify the efficacy of transnational political organizing in the United States, where the Filipino American activist embodies an emergent racial consciousness grounded in knowledge about the interconnectedness of US colonialism and racism. Such studies generate reflections about martial law that position Filipino America as a nucleus for expansive transnational connections.

While the Bantayog incorporates the Filipino diaspora in the United States within its invocation of Philippine national history, the United States itself remains an aporia, a peripheral presence that lingers on the edges of the memorial but does not fully materialize within its conception of dictatorial power. The memorial frames the dictatorship as a national dilemma rather than a quandary about state and imperialist power, even though Marcos enjoyed US support during much of his reign. The US-based histories, on the other hand, overdetermine Domingo and Viernes as Filipino American. The proclamation of an already coherent and uncomplicated Filipino American subjectivity attends neither to the terms of its formations during the Marcos era nor to the risks of its invocation as such. Even as both memorializations situate the assassination as part of a wider story about martial law, the declaration of its importance often embeds Domingo and Viernes within the discourses that have come to define the study of the dictatorship. The two men become recognizable only within the parameters of these limited frames. More importantly, their recognition elides other forms of sociality that materialize within and between the pathways of transpacific relations.

How do these narratives memorialize Filipino America? How do they remember martial law and dictatorship in ways that idealize the nation and the transnational? In what ways do these ideals inhere through specific conceptualizations of race, gender, and subjectivity? How might one begin to rethink these formations in order to reimagine authoritarianism not as aberrational to but as a critical function of liberalism? How can we reimagine Filipino America to highlight other forms of exclusion and belonging that impart insight into the continuity of colonial modernity in shaping our discourses of subjectivity?

This book turns to Filipino America as a kind of postcolonial memorialization, a project that suspends an event or the experience of an event as a cohesive recollection while it moves other moments of Philippine-US collaboration inside and outside visibility. To apprehend it in this way rather than treating it as a static category of racial or ethnic difference is to point to it as a nexus for laying bare the collaborations of Cold War politics—the intertwining programs of dictatorship, colonial and imperialist war, and liberal reform—that make race and gender legible as distinct forms during specific periods. Rather than privilege a set of answers about the Filipino relationship to America, this memorialization helps resituate Filipino America as a persistent question about the terms that surround its invocation. I begin here to destabilize the familiarity of Filipino America, to disrupt its cohesion, to engender a different critique and politics of Filipino and America that is attuned to the discourses of raciality that encircle Philippine-US dictatorship.[12] More significant than revealing the truth (or what Lisa Yoneyama calls the "how much" of history) of dictatorial violence, I treat dictatorship as a consequence of empire, one whose legacies manifest themselves in the very discourses by which we come to remember it.

The year after the assassination, Dorothy and Fred Cordova founded the Filipino American National Historical Society (FANHS) in Seattle, providing a home for the collection of archival documents and the showcase of Filipino American culture and history.[13] The organization was the culmination of the Cordovas' decades-long work to establish programs dedicated to the two-pronged project of Filipino American cultural preservation and identity formation among Filipino American youth. Fred Cordova's 1983 pictorial history, *Filipinos: Forgotten Asian Americans*, showcased the collection by including two centuries' worth of photographs and oral histories. It serves as one of the first composite histories of Filipinos in the United States. In its opening pages, Cordova dedicates the book to "Filipinos, who are forgotten Asian Americans, forgotten Filipino Americans, forgotten Pinoys, forgotten Americans."[14] For Cordova, Filipinos' elision not only from US national history but also from the minoritized discourses of Asian American history conveys the specificity of Filipino American abjection. The underlying task here, to remember forgotten Filipinos, is not simply an attempt to recover something that was lost. To remember is to conceptualize Filipino America as the emergence of a once-marginalized form of Filipino subjectivity whose expression heralds the arrival of a distinct racial formation.[15] Within the broad reaches of US history, the Filipino and the US colonial history of the Philippines are often rendered insignificant if not entirely erased. Yet Filipino America in Cordova's collection marks the transformation of the Filipino, no longer a "little brown brother" or an immigrant "alien," from the object of US exclusion to the subject of US multiculturalism.[16] The invocation of a Filipino American "national history," more specifically, attempts to resolve the incommensurability that has characterized a Filipino ontology within US colonial epistemologies and US citizenship.[17]

While the ongoing work of FANHS illustrates the immensity and generosity of the Cordovas' historical and cultural projects as well as the "integrity and strength of local experience and knowledge" that such projects encapsulate, the declaration of a Filipino American national history reappears elsewhere and is worth untangling.[18] The invocation of a national history privileges a unidirectional diasporic trajectory that positions the United States as both origin and final destination, arranging Filipino America within the temporal and spatial parameters of the US nation form. Cordova's history begins with descriptions of the "Louisiana Manilamen" and ends with the Filipino American soldiers of World War II, bookended by historic firsts. Contextualizing contemporary migration as a product of US conquest, empirical studies of the Filipino diaspora in the United States in the 1960s and 1970s have often followed such an approach.[19] These explorations, however, consider the Filipino experience in the United States through an additive model that situates Filipino America as the accumulation of historical experience in which history overdetermines the effects of coloniality. By concealing the overlaps and intersections that have constituted such migrations, these studies fail to address the limitations of this empiricism. In the epilogue of his book, Cordova writes, "We waste precious time in perennially asking these questions about ourselves among ourselves but never listening to ourselves for the answers which should come from within ourselves in our search for ourselves."[20] National history "answers" this slew of historical inquiries. The equation of Filipino America with national history irons out the tensions that invisibility provokes, conflating racial subjectivity with racial arrival.

The promise of a national (as well as a transnational) history establishes Filipino America as an already cohesive and coherent formation, constantly sewing its seams even as they threaten to come undone. FANHS's origin story absents the assassination of Domingo and Viernes, killed by Marcos associates in the same city where the Cordovas founded the organization.[21] This is not to argue that FANHS is responsible for attending to anything and everything having to do with Filipinos in the United States. It only suggests that the theorization of invisibility as the defining characteristic of Filipino American raciality renders the assassination illegible within the epistemological frame of Filipino American national history. Such a framework would assume a distinct experience and subjectivity that positions a cohesive national history as the prescription for the injury of invisibility. The absence that invisibility imparts obscures a dialectical struggle between the visibility afforded by historical and political recognition based on racial difference and the materiality that recognition elides. Where Filipino American national history might foreclose other subjectivities that exceed its articulation of belonging, the assassination unsettles Filipino America by unraveling it from the subject of national history and revealing it as the condition of living under both Philippine authoritarianism and US liberalism. The labor struggles between Filipino and other Asian workers and US agribusiness in the US West during the period, for instance, reveal a critical contradiction of US multiculturalism. Continuous assaults on immigrant labor in the 1970s and 1980s, misaligned with the civil rights legislation of the late 1960s, highlight the ways that the imperatives of racial capitalism always underscore the celebratory declarations of liberal progressivism.[22] Labor policies under the Marcos regime transformed Filipino labor into a capacious vehicle for facilitating the movement of multinational capital within the country while rendering Filipinos themselves subject to the restrictions of martial law. Filipino workers' struggles pinpoint the disjuncture between the promise of freedom, on the one hand, and the actualization of that freedom, on the other.

Claims for subjectivity often absorb acceptable difference within US national discourses in ways that sustain liberal race projects.[23] While political representation attempts to address the invisibility that Cordova described, it fails to attend to the myriad forms of power and violence that have constituted Filipino colonial and diasporic formations.[24] I argue for an incessant interrogation of the subject that highlights its racialized, classed, gendered, and sexualized constitution. However, I also insist that the study of subjectivity is imperative for understanding the interconnectedness of seemingly oppositional modes of state governance that cohere as colonial modernity. The "achievement of subjectivity" as an epistemological endpoint occludes the radical possibilities inherent in the study of Filipino America.[25] By unhinging the Bantayog, the narratives of Domingo and Viernes, and FANHS from the contours of heroism and self-determination that shape them, these projects reveal Philippine-US dictatorship as a crisis where the representation of that crisis is the ground on which one can contend with the multiplicity and extensiveness of state and imperialist power.

Even as these narratives reframe the lives of Domingo and Viernes according to the parameters of national history projects, Domingo's and Viernes's intellectual and political work confounds the bounds of these arrangements. That the two men are visible, recognizable, and knowable is precisely the point: this visibility, recognizability, and knowability reveal the ways that we come to know the past and the means by which the past comes to be made known to us.[26] The heroization of Domingo and Viernes as martyrs of the transnational anti–martial law movement functions through a conceptualization of power as coercion and suppression, and freedom as the absence of power. When such heroization operates through national memory projects, it reinforces the supremacy of the masculinized citizen-subject as a mode of self-determination and the historical agent of national progress, one who acts bravely in order to access rights afforded by the state, rights that are limited only in their distribution, not in their constitution.[27] This subject is the vehicle through which the republic functions as a benefactor of the people; at the same time, he is the modality by which challenges to the state also gain political legibility. Heroization is a memorial in itself, a way to personify politico-juridical law; and in transmogrifying the labor and energies of a people, it contains difference in the production of the subject of modernity.

Challenging the overdetermination of political unity that the memorials underline, I read this heroization as an attempt to remember the production of death but not the widescale management of life that leads to such death, let alone the language by which we conceive of and name that life.[28] Beyond a conceptualization of power as suppression, I point to the inextricability of state and imperialist power that is multimodal, multivalent, and expansive and that operates as much through repression as through acts of false liberation. Interrogating forms of subjectivity that materialize as state recognition emphasizes the criticality of other social forms, often rendered feminized and queer, that are not simply invisibilized or marginalized by dominant forms of citizenship and belonging but rendered incommensurable and expendable by these parameters. These tempting versions of political subjectivity that cohere within strictures of global capitalism foreclose the creative possibilities necessary for social disruption and upheaval. I search for ways to name the dead and the living that do not overdetermine their being and becoming in the world.[29]

* * *

Postcolonial Configurations is about dictatorship, coloniality, and subjectivity. Interrogating Filipino away from America to explore the processes by which the two were defined, redefined, and sutured during the Marcos dictatorship, this book proposes "postcolonial configuration" as a modality for reconsidering the continuous and perplexing relationship between Filipino and America throughout the Cold War. A configuration is a racial and gender formation that becomes recognizable, namable, and legible at the intersections of overlapping state and national forces. These forces are transpacific collaborations that invest in development and modernization and take shape as authoritarianism, liberalism, and imperialism. This means that "binational" partnerships orchestrated by the Philippine and US governments are rarely, if ever, equitable alliances or strictly confined to "foreign policy." Rather, the distinct political orders of dictatorship and representative republicanism—what Hannah Arendt has described as the long-standing "affinity between democracy and dictatorship"—are often framed as oppositional state systems but are shaped by a more intricate geopolitics that make each integral to the other's function.[30] A configuration identifies subjectivity as the critical avenue for identifying and comprehending this affinity. Subjectivity consolidates postwar, postcolonial anxieties in the Philippines and the United States into cohesive, portable forms. Distinct from calls for and investments in new archives, new histories, or new ways to consider the transnationality of Filipino America, configuration offers a different way to contend with the ongoing significance of the Filipino to, within, and alongside America. It is less interested in defining what Filipino America is, is not, or should be. Rather, configuration allows the incongruencies and incoherences that shape the Filipino relationship to America to guide other inquiries into state and imperialist power.

This book decenters the usual figures of Filipino American national history not to recuperate new ones but as a way to point to other socialities that often fall by the wayside of Filipino and Filipino American studies as well as studies of dictatorship in the Philippines and to offer other ways to consider the legacies of US-backed authoritarian regimes. It mines old figures for different lessons to explore the ways that colonial epistemologies continue to bear on knowledge production.[31] To unmake a configuration is to interrogate the logic of wholeness—of subjectivity, nation, and culture—and the violence that often underlines it.[32] Unmaking traces the fissures that always constitute the projection of cohesion to reveal what Frantz Fanon has called the "empty shell, a crude and fragile travesty of what it might have been."[33] Unraveling the seams of wholeness exposes other expressions of lifemaking that have always been, knowledges of the world that are suppressed yet continue to make themselves known in some way even if they fail to bind together into recognizable forms.[34] Unmaking seeks neither recovery nor revision; instead, it attempts to inch closer to articulating a Philippine historical experience.[35] I propose that we risk losing Filipino America as an object of recognition or recuperation, or as the center of intellectual work, in order to catalyze other points of political possibility. This is not an attempt to dismiss the concrete ways that diasporic experiences engender important forms of recognition.[36] It only wrestles with the tenacity and dynamism of coloniality to shape our language for ourselves.[37] It is, above all, an effort to envision other ways of thinking alongside and inhabiting the world.

THE FILIPINO QUESTION

The Filipino question has long organized colonial historiography. After its defeat in the war of 1898, Spain ceded the Philippines to the United States for $20 million. The war between the US military and Philippine forces that followed this cession resulted in the loss of over 500,000 Filipino lives (nearly a million by some accounts) and the formal declaration of US colonial tutelage over the archipelago. The period of US colonization, officially from

1898 to 1946, saw the development of a US governmental system in the Philippines as well as the rise of public institutions that would outlast the colonial era. In the first decades after the war, Filipino workers migrated to the United States as US colonials, serving as a new laboring body in the United States, particularly in Hawai'i and along the West Coast, that helped to manage agricultural development and industrial expansion and mitigate the ongoing effects of emancipation, immigration, exclusion, and burgeoning labor movements. Filipino workers moved to and from the United States until the Tydings-McDuffie Act of 1934 granted commonwealth status to the Philippines and designated US colonials as new foreign aliens.[38] By the time Domingo and Viernes organized Filipino cannery workers in Seattle in the late 1970s, these laborers had long been navigating what Rick Baldoz has called "transpacific traffic," the movement of people and goods that followed the rise of US overseas empire as well as the expansion of US capitalism alongside empire.[39]

Filipino raciality in the United States has been constituted precisely by the conditions attached to the early decades of Philippine sovereignty. The years that defined the Philippine commonwealth also structured the exclusion of Filipino colonials from the United States. Yet exclusion, in terms of immigration mandates as well as the violent attacks on Filipino migrant workers in the 1920s and 1930s along the US West Coast, operated not as antithetical to the US "benevolence" represented by the granting of commonwealth status and later independence but as an important extension of it.[40] The violent struggles illustrated by the race riots in Exeter and Watsonville, for example, evidenced the dangers of the project of inclusion, however tentative, of colonial subjects into the national body.[41] The categorization of the colonial subject as foreign alien mandated by Tydings-McDuffie made possible the removal of the Filipino from the US ideal of racial homogeneity while maintaining the project of US benevolent empire, what the Insular Cases evidenced as "foreign in a domestic sense."[42]

During World War II, the Philippines operated as the stage for the Pacific Theater, an interimperial war between Japan and the United States for control over Asia and the Pacific. After the Japanese imperial occupation of the Philippines during the war, the Allies' victory returned control of the archipelago to the United States. With the US declaration of Philippine independence in 1946, colonialism took different shape. Washington orchestrated a series of economic and political mandates that severely restricted the reach of Philippine sovereignty. The postwar, postcolonial period saw the repeated failure of US promises to the Philippines: the revocation of benefits for Filipino veterans who fought for the US military during World War II; the US management of the Philippine economy through the Bell Trade Act (and the subsequent Laurel-Langley Agreement); and the fortification of the US military in the country through the Joint US Military Assistance Group. The Bell Trade Act tied the Philippine economy to US investments, and the Military Bases Agreement of 1947 ensured US military control over the Clark Air Base in Angeles City and the Subic Bay Naval Base in Olongapo. Throughout the 1950s, when the Philippine government, together with the US Central Intelligence Agency, waged a vociferous battle against the Hukbalahap (Hukbo ng Bayan Laban sa Hapon, or People's Anti-Japanese Army) resistance, such collaboration further entrenched the nation within the geopolitical program of US imperialist war, while the Filipino people languished under the control of a deepening oligarchy.

To argue that US politics has compromised Philippine independence is to restate a well-known fact. What is important to emphasize is that Philippine leaders' struggle to define national sovereignty against such realities produced an array of political projects that attempted to resolve these contradictions. While President Ramon Magsaysay distinguished himself as "America's boy," Carlos Garcia advanced a Filipino First stance. He implemented an isolationist policy that mediated continuous US efforts to saturate the Philippines with US imperial programs, what he described as "a new Asia policy for the Philippines."[43] US neocolonialism also compelled Filipino intellectuals to expound on the effects of postcoloniality on the Filipino condition. At the Bandung Conference in 1955, statesman Carlos Romulo ruminated on the Philippines' global position to express the possibility of renewed affiliations between the Philippines and the Third World. While, as Augusto Espiritu has written, Romulo was a staunch anticommunist and clear Washington ally, his articulation of Afro-Asian affiliation at the meeting defied any easy subservience to the Philippines' former colonizer. He supported the conference delegates and their decolonial aspirations.[44] The conference challenged Romulo to distinguish a Philippine sovereignty that, while in tension with its alliance with the United States, was accountable to the decolonization struggles of nonaligned nations.[45]

Certainly, by 1955, the United Nations and its financial arms became extensions of Western hegemony, especially their deployment of an integrationist paradigm that espoused widescale international cooperation.[46] It was in the spirit of this liberal internationalism that the US military sanctioned the continued occupation of nations in the Pacific, Asia, Latin America, and Africa as part of a broader effort to protect the "free world" against the threat of communism. US military offensives continued throughout the Mariana Islands, Samoa, and the Marshall Islands. The Korean War and the Vietnam War violently bifurcated Norths from Souths in an effort to maintain the US stronghold over Asia. In the decades that followed these wars, the rehabilitation of Asia through the continued reconstruction of Japan, South Korea, Taiwan, the Philippines, and other countries channeled multinational investment into these nations in ways that kept them tethered to the ebbs and flows of global capitalism. Neoliberalism as a practice of deregulation and privatization throughout the 1970s and onward functioned precisely through these ongoing alliances between the US and other Western governments and the national administrations of decolonizing nations. The inherent contradiction of a free world organized by these systems of structural adjustment is what Aihwa Ong has termed "neoliberalism as exception."[47] Such political arrangements heralded the emergence of a new world order, yet they also rearranged past forms of coloniality into new frameworks of modernity.

While Filipino migration to the United States continued to be restricted in the first decades following independence, the 1950s and 1960s saw the institutionalization of the Exchange Visitor Program, which facilitated the mass migration of Filipino nurses and other professionals to the United States. Catherine Ceniza Choy has written extensively about the "multidirectional and interdependent" nature of such migration, noting that the program shared similarities with earlier US colonial education programs that dominated the early half of the twentieth century in the Philippines.[48] I note it here to pivot away from the notion that Filipino migration to the United States unabatedly continued since the early years of US colonization and, rather, to emphasize the extent to which shifting US-Philippine relations in the postwar period shaped distinct racial formations. Both the unfair treatment (lower wages and difficult work hours compared to their white counterparts) that Filipina nurses experienced in the United States and the remittances they sent back to the Philippines showcase the ways that Filipinas' position in the United States during the period articulated both the tentative racial pluralism of the early US Cold War and the burgeoning dependency of the Philippines on Filipino labor migrants generally and gendered labor specifically.[49] These formations reflected the myriad anxieties about the scope of US overseas empire as well as the shape of Philippine sovereignty. While this racial position drew from the longer legacy of Filipino migration during the colonial period, it also pinpoints a subjectivity that emerged from a nascent postwar, postindependence politics.

Writing in 1959, Renato Constantino admonished ineffectual "Filipino-American" leadership (by which he referred to Filipino leaders beholden to the United States), asking, "Is it any wonder that having regained our independence we have forgotten how to defend it?" Demanding a distinctly nationalist education, Constantino insisted that "the new demands for economic emancipation and the assertion of our political sovereignty leave our educators no other choice but to re-examine their philosophy, their values, and their general approach to the making of the Filipino."[50] I am drawn to Constantino's invocation of the Filipino in 1959, over a decade after independence, as a *question* about the shape of subjectivity in relation to the ongoing nature of coloniality.[51] Within Constantino's essay, it is "the making of the Filipino" that provides an entryway for exploring both this continuity as it seeped through the crevices of national culture and the "philosophy," "values," and "general approach" that constitute this culture. Relatedly, Nick Joaquin, in 1988, proclaimed that "the identity of a Filipino today is of a person asking what is his identity."[52] Joaquin treats "Filipino identity," like Constantino, as a quandary unto itself. The problem of Filipino identity has long organized concerns about authenticity and progress: What belongs to the Filipino, and what belongs to the foreigner? What must the Filipino keep, and what must the Filipino throw aside? For Joaquin, subjectivity—framed here as identity—offers a medium for charting a genealogy of nationalism rather than upholding the certainty of the nation itself.[53] Denise Cruz has noted, however, that the politics of Philippine nationalism in the postwar era took shape precisely through the mediation of women's bodies and lives. This "male cultural nationalism" cohered through shifting ideas about a woman's role within the nation.[54] The Filipino question is an epistemological one whose positing and answer have often occluded the ways that masculinized conceptualizations of the nation as well as the gendered labor of "women's work" undergird every invocation of Filipino identity. Insofar as the Filipino evokes a persistent query, attempts to answer it also reflect the expanding contours of state and colonial power as they are embodied through changing forms of racialized and gendered subjectivity.

Several studies have explored the "Filipino" as a social category that emerged during the era of Spanish colonization to differentiate Spanish officials and *indios* from mixed-race mestizos. Early US census records in the Philippines illustrate the means by which colonial tutelage homogenized native difference to produce "a people."[55] The overdetermination of Filipinos as a distinct creolized *race* drove the colonial discourses of modernity. In his theorization of "race as praxis," John D. Blanco contends that "race attempts to lay claim to a knowledge or science of *history*. It not only attempts an account of human difference, but it does so in and through a narrative whose function it was to inform the prudence of colonial practices—decrees, policies, and their enforcement or disregard."[56] The utility of Blanco's discussion here is its theorization of race not as the fact of difference but, rather, as a struggle between colonial knowledge production of which race is a part and the myriad challenges to that order. The question of the Filipino is, above all, an inquiry into race as the representation of coloniality. If, indeed, the problem of race in the Philippines at the end of the nineteenth century reflected the transformation of colonial policy into an articulation of human difference, the period of independence traces the transformation of that question into a language of postcolonial sovereignty.

This is to argue that the postcolonial does not mark colonialism's end but signifies the distinct expression of modernity enabled by the *declaration* of colonialism's end. Ferdinand Marcos and his administration recuperated the Filipino question as a vehicle for organizing an authoritarian politics that attended to the crises of the period—governmental corruption, civil insurgency, communist infiltration, and the Vietnam War, for instance. For Marcos, elected to the Philippine presidency in 1965, the proclamation of the postcolonial advanced new discourses of state governance emboldened by the language of modernity.[57] Through his political rhetoric of national progress, Marcos emplaced the Filipino within the prescriptions for global capitalist integration mediated by the integrationist paradigms of postwar international financial institutions. The regime's modernization program, for instance, materialized as urban renewal projects, the advancement of public health programs, and the celebration of national culture, often guided by UN mandates and US aid. Marcos consolidated the tensions that had long defined decolonial theorizations of Filipino subjectivity into a pronouncement of national identity that declared the realization of a true sovereignty shaped by the international politics of the Cold War. I define authoritarianism in this way as a system of governance—or "art of government"—that consolidates decolonial and anticolonial discourses and resistances into an evocation of national sovereignty that presents the state as the guarantor of postcolonial self-fulfillment and sanctions extrajudicial power as the means of defining and protecting the project of self-determination.[58] It was not simply that Marcos was a US-backed dictator; the shifting logics of US hegemony, rooted in a politics of counterinsurgency and neoliberalism, shaped his articulation of a new nationalism whose consequences would reverberate well after his deposal.

In his 1969 State of the Nation address delivered four years after his election to the presidency, Marcos introduced New Filipinism—later, the New Society—as a program for national modernization. New Filipinism produced a postcolonial discourse that concerned itself with rectifying national injury by supplanting colonial institutions and ideologies with new edifices (figurative and literal) that promoted economic and political self-sufficiency.[59] While the New Society materialized as a set of policies and reforms, Marcos's proclamation of a new nationalism often relied on a historicism that claimed the maturation of the colonial object into a political agent that might finally claim the telos of sovereignty. The New Society announced the arrival of the Philippines to modernity, where the Philippines inhabited a world stage of independent nations and participated in its program of global exchange and goodwill. This was a declaration riddled with paradoxes. Adopting the language of decolonial struggle and Third World affiliation, Marcos identified Filipino subjectivity as a profound site of crisis. In his speech, he described "Juan Tamad" as the archetypal figure of Filipino degeneracy that signified the languid state of the Filipino in the world. Attuned to the sweeping force of decolonial movements around the globe, which condemned racial subjection as an operation of colonial domination, Marcos positioned the rectification of the racial subject as a critical focus of political reform, deploying raciality as an avenue for symbolizing the national predicament that Marcos declared himself as uniquely fit to address. Raciality here is not only an "account of human difference" but a vehicle for managing difference through the distinct expressions of and programs for global exchange. Imploring the Filipino people to wage battle against this image by practicing Filipino ingenuity, he promoted modernization projects that would remedy Filipino abjection. For Marcos, the solution to the crisis of Filipino subjectivity was social welfare, infrastructural reform, and rural development; but these projects failed to improve the lives—indeed, they worsened the life conditions—of a vast majority of Filipino people.

By 1972, Marcos declared martial law. He consolidated the branches of governance into his executive power, suspended the writ of habeas corpus, censored the press, and tortured and disappeared his political critics. More than a point of political and historical exception, martial law is a palimpsest, a symptom of and response to the colonial century. In his justification of martial law, Marcos warned the Filipino people that radical insurgents threatened to destroy the nation. He framed martial law as an instrument for containing a growing movement organized by the communist left. In his justification of martial law, Marcos proclaimed that he was waging a "revolution from the center," a people's rebellion that would save the nation from external threats—even as that "revolution" kept that very people under political arrest. In this way, Marcos's declaration of martial law was also an attempt to delineate "the people" from enemies of the state. The former was no given: martial law effectively defined Filipino subjectivity against the nation's others, a general category that required state force to materialize this abstraction into detail, a materialization that simultaneously elevated and disciplined the country's most marginalized populations.[60] To illustrate, Melisa S. L. Casumbal-Salazar notes that "Philippine indigenous subjectivity is aporetic to the extent that it is predicated on simultaneous, contradictory claims—to territoriality and non-territoriality, singularity and commonality, and both resistance to and inclusion within the time-space of the nation."[61] The state's identification of indigeneity veers between an articulation of its heterogeneity and its singularity, at once proclaiming the cohesion of the nation and using national law to dispossess Indigenous people. For Marcos, Filipino subjectivity garnered specificity through the shifting signification of the racial other, often Indigenous, often Muslim. Set against Indigenous, Muslim, and other peoples excised from the nation, Marcos's enactment of race reconstituted the Filipino as the postcolonial subject of modernity.

THE RACIAL COLD WAR

In response to the defeat of fascism and totalitarianism at the end of World War II, the United States renewed its commitment to civil liberties, pluralism, and free-market capitalism. The adherence to these commitments also defined inclusion into an international body. The 1942 Declaration of the United Nations proclaimed that the "complete victory over [UN] enemies is essential to defend life, liberty, independence and religious freedom, and to preserve human rights and justice in their own lands as well as in other lands, and that they are now engaged in a common struggle against savage and brutal forces seeking to subjugate the world."[62] Emerging as a response to these "savage and brutal forces seeking to subjugate the world," this international philosophy provided the ideological backing to support the formation of the United Nations, the International Monetary Fund, the World Bank, the United States Agency for International Development, and other institutions of international governance led by the United States and its allies. As these organizations structured the terms of nationhood and economic stability for decolonizing governments, the discourse of life and liberty that had previously underpinned the mandates of colonial administrations now outlined the terms of global integration. Liberalism transformed colonial power into international governance.[63] In his theorization of "Asia as method," Kuan-Hsing Chen argues that "the cold war mediated old colonialism and new imperialism."[64] Indeed, the Cold War not only facilitated the transformation of coloniality into twentieth-century globalization but also saw the construction of programs whose operation rendered these processes invisible.

International institutions, through which the United States and western Europe monopolize the terms of global integration, disperse the terms of coloniality through the law. This law often underpins state violence as the justifiable means to an end. The law is not an end divorced from violence but a process that unfolds through it insofar as, Walter Benjamin writes, "lawmaking is power making and, to that extent, an immediate manifestation of violence."[65] Where these liberal declarations denounced tyranny, these institutions rewarded nationalist governments that aligned themselves with international mandates even as they defied the doctrine of life and liberty that liberalism denounced. US pronouncements against totalitarianism as the originary violence of the post–World War II era made room for the formation of authoritarianism in the decolonizing world.[66] The rise of authoritarian regimes at the end of the war did not necessarily contradict the aims of Western liberalism; they often emerged in tandem with its principles. By the time Marcos declared martial law in 1972, authoritarianism had already become a key feature of US-backed regimes in Asia. US support of the Marcos regime, like its defense of the Park Chung Hee administration in South Korea and the military occupation of Taiwan, illustrates the degree to which authoritarianism and extrajudicial violence served as modalities for liberalism's function. The rise of the United States as the leader of the postwar free world required the legitimization of necessary violence throughout Asia in an effort to contain leftist insurrection and communist encroachment.

Authoritarianism operates as a postcolonial state of exception that betrays the central paradox of liberalism's operation, the contradiction to its promise of life and liberty. As a state of exception, authoritarianism is, as Giorgio Agamben writes, "not a special kind of law (like the law of war); rather insofar as it is a suspension of the juridical order itself, it defines law's threshold or limit concept."[67] While US state reports often reprimanded Philippine authoritarianism in the later years of Marcos's presidency as the obverse of freedom, it also sanctioned it as both a necessary force in the curtailment of communism and a reminder of the exceptionality of American democracy. The actuality of authoritarianism also demonstrated the US urgency to extend this freedom elsewhere.

Alongside the advent of the New Society in the Philippines, Lyndon B. Johnson's Great Society platform in the 1960s promised an unprecedented era of US progressivism. Resistance movements in the United States, particularly Black and Third World social movements, articulated important connections between Indigenous, Black, and brown struggles for liberation and decolonization movements throughout the world. This political work to materialize a human rights apart from state articulations of citizenship was, at times, incommensurable with US civil rights law that aimed to preserve the sanctity of US institutions. Yet the declaration of the "great" extracted the language of unprecedented struggle into a paradigm of liberal progress. In his study of Black social movements that followed World War II, Cedric Robinson noted that the class war that followed the political struggles of the 1960s "reconfigured anticommunism into a race discourse on the rule of law."[68] The intimidation, surveillance, and policing of leftist activists rearranged anti-Black policies into US Cold War counterinsurgency programs in ways that further dispossessed the Black working class yet also generated the conditions for new social movements. Civil rights reforms emerged from the international politics that constituted the US Cold War.[69] Jodi Melamed attends to the ways that the US government used the racial crises of the 1960s and 1970s to construct a transnational politics that maintained its geopolitical dominance.[70] Progressive racial policies were couched in the discourses of Cold War anticommunism and mitigated political tension within the United States while intensifying militarized imperialism outside it.

Johnson's invocation of greatness signified the US defeat of fascism, the challenge to global injustice, and the emergence of the United States as the rightful leader of the free world. At the same time, this pronouncement of greatness relegated US colonialism to empire's past even as the United States as empire of the present continued its imperial and neocolonial occupations. The discourse of equality for colonial subjects has often organized the terms of political struggle in ways that tether social movements to the investments of empire.[71] Throughout the book, I analyze US liberalism as the political philosophy and practice of extending individual recognitions and rights and expanding the scope of free movement and trade to curtail collective calls for self-determination. Liberalism brushes up alongside authoritarianism in its attempts to govern the terms of political agency. It also guides an American exceptionalism that espouses an aggressive anticommunism that legitimizes militarization and occupation. Within these articulations of authoritarianism and liberalism, configurations become ways to disperse the urgencies of racial crises within the parameters of state recognition.

In 1965, Johnson signed into law the Hart-Celler Act (or the Immigration and Nationality Act), eliminating nationality as a prerequisite for immigration to the United States by ending the US national quota system. As others have already noted, the act did not intend to radically alter the demographic makeup of the United States, only to stand in as a model of liberal, anticommunist reform during a Cold War in which superpowers jockeyed for Third World favor. It did, however unintentionally, offer a pathway for people, especially those from Asia and Latin America, to enter the United States. The act importantly increased the size of the Filipino diaspora in the United States, shaping the contours of Filipino America into a recognizable political body.[72] No longer restricted by the provisional and exclusionary mandates of earlier US immigration law, the post-1965 Filipino migrant to the United States gained access to an unprecedented legal pathway to US citizenship. Much scholarship that addresses post-1965 Filipino diasporic formations in the United States does well to acknowledge that both a legacy of Filipino movement between the colony and the metropole and the social conditions under martial law in the Philippines spurred migration from the Philippines to the United States in the late 1960s and throughout the 1970s. But apprehending the Filipino diaspora in the United States in this way establishes the language of US legal reform as the primary discourse with which to articulate its emergence. This conceptualization of the post-1965 Filipino immigrant allows US legislation to imagine this figure into being notwithstanding other politics and subjectivities established and foreclosed in its formation.

In 1974 (on May Day, no less), the Marcos administration instituted the Labor Code of the Philippines. The code formally legalized policies to govern labor within the country but also effectively defined labor export, for the first time, as a critical component of the Philippine political economy. One of its objectives was "to insure careful selection of Filipino workers for overseas employment in order to protect the good name of the Philippines abroad."[73] While the code aimed to protect Filipino contract workers from "exploitation" and "discrimination" in their countries of employment, it also required the remittance of "foreign exchange earnings" back to the Philippines. Whereas the Hart-Celler Act pronounced the momentous subsumption of national difference into the exceptional American nation, the labor code identified this difference as a key to Philippine aspirations. The code's address of exploitation and discrimination aimed to protect migrants from what it perceived to be the effects of national difference while it rendered their labor distinctly consumable and expandable. Taken together as Cold War policies, both the labor code and the immigration act organized the distinct recognition of the Filipino as a facet of a Cold War globality that empowered the former colonial subject only to the extent that such policies also ensured the continuity of migration and labor extraction.[74] That the Hart-Celler Act determined the bounds of Filipino America at the same time that the site of Filipino labor was made boundless reveals the ways that national reform capitalized on racial difference in the service of transnational cooperation.[75] The emancipatory project of citizenship is the site on which state power reorganizes the terms of belonging alongside the movement of labor and the circulation of capital. Lisa Lowe notes that "immigration law reproduces a racially segmented and stratified labor force for capital's needs, inasmuch as such legal disenfranchisements or restricted enfranchisements seek to resolve such inequalities by deferring them in the promise of equality on the political terrain of representation through citizenship."[76] This transnational management of racial difference, especially through the inclusion and protection of that difference, negated the unresolved tension of Filipino raciality by saturating it within the juridical framework of international integration.

Earlier attempts to contextualize the epistemological formations of Filipino America point to the ongoing legacies of colonialism in shaping the bounds of Filipino America. Yet an interrogation of the terms of Filipino America, I insist, requires a study of the precise ways that the Cold War fashioned *new* discourses of race to shape the Philippine-US relation. In his discussion of the contentiousness of Filipino American subjectivity, Oscar Campomanes explains that "this unique burden on US Filipino politics of emergence and recognition is at its heaviest, and the Filipino American difficulty in pursuing this politics at its most vexed, at the precise moments when US Filipino nominative or identity formations are structured by such irreconcilable Philippine-US nationalist antagonisms and nativistic narrations."[77] Campomanes directs attention to the timeliness of a "U.S. Filipino politics of emergence and recognition" that actually constitutes the shifting politics of US-Philippine neocolonialism. This notion of Filipino America interrogates identity as it embodies an ongoing struggle between the aims of the Philippine state and those of US geopolitical programs.

Moreover, in his study of the genocidal logics of the Filipino American condition, Dylan Rodriguez writes that "post-1965 Filipino Americanism is, from its moment of articulation, a material discourse and self-consciously popular cultural formation that intends a communion of desires, historical identifications, and political allegiances."[78] Rodriguez succinctly draws attention to Filipino American civil recognition as having emerged from an ongoing US colonial and genocidal war. Such a theorization points to the limitations of a Filipino American politics of recognition.

While Campomanes and Rodriguez offer lucid interrogations of Filipino America as an effect of coloniality, I contend that Filipino America is a distinct predicament of *post*coloniality. The configuration as the subject of modernity (and no longer the object of coloniality) gained motility and currency across geographies, nations, and governments in ways that served the aims of collaborative regimes and economic markets. In addition to its function as a mode of "self-comprehension" produced from "an extended monologue of radicalizations," Filipino America emerged within a politics of international integration and global capitalism that managed the modernization of the Third World.[79] Postwar, postcolonial state collaborations between the Philippines and the United States often used the law to invest in and make legible new social formations that set the terms by which Filipino America cohered as a form of civil recognition. Where Filipino America has often come to name a consequence of colonial intrusion, the articulation of the Philippine-US relation as a postcolonial state of exception makes visible the necessity of the Filipino to America. Where the coherence of Filipino America as a category of racial difference or of cultural belonging obscures the space between Filipino and America in exchange for its recognition, authoritarianism points to that space as liberalism's threshold, the gap that must be closed in order to guarantee empire's extension and maturation.

Few studies position Filipino America or the Philippines as critical sites of engagement for an exploration of Cold War politics.[80] While the Philippines was instrumental for US military operations during the war in Vietnam, it bypassed the proxy wars that characterized the devastating US assaults in Vietnam, Cambodia, and Laos.[81] If critical scholarship seeks to uncover the events and sites that are obfuscated by the persistence of US Cold War historical narratives, how too might such studies reinforce the need to recover the truth of the conflicts in ways that delimit other possibilities for its interrogation? The elision of the Philippines from this body of scholarship reflects some of the problems associated with the apprehension of the conflict and period. In addition to the state and international policies that constituted the US Cold War, the intellectualism that emerged from the period also established epistemologies for comprehending its politics. The rise and institutionalization of area studies, for instance, drew from an orientalist objectification of the colonial other to legitimize academic expertise that transformed the discourses of colonialism into a rhetoric of containment and integration.[82] These studies of Asia and the Pacific theorized these regions as distinct, contained, and unlinked to histories of colonialism, imperialism, and empire. This regionalism marginalizes the Philippines to the local rather than underlining it as a central site of engagement. It refuses the political connections between the Philippines and the rest of Asia during the Cold War, delinking its importance to the formation of Cold War ideologies. Similarly, while the study of Filipino America often assumes the United States as the privileged site of analysis, such an assumption relegates both Filipino and America as static objects and sites rather than as provocations to interrogate the other formations that emerge in their invocation and the rigidity of their political and intellectual borders. Instead, reconsidering Filipino America as an inquiry into the "layering, erasures, and reinscriptions of histories, spaces, and cultures," as Martin Manalansan and Augusto Espiritu encourage, challenges the determinisms of Cold War knowledge production.[83]

Dominant conceptualizations of the Cold War as a battle between "the two imperial hegemons" obscure the magnitude of "struggles to obtain or vanquish racial domination."[84] Upending a Manichean conceptualization of the Cold War as a struggle between the United States and the Soviet Union, I name the racial cold war, following Yoneyama's lowercase designation, not as a historical period but as a multistate governmentality in which authoritarianism and its paradigms of order, sovereignty, development, and modernization align with republicanism and its operations for progressivism, reform, and militarism to resolve and organize the colonial problem of raciality, where raciality also operates through gender and sexuality.[85] The racial cold war shifts the focus of study from the exceptionality of the historical period to interrogate the complex production of Cold War subjects as configurations that outlast the period.[86] In doing so, it presents an alternative analytic for contending with coloniality in the Philippines that notes the ways that the progression of international politics after World War II comes to bear on the earlier Filipino quandary.

The racial cold war highlights a set of transpacific politics to study the ways that proclamations of newness reorganized historical coalitions into different political arrangements that could operate within the shifting landscapes of the postcolonial epoch. The racial cold war necessitates transpacific critique to challenge the disciplinary boundaries that emerged as the product of Cold War knowledge production or, as Jodi Kim has written, to point to the Cold War as "a structure of feeling, a knowledge project, and a hermeneutics for interpreting developments in the 'post–Cold War conjuncture.'"[87] Rather than revise US Cold War history to include a consideration of the Philippines (that is, to have the US Cold War bear on the Philippines), this study conceives of national and postcolonial politics as integral to each other's unfolding.

THE CULTURE OF COLD WAR MARTIAL LAW

Through the racial cold war, state programs assembled configurations that advanced modernization and globalization and quelled resistive claims against the state. As the state and its laws construct these forms of representation, it is less interested in people's self-determination than it is in the consolidation of political power, the suppression of dissent, the accumulation of land and capital, and the monopolization of the terms of justice. A configuration captures the historical nuance of colonial subjectivity by pinpointing who, what, and why governments invested in the transformation of subjectivity during distinct periods. A configuration allows one to trace the means by which racial difference surfaces as a subjectivity that claims ownership over that difference to access promises of recognition, representation, and capital. Most importantly, it makes visible the dialectical relationship that constitutes any formation of subjectivity to challenge the overdeterminations that suffocate the expression of historical experience.

Culture is a site of struggle not only between dominant and subordinated articulations of experience but also against the idea of culture as the mere symbolic expression of racialized difference.[88] Throughout this book, culture is both a mode of expression for state power (as in "national culture") and the emergent forms of lifemaking that are obfuscated by or exceed that power.[89] This is what Raymond Williams has described as a "whole actual life, that we cannot know in advance, that we can know only in part even while it is being lived."[90] Each chapter situates official state records with and against cultural texts to explore a culture of cold war martial law. These texts tackle martial law and dictatorship yet often fall outside a conventional archive of martial law insofar as they treat dictatorship not as a singular event but as a set of historical, political, social, and cultural studies, as facets of broader concerns about memory, labor, and subjectivity. Expanding the time and place of dictatorship and the Cold War beyond the frame of 1947 to 1989 and outside only the Philippines and the United States, the texts consider other sites for locating and contending with Filipino America. They reveal the ways that Filipino American subjectivity finds fruition and coherence not only within the borders of the United States but also, and especially, in the spaces of migration and movement in ways that often refuse the impulse of diasporic conclusion or homeland return. Their conceptualization of time and space, power and resistance, and remembering and forgetting illuminate other subjectivities, affiliations, and relations. This body of literature reflects a continuous tension between the construction of wholeness and the ongoing work to refuse it.

These texts illustrate the complexity of postcolonial configurations. Each chapter explores the formation of a particular configuration and then charts a path for unmaking it. The first chapter interrogates "national culture" as it named state fictions that consolidated postwar memories of US colonial and imperial wars into discourses of Cold War national identity. Lowe has noted of US national culture that "where the state is unable to accommodate differences, it has fallen to the terrain of national culture to do so."[91] Both Marcos's and Johnson's separate but linked conceptualizations of national culture declared the end of colonial time in order to narrate progressive national histories that justified civil rights programs as well as new nationalisms. In this way, national culture offers a mode for tracing the transpacific geopolitics that organized the Philippine-US alliance as well as the diasporic Filipino subjectivities promised by these renditions of culture. In the second half of the chapter, I read Eric Gamalinda's 1990 novel *Empire of Memory* to highlight the importance of Gamalinda's notion of "memory as anti-history." Memory as anti-history theorizes national culture as a site of reckoning and disrupts the linear temporality of national historiographies that are instrumental for solidifying hegemonic notions of subjectivity.[92]

In the second chapter, US immigration reform and Philippine state investments in migrant remittances produce the *balikbayan* or Filipino return migrant to the Philippines as an emblem of national and historical progress as well as transpacific state collaboration. Much scholarship on the balikbayan focuses on the sociological development of the balikbayan and the early formations of the Philippine remittance economy. This chapter reconsiders the balikbayan as a distinct Cold War formation that inheres not only through the regime's development policies but also through the liberalization of US immigration reform. Analyzing Philippine-US transportation policies, the nationalization of Philippine Airlines, and the Marcos regime's urban development programs, my analysis focuses on the ways that the racialized and gendered constitution of the balikbayan set the terms for the displacement and dispossession of Manila's poorest communities. I also consider features from the Marcos-era publication *Balikbayan Magazine* to envisage the balikbayan as a distinct historical agent that materializes the logics of Cold War modernity.

Tracing the rise of the New Filipina as a discourse that emerged from the Marcos regime's investment in women's empowerment as well as international mandates for women's rights, the third chapter considers the avenues through which the state recognition of Filipina women as new political agents facilitated the extraction of women's labor and the feminization of the national economy. It argues that the Marcos regime's distinction of the New Filipina as connected to yet distinct from earlier ideas of women's roles in the Philippines aligned with international declarations for women's rights that characterized the postwar neoliberal mandate imposed on decolonizing nations. The chapter studies Lino Brocka's 1976 film *Insiang* to analyze the filmmaker's social realism as a technique for visualizing and apprehending the gendered violence of the authoritarian state. Brocka's strategies for showcasing the universal delineated the distinct and repressive forms of gendered violence under the Marcos regime.

The fourth chapter argues that the Marcos regime's articulation of Filipino raciality functioned, in part, by translating the tenets of international humanitarianism into a model of Filipino subjectivity that could be transformed into global reproductive labor. The gendered work of the Filipino humanitarian at the Philippine Refugee Processing Center functioned to rehabilitate the refugee. The chapter discusses the ways that Filipino humanitarianism drew from Marcos's own conceptions of the human and humanism as well as from US colonial understandings of the efficacy of Filipino service work. Focusing on English teacher Ruby Ibañez's letter published in a journal of refugee instruction, I analyze the ways that the refugee processing center extracted the labor of the Filipino teacher in the service of refugee rehabilitation. But I also trace the ways that Ibañez unmakes the configuration of her subjectivity by charting affiliations between the Filipino teacher and the refugee student that confound the paradigms of global humanitarianism.

Returning, in the conclusion, to memorialization and the work of memory, I point to a politics of reckoning to reconsider the legacies of dictatorship in the present. Filipino American cultural production continues to turn to the martial law era as a site for contending with ideas of becoming and being.[93]

Vince Gotera's poem "Three Sonnetinas" and R. Zamora Linmark's poem "What Some Are Saying about the Body" direct attention to subjectification as a mechanism for consolidating energies, stories, and lives into forms of political recognition that adhere to colonial conceptions of humanity and state mandates of citizenship. Importantly, they also invigorate the crevices of subjectivity as sites of potential.[94]

A configuration must be unmade to reveal its making. It must be undone from, as Benjamin writes, "the utopia that has left its trace in a thousand configurations of life."[95] Unmaking helps identify the processes, procedures, and systems that transform difference and experience into juridical frameworks that iron the tensions and complexities of that difference by consolidating them into cohesive forms under the law. Unmaking offers a modality for historicizing and interrogating social formations and for imagining other subjectivities that are not tied to the prescriptions of empowerment, emancipation, and liberation defined by modernity. Unmaking assumes not cohesion but disorder in ways that uncover the labor and energies that constitute solidity, directing attention to the inherent instability of each arrangement. In revealing the ways that configurations uphold and confound the operations of authoritarianism and liberalism, unmaking turns to other forms of life and living that refuse the promise of historical agency. Unmaking searches for a language to describe the ways that people create other lifeworlds—the sites, spaces, and places that are not always recognizable within the framework of the dominant or the historical but that are essential to living.[96] While they are often born of power and violence, these lifeworlds also make legible resistances that might otherwise remain undetectable if all we ever search for is the "transparent I."[97] This insistence on interrogating the politics of Filipino America is not an attempt to denounce the kind of solidarities and kinships it enables but, rather, a struggle to forge other critiques and imaginations.

ONE. THE FICTIONS OF NATIONAL CULTURE

On September 16, 1966, as part of their state visit, Philippine president Ferdinand Marcos and First Lady Imelda Marcos joined US First Lady Lady Bird Johnson, John D. Rockefeller, and other US dignitaries at the opening night of the new Metropolitan Opera House (figure 1.1). The evening included a performance of Samuel Barber's *Antony and Cleopatra*. In a *New York Times* photograph of the evening, President Marcos gazes at Imelda Marcos while she stares directly at the camera. Johnson laughs as Rockefeller whispers into her ear.[1] The event marked the completion of the newest addition to the grand Lincoln Center for the Performing Arts complex. A new massive presence in New York City's Upper West Side, the privately funded complex coincided with a growing federal investment in the "arts and humanities." The new building, according to Johnson, exemplified the "'gaiety ... splendor ... excitement'" that would usher in a "'Golden Age' in the history of the Metropolitan Opera.'"[2] With the closure of the old opera house on Thirty-Ninth Street, which had opened in 1883, the new structure boasted the capacity to hold larger productions. Along with its counterparts, it marked a new interest in the formation of an American "national culture." Imelda Marcos, impressed by the center's grandiosity, returned to the Philippines with her own plans to construct a cultural center in Manila. Much important work has explored the role of US cultural propaganda during the Cold War.[3] Several of these studies note the significance of the arts and humanities to the presentation of American cultural values of

FIGURE 1.1 Dignitaries at the September 16, 1966, opening night of the new Metropolitan Opera House. Photo: Jack Manning/*New York Times*.

self-expression, pluralism, and independence that operated through a US politics of imperialism and anticommunist war. For Washington, the articulation of racism as the exception to national greatness situated race within discourses of national progress to legitimize the advancement of transpacific collaborations in the name of modernity.

This same week, at the order of President Marcos and following a series of negotiations with Washington, the largest faction of the Philippine Civic Action Group (PHILCAG), a contingent of the Philippine Army, arrived in Vietnam to set up a base camp in Tay Ninh Province.[4] The arrival of PHILCAG in Vietnam signaled Marcos's apparent commitment to US president Lyndon B. Johnson and his Free World Military Force, an alliance of military units from various nations assembled under Johnson's directive to support the US war in Vietnam. What might one make of this confluence of events in New York City, Manila, Washington, and Tay Ninh? How can one read them not as happenstance or foreign policy or a mere sequence of events but as the very fabric of transpacific war? What is the significance of these encounters: What leads do they offer, which paths do they ask us to follow, and what possibilities do they hold?

Eric Gamalinda's 1992 novel, *Empire of Memory*, also begins in 1966 on Philippine-American Friendship Day, the day that Marcos "urged Filipinos to 'recall the lasting and valuable friendship between America and the Philippines.'"[5] The novel follows Al and Jun, officers of the Marcos regime's censorship office, as they work to fabricate the Marcoses' family genealogy. Al begins by narrating retrospectively, offering memories of a period when Marcos officials worked to "produc[e] a pastiche of idiosyncrasies culled from various texts, ranging from the manner of circumcision among native Tagalogs, to all the available ejaculations, to saints real and not . . . little details to embellish his book of anti-history (as he sometimes called it)."[6]

Drawing from earlier studies to interrogate the underlying political investments of Cold War cultural exchange, this chapter reads Gamalinda's novel to reconsider national culture as a configuration of empire and authoritarian statecraft. Forms of Philippine and US national culture elevated new cultural objects to narrate the transformation of the nation and the citizen while consolidating memory about the colonial and imperialist wars that preceded and operated concurrently with this transformation. By highlighting the ways that the state manufactures national culture, the novel uses other creative forms to unravel state investments in these fictions. It threads together an array of texts to showcase national culture as an accumulation of "fragments of documents" and "notes taken for [Al's] video of the mysterious, demented Kristo of Akeldama."[7] More than simply historical fiction, memory functions within the novel as "anti-history," which positions culture as the very site of tension and struggle between official state narratives and forms of lifemaking obfuscated by these configurations. By interrogating the lines that separate fact from fiction and history from memory, the novel explores the means by which the racial cold war operates, in part, through a continuous rearticulation of colonial and national violence.

THE GREAT SOCIETY

One year before the opening of the new opera house, President Johnson approved the US Arts and Humanities Act of 1965. Following the recommendations of the newly organized National Council on the Arts, the act established a federal endowment for the arts and humanities, laid the groundwork for the formation of national arts societies, and encouraged other institutions, especially educational institutions, to implement arts and humanities programs within their jurisdiction.[8] For the first time, and amid the backdrop of the Cold War, the act pronounced an official national culture, wherein culture identified the customs and traditions of the nation while signifying its ideologies. The act conceived of the arts and humanities as an avenue for "social uplift [and] American freedom and democracy" as well as the instantiation of a "moral force in the age of affluence."[9] As scholars of the cultural Cold War have ascertained, these claims of a distinct "American culture" also tasked culture with the charge of defensive propaganda. Anti-American Soviet propaganda coincided with anti-imperialist sentiment throughout the postcolonial world and tested the image of the United States as a beacon of democracy by highlighting the racial struggles of the period. In turn, the circulation of an American culture aimed to impress the supremacy of American talent and goodness onto the rest of the world. Throughout the Cold War, the US State Department highlighted the superiority of American artistry as well as the range of self-expression that was possible in the United States. The department's commission of Black artists and performers abroad as well as its enthusiasm in bringing cultural producers from other countries to perform in the United States (especially at the Lincoln Center) evidenced proof of US multiculturalism as news of racial violence in the United States was broadcast around the world.

The act was one arm of Johnson's broader Great Society campaign, a stratagem that rested on a conceptualization of the *outdatedness* of US culture and insisted on the progressiveness of US politics. This platform made visible a disjuncture between what the nation claimed to be, what it was, and what it could someday become. Justifying the urgency of the act, Johnson explained that the greatness of a nation is a measure of time or longevity. He warned, "In the long history of man, countless empires and nations have come and gone. Those which created no lasting works of art are reduced today to short footnotes in history's catalog."[10] Johnson appeared to heed the caution of a 1964 report prepared by the Commission on the Humanities, which warned that the failure to cultivate the national humanities poses "a danger that wavering purpose and lack of well-conceived effort may leave us second-best in a world correspondingly impoverished by our incomplete success."[11] The act worked in conjunction with the Civil Rights Act of 1964, which ordered the transformation of US society through the eradication of "poverty and racial injustice" at home to align the nation with the time of modernity. Addressing the nature of this injustice in a speech that he delivered at Howard University in 1965, Johnson explained that

"American Negroes" had been forced to inhabit "another nation: deprived of freedom, crippled by hatred, the doors of opportunities closed to hope."[12] For Johnson, differentiating Black Americans as "another nation" highlighted the discrepancies between US proclamations of equality and its actual manifestations. In doing so, he defined injustice as the exclusion of African Americans from the temporality of US progress and not as the persistence of anti-Blackness to the progression of US state formation—what Jodi Melamed describes as the "portray[al of] race as a contradiction to modernity rather than one of its structuring conditions."[13]

The realization of racial justice in the Great Society required the reclamation of this *other* nation by the one US nation. Historicizing the formation of African studies in the United States as a Cold War tension between Black struggles during the 1960s through the 1980s and US state operations on the African continent, Lisa Brock writes that the "liberal and sanitized 'national inclusion' of the black experience in the United States was slowly and unevenly added to curriculums[, and t]he result was a less politicized and a more cultural engagement with the diaspora."[14] Indeed, Johnson's identification of an other nation illuminated a certain kind of inequity in the service of national posterity while it undercut Black challenges to the nation itself. To be sure, Johnson's identification of this temporal exclusion as the "one huge wrong of the American Nation" delineated a moral framework that sought to atone for past mistakes only insofar as that call for justice might advance the accumulation of historical time to actualize American exceptionality in the present. The discursive and juridical articulation of racial justice strove to advance the continuous progression of historical-national time, and the restitution of this time fulfilled the necessary prerequisite for the assertion of the United States' moral imperative elsewhere.

US multiculturalism denotes a plurality that conflates race with a shallow inclusion within the nation. The nation's claim to multiculturalism requires that national culture devour the contradictions of raciality (that is, between the proclamation of equality, on the one hand, and the continuity of the structure of racial disenfranchisement, on the other) by immersing it within the temporal framework of US overseas empire. Integral to the coherence of national culture as such is the deployment of race as a form of difference that can (and must) be incorporated within a pluralistic nation. While its focus on the national presents culture as specific to the nation, its efficacy depends on its transnational circulation and consumption. In her incisive theorization of the racial liberalism that emerged in the wake of the US Cold War, Melamed has described this as a "racialization [that] displaces its differential value making into world-ordering systems of difference [by] concealing its performative work with its constantive work." At the same time, such conflation offers the necessary conditions for the extension of colonialism, imperialism, and war. Racial liberalism was "as much geopolitical as racial," and "official antiracism now explicitly required the victory and extension of US empire, the motor force of capitalism's next unequal development."[15] The US declaration of exceptionality, through its pronouncement of national culture, was intertwined with its assertion of multiculturalism, where multiculturalism positioned liberalism in contradistinction to racialized communist threat elsewhere. The reparation of this dialectical tension between multiculturalism and raciality sought to actuate the national "greatness" on which US proclamations of exceptionality relied. That any claim of multiculturalism is false is not the point; rather, its presentation within Great Society frameworks functioned as the operative modality for adjudicating US militarization and imperialism outside the nation.

Johnson's use of national culture often moved well beyond the arts and humanities to supply a discourse for employing racial pluralism and national progress in the service of US overseas empire. Johnson identified the Vietnam War as a point of origin for delineating the rise of the United States as the leader of the free world. The presentation of Vietnam as the new nexus of threat and possibility in Asia rested on the progression of historical-national time. In a 1976 speech on the US war in Vietnam, Johnson described the war as an effort to fulfill "the desires of the South Vietnamese people for self-determination and for peace, for an attack on corruption, for economic development, and for social justice."[16] The war, in his estimation, was not simply a question of communist containment but also a matter of Vietnamese self-determination and "social justice." Social justice reorganized the discourse of war by rearticulating the conflict not as a matter of empire but as one of decolonization rendered in the abstract.[17] In this speech, Johnson also praised Marcos, who had warned of the attempts of the "Red Chinese to gobble up all of Asia," and South Korean president Park Chung Hee, who had expressed the danger of the "direct and grave menace against the security and peace of free Asia," to showcase the growing support for the increasingly unpopular US war in Vietnam from Asian leaders, especially those from formerly colonized and occupied countries like the Philippines and South Korea.

National culture became integral to the administration's foreign diplomacy, functioning as a mode of transnational exchange. During the 1966 Manila Summit, Johnson and national leaders from South Vietnam, the

Philippines, South Korea, Thailand, New Zealand, and Australia convened to organize a plan for "peace" and "freedom" in Vietnam. The meeting ended, according to Lady Bird Johnson, with a "feast of the picturesque and colorful, of ancient history, and vivid colorful emotions."[18] This Barrio Fiesta, a grand Filipino celebration, culminated with a performance by the Bayanihan dance troupe and "general dancing among the three thousand guests" to the tune "of all our countries—'Waltzing Matilda' for Holt of Australia; 'Arilang' for President Park of Korea; 'Deep in the Heart of Texas' for us; the Maori Farewell Song of New Zealand for Mr. Holyoake."[19] The US First Lady contemplated, "I hope someday I will look at it and think that this was a night not only of pageantry, color, and vivid entertainment, but also the night when something important began."[20] Popular conceptualizations of national culture often characterize the task of culture as gendered work assigned to first ladies. Christine Bacareza Balance has described this cultural work as that which "[supplements] their husband's roles as lawmaker and public speaker with their own responsibilities in the realms of civic work and 'feminine arts' such as hosting, redecorating, entertaining (through dance or song), managing staff members, and organizing events."[21] The perception of culture as women's work minimizes its importance to foreign policy, which is characterized as the masculinized duties of national defense and international negotiation. However, as Keith Camacho has shown, national culture provides the necessary frame for legitimizing militarized aggression as "peace."[22]

The US First Lady's reflection of the performance as the beginning of "something important" presents a transpacific consensus around the war. Her emplacement of each nation as equally invested in the war's progression illustrates the affair as an unprecedented coalition even as that partnership was constituted by the uneven legacies of US colonialism and imperialism. Her presentation of cultural celebration mirrored the strategy of the president's "More Flags" operation, which employed allied transpacific nations to send aid as well as combat and noncombat troops to Vietnam in an effort to present a broad consensus around the war. "More Flags" exhibited a seemingly easy coalition of nations while depending on and strengthening US military and economic programs in specific countries organized by the logic of postcolonial development under US empire. South Korea's massive involvement in the Vietnam War, for instance, was motivated by the anticommunist and developmentalist politics of the Park Chung Hee regime, itself guided by the rise of Korean patriarchal nationalism in the aftermaths of Japanese occupation, US militarized industrialism of the Cold War, and

FIGURE 1.2 Philippine First Lady Imelda Marcos and US president Lyndon B. Johnson dance at the Barrio Fiesta in Malacañang Palace on October 25, 1966. Photo: Yoichi Okamoto/Lyndon B. Johnson Presidential Library, White House Photo Office.

the legacies of the US war in Korea.[23] Further, while the Philippines' deployment of PHILCAG to Vietnam was initiated under President Diosdado Macapagal, Marcos's agreement to maintain Philippine troops in Vietnam was attached to an approximately $50 million US aid package to support Marcos's development plan that aimed to expand the Philippine military and its counterinsurgent security programs.[24]

As part of her cultural work, Imelda Marcos sang each of the national songs alongside the Bayanihan troupe's dance performance.[25] This performance of Philippine "color" acknowledged national difference only insofar as that difference stood as secondary to the transpacific military alliance. It blurred the distinctions of locality to call the globe into its enunciation.[26] As Bayanihan encouraged guests to dance to the sound of "all our countries," the fiesta staged national culture as a presentation of a new geopolitical landscape that blurred the historical and political routes that facilitated these encounters (figure 1.2). The first ladies' gendered work established continuity between the present national discourses of peace and the histories of colonial and imperialist war.

National culture constructed state fictions that consolidated the contestable memories of the postwar period, those of destruction, reconstruction, redress, and rehabilitation, within cohesive narratives of global cooperation.[27] The fiesta worked in tandem with President Johnson's political focus on Vietnam to construct a "new Asia" where "Asians take up the burden [the United States] ha[s] been carrying—on the battlefield—and in the farms."[28] He described a horizontal transpacific alliance that rearranged the weight of responsibility for imperialist war.[29] In delineating the importance of the Philippines and South Korea to the liberation of Vietnam, his speech positioned Vietnam as the object of a new globality through which the Philippines and South Korea might exercise their muscle. Philippine and South Korean participation in the war effort evidenced the capacity of the formerly colonized to progress toward a sovereignty aligned with the political and economic investments of US expansion. In this objectification of Vietnam as the location of Asian postcoloniality as well as the herald of Philippine and South Korean national arrival, the speech also legitimized the earlier US colonization and occupation of the Philippines and South Korea as a vehicle for the realization of a new world order that enlivened, as Johnson declared, the "world of Asia and the Pacific . . . through a critical transition—from chaos to security, from poverty to progress, from the anarchy of a narrow nationalism to regional cooperation, from endless hostility . . . to a stable peace."[30] The Philippines and South Korea were the Vietnams of an earlier period: the past "chaos" that once characterized their relationship to the United States shifted into a cooperation and stability guided by US military operations in Angeles City, at Subic Bay, and at the thirty-eighth parallel. This herald of postcolonial sovereignty elided the ways that these alliances established the conditions within which authoritarianism might emerge, wherein the nascent dictatorships of the Philippines and South Korea functioned as the conditions of US liberalism's possibility in postwar Asia.[31]

THE NEW SOCIETY

During the Marcoses' 1966 US state visit, Imelda Marcos dedicated the popular song "Dahil Sa Iyo" ("Because of You") to Johnson at a reception hosted by the Philippine embassy. The ballad follows the speaker as she narrates that the object of her affection has saved her from a life of hardship and sorrow. Analyzing the First Lady's performance, Balance notes that it "became one of many romanticized musical urtexts that performed the Philippines' dependence upon the United States when, in reality, the Cold War political relationship between the two nations was more aptly codependent."[32] Balance's study of the song traces its origin to nineteenth-century Filipino displays of enactments of suffering and pity in the name of the mother country. While the First Lady's romancing of Johnson performed a gratitude toward him and a dependence on US patronage, it also enacted a certain arrival for the Philippine nation made possible by US support. Marcos usurped the suffering and pity of the ballad to mark this "codependence" as the start of a new relationship with the United States. In this instance, "Dahil Sa Iyo" was not only a song of indebtedness; an unprecedented act for a First Lady to perform in this way during a state visit, her rendition emphasized the distinct transformation of the speaker herself rather than the secondary role of her lover.[33] The First Lady's excessively dramatic performance of the song repositioned the singer, rather than her object of affection, as the protagonist of the romance. The song announced the advent of Marcos herself to the global stage, eclipsing Johnson from view. For his part, Marcos delivered a speech that commended the US president as the "man who has guaranteed security" for Asia. He also noted a "new dimension" of the US-Philippine partnership that illustrated "compassion . . . mixed with a sense of humor."[34] As the Marcoses expressed enthusiasm and vitality through song and speech, they conveyed a new ethnonationalism that revised a long-standing relationship to the United States, not as one based on colonial subjection but as one based on mutual respect. These enactments of cultural exchange were so powerful that Johnson conceded that he "'forgot the differences in our sizes and the sizes of our countries.'"[35] Impressed by the Marcoses' displays of charm and goodwill, he noted that the Philippines had taken its place alongside the United States as an equal partner and was no longer bound by US interests. While this was, of course, far from reality, cultural exchange aestheticized and performed a national emergence where the new eliminated the old and where empire transformed itself into a web of transnational collaboration. It provided a shared language of modernity between the former colonizer and the colonized that operated within a new global order and fortified the liberalism that structured US neocolonialism.

The Marcos regime's affiliation with Washington did not simply signify an uninterrupted continuation of US-backed Philippine presidencies even as the Marcoses themselves performed indebtedness in these ways. By 1966, Marcos had already begun to name his own political legacy, distinguishing it at first as New Filipinism and then later as the New Society.[36] Marcos's adherence to the "new" advanced a discourse of postindependence national sovereignty that, despite its enjoinment to Johnson's alliance of free nations, committed itself to incremental shifts away from the United States through a political alignment with Asia and the Third World, various redevelopment and modernization projects, and a reconceptualization of Filipino raciality. In Marcos's own political maneuvering with Johnson, he insisted on the US payment of war reparations, the revision of the US military bases agreement, and the administration of US benefits promised to Filipino World War II veterans. While such demands remained largely at the level of rhetoric and were often guided by political pressures at home, Marcos framed these grievances as methods that would spur the "reorientation of our people's idea of themselves and of their capability." Marcos rearticulated Filipino subjectivity in contradistinction to the colonial objectivity that had, in his estimation, long characterized a Filipino ontology. In his study of the New Society as an interpretation of a broad global movement for decolonization, Patrick Flores explains that "Marcos invoked meetings and declarations such as the Bandung Conference (1955), the Algiers Charter (1967) and the Lima Declarations (1972 and 1975) by way of context."[37] These references tied Marcos's governance to Third World declarations of anticolonial liberation that presented political and economic alternatives to frameworks of modernity that organized the colonial century. The regime's consistent pronouncement of political sovereignty in these ways employed a postcolonial structure of feeling to legitimize his political acumen as a necessary vehicle for Philippine decolonization.

Marcos also established collaborations that further entrenched the country within the kinetic affairs of imperialist geopolitics. In 1971, Marcos instructed officials to reflect on the state of the Philippine-US relationship and to consider advancing partnerships with socialist nations to address "the urgent need to intensify our export outlets."[38] He declared that "the most important developments of the past year in Southeast Asia are the following—the decreasing American presence in Asia, the assumption by Japan of a more active economic role in Asia, the fresh diplomatic offensive by the People's Republic of China, and the intensification of regional cooperation among the smaller powers in Southeast Asia."[39] Throughout the 1970s, Marcos's foreign and economic policies sought to expand the nation's relationship with China and the Soviet Union to capitalize on these markets during periods of global economic instability.[40] Yet while Marcos insisted that the nation redefine its relationship to socialist countries, he also identified socialist, communist, and leftist insurgents as "lawless elements" who sought to undermine the republic by waging a war against the Filipino people.[41] When he declared martial law in 1972, he described it as a critical measure "to maintain law and order throughout the Philippines, prevent or suppress all forms of lawless violence as well as any act of insurrection or rebellion and to enforce obedience to all the laws and decrees, orders and regulations promulgated by me personally or upon my direction."[42] Marcos suspended the "Filipino people" at the threshold of law and chaos only to tether the "masses" to the ebbs and flows of transnational finance.

The regime tasked national culture with reimagining the condition of Filipino postcoloniality in ways that helped to reposition martial law as the effort to manage economic and political crises. As early as 1969, Marcos had described the Filipino condition as the signification of the "frustration, resignation, cynicism and indolence . . . complacency, and . . . indifference" that followed centuries of colonial rule. This rectification of this ambivalence required nothing short of the complete "metamorphosis" of Filipino subjectivity.[43] With *Tadhana: The History of the Filipino People*, published in 1977, Marcos and his team of ghostwriters, not unlike Al and Jun in Gamalinda's *Empire of Memory*, fabricated an extensive history that traced the emergence of the nation to an indigenous prehistory and identified the Marcoses as the true and fateful leaders of the Filipino people.[44] *Tadhana* illustrates the definitive role of historiography in legitimizing the regime's authoritarian state. In his illuminating study of the construction of *Tadhana*, Rommel Curaming describes the ghostwriters as a team of scholars and intellectuals whom Marcos paid to complete the project. Curaming discusses the text as a consolidation of liberal and authoritarian elements that evidence the ways in which "the opposition between political interests and 'good' scholarship might not be as strict."[45] Primarily concerned with "national identity, national unity and national self-determination," *Tadhana* linked the "external" revolution of 1896 that produced a nascent national consciousness with the "internal" revolution of the New Society that marked a "turning point" in a postcolonial consciousness. According to *Tadhana*, Marcos himself manifested the sovereignty that national hero Jose Rizal originally theorized but which was never realized until his own arrival.[46]

Reflecting on his early education around foreign events and leaders, Marcos asked, "Where was the Filipino in all of this?" By posing the question as such, Marcos not only centered the concern over national becoming as the focal point of Philippine history; he also, more importantly, set the terms for its final, definitive answer. In a speech that he delivered at the National Historical Institute, he explained, "[Filipinos] have always identified ourselves with the Big Powers. This again is something which Rizal, Mabini, Luna and the rest of the writers ascribed as the reason for our national weaknesses. But the colonizer, the dominating race, is long gone. We are now responsible for ourselves."[47] Recall that Johnson's description of historical-national time identified racism as a barrier to its realization. *Tadhana*'s portrayal of national history framed colonization as a long interruption of the historical-national time sparked by the nationalist revolution of the nineteenth century. For Marcos, the solution to the predicament of Filipino abjection caused by such interruption was the reclamation of historical agency from the time of empire. His exhortation to Filipinos to take "responsibility for ourselves" encouraged a disidentification with the "Big Powers" and defined Filipino agency as the capacity to fully participate in the construction of universal historical meaning.

While *Tadhana* situates the conflicts of revolution within historical-national time, it also situated the Filipino within empty, homogeneous time:

> History, instead, is a continuous process—a fact that becomes even more evident if one recalls that Hegel himself pointed out, and his disciple Benedetto Croce emphasized, that history is the story of liberty, no matter how much we may quibble over the nature, the extent and even the desirability of this human ideal. There is indeed a relentless thrust toward human liberation in history. But alongside this thrust and basically informing it, another ceaseless movement can be perceived—a dialectical interaction between East and West, which destroys the Hegelian notion of human civilization rising like the sun in the East ... and setting in the West.[48]

Marcos argued that the "dialectical interaction between East and West" informs the process of "human liberation." Interrogating Hegel's theorization of human civilization beginning in the East and ending in the West, Marcos declared, "We would be endorsing Hegel's theory if we did not undertake to write our own history." For Marcos, "our own history" is not a denial of the West but, rather, an equilibrium between two opposing ends. Filipino subjectivity is a "continuous process" that concludes with an acknowledgment of the Filipino's natural position within the binary. While he described this equilibrium as a necessary function of national development, it more adequately established a discourse by which Filipino subjectivity could be made to inhabit an emerging globality. The narrative arc of *Tadhana* adopted as its telos a modernity shaped by the political and economic investments of the Cold War, where the "East" in fact functioned as the object of modernization. Where the text describes "Filipino alienation" as the colonial removal of the Filipino from the pages of history, the reconstruction of historical-national time emplaces Filipino subjectivity within the global time advanced by modernity, removing the Philippines from the "waiting room of history."[49] The Filipino's possession of national history and the attendant realization of national self-determination would, according to Marcos, lead to the "withdrawal of the curtain of seclusion" and the activation of Philippine participation alongside its "geographic neighbors and kinsmen."[50] Such partnerships would enable the "free flow of men and ideas through international travel and exchanges," especially important "for Asians ... if we are to tear down the walls of ignorance and intolerance built by the colonial past."[51] Such ideas underlined Marcos's commitment to the capitalist restructuring of postcolonial Asia and the Pacific.

Marking both the end of racist, colonial war and postcolonial arrival, Johnson and Marcos employed the "great" and the "new" as maneuvers for pronouncing the present as points of origin for political emergence. Cultural exchange established new regimes of obfuscation and foreclosure, reconsolidating the past within the expressed urgency of the present.[52] In his study of postwar commemoration in Guam, Camacho notes that such forms of postwar commemoration move from the celebration of rehabilitation to the extolling of modernization. He explains that "the most internationally visible commemorations of the war in the Pacific include the remembrance of its 'beginnings' and its 'end.'"[53] The great and the new expressed different constitutions of sovereignty during the Cold War. Referencing Marcos's 1965 pronunciation that the Philippines "can be great again," Flores explains that the "fantasy of greatness gained ground and took flight because it was imbricated in the discursive densities of development, identity, and democracy. To be great may have meant to emerge, to fulfill the project of rendering the self coherent and to guarantee opportunities of equality to everyone."[54] As this signaling promised new political courses of action, it reorganized the past in the service of the present, managing the direction of postcoloniality within the paradigm of global liberalism. Johnson's aspirational statement of forgetting the "differences in our sizes" exchanged memories of US colonial war and governance for a transpacific commitment to the imperial reorganization of Asia and the Pacific. The Cold War Philippine-US coalition took root from this shared vision of emergence.

THE CULTURAL CENTER OF THE PHILIPPINES AND
THE TERMS OF POSTWAR REHABILITATION

National culture produced and reproduced state fictions that heralded the newness of the political moment as the beginning of a new world order wherein a new global threat also produced new possibilities for international cooperation. Marcosian historicism advanced the regime's promulgation of national culture as a medium for translating the language of the political economy and Cold War modernity into authoritarian power. Cultural programs offered to the nation the unprecedented opportunity to cohere with the historical-national time that Marcos outlined in *Tadhana*. The Cultural Center of the Philippines (CCP), Imelda Marcos's "Lincoln Center," concretized national culture as the actualization of the president's "principle of self-help" or self-determination for a new postcolonial sovereignty.[55] A "sanctuary for the Filipino soul," the CCP threaded history and culture to represent Filipino subjectivity "as a mode of agency ... an expressive force."[56] The CCP complex boasted a performing arts center, the Manila Film Center, the Coconut Palace, the Philippine Convention Center, and other buildings that, together, aimed to initiate a "cultural Renaissance" and elevate "national art." From the street, the CCP arose as a massive presence, clearly distinguishing itself from the older buildings of the area. The complex itself, designed by architect (and later National Artist) Leandro Locsin, endeavored to signify the peak of Philippine modernity. It was part of what Gerard Lico has described as the Marcoses' "edifice complex," their fixation on concretizing political power through the construction of grand buildings throughout Metro Manila.[57] Characteristic of Locsin's designs, the complex stood as an homage to postmodernism, a style that became an important symbol of the regime's power. Along with the complex, the First Lady instituted a number of artistic programs that aspired to connect the Filipino to himself.[58]

The CCP traces its roots to the Philippine American Cultural Foundation, an office that the Philippine government established in 1962 in partnership with the US Information Agency of Cultural Affairs, to generate a "national culture" in the Philippines.[59] The collaboration resulted in the creation of a "binational cultural center in Manila as a living memorial to Philippine-American friendship."[60] This partnership drew from a longer history of US colonial urban planning and architecture that began in the wake of the US war in the Philippines at the turn of the twentieth century. Daniel B. Burnham's architectural plans for Manila during the early years of the US occupation ordered the reconstruction of the city to make it amenable to US and other foreign visitors, what Rebecca Tinio McKenna has described as "the transformation of Philippine pasture into American pastoral."[61] Seeking to eliminate the residues and dregs of the ousted Spanish empire, Burnham suggested the elimination of Intramuros, the walled area of the capital. He mandated that the moat around Intramuros "be drained and filled, as the Habsburgs had done with the moat in Vienna, and planted with trees to provide a useful and novel elongated park."[62] According to Burnham, Manila, was "'to become the adequate expression of the destiny of the Filipino people as well as an enduring witness to the efficient services of America in the Philippine Islands.'"[63] The beauty of Vienna synonymized American modernity with the universal aesthetic of western Europe. Even as many of these US colonial buildings were razed during World War II, the US insistence to build a "binational" cultural center in 1962 attempted to commemorate US colonial planning and ingenuity while making invisible the bookended wars that both instigated and destroyed the capital, mediating "memory through its very absence."[64] The naming of the foundation as binational rather than singularly American pronounced the solidity of Philippine sovereignty even as the attempt to establish "national culture" began as a US geopolitical endeavor.

During the Marcoses' US state visit in 1966, the first couple convinced President Johnson to spend $3.5 million of a $28 million Special Education Fund on the construction of the CCP in exchange for Philippine military support in Vietnam.[65] The Special Education Fund was reserved for the reparation of war damages incurred by the Philippines during World War II. "Postwar rehabilitation" was a contentious category, one that attempted to reorganize memories about war, itself a discourse fraught with the struggles of national independence, the gravity of Manila's destruction, and the role of the United States in structuring postindependence governments. In a report prepared by Ernest Schein, the former Chief of Public and Private Claims of the Philippine War Damage Commission, Schein described the incommensurability between the war commission's account of war damage and Filipinos' own articulations of loss and grief:

> The most common claims before the Commission were based upon total or partial destruction of small homes; simple tools; work animals; mostly carabao, pigs, chickens; and stocks of wood. These were usually inadequately identified. Not all of the claimants had the patience or artistry of one from Dipolog, Zamboanga, who not only enumerated his personal belongings and

described them in detail, but portrayed them with rare skill in drawings, some of them colored. He elaborated upon each item with such detail as "muslin (cocoa) blanket bedspread combination, beautifully embroidered by my wife; when we arrived in Cebu the work was done; she was a school teacher, but when I took her to Cebu she stayed at home to comfort her life companion."[66]

The commission's valuation of war damage focused on the cost of "repairing, reconstruction, or replacement."[67] Schein noted, however, that the failure of rehabilitation emerged in its incapacity to conceive of Filipino life beyond or in excess of the abstract value identified by the commission. Where he faulted the claimants' "inadequate identification" of lost items to their lack of "patience or artistry," the passage also reveals the narrow logics of the commission's adjudication of damage. For instance, the claimant from Dipolog articulated both the incomprehensible loss of war—Raymond Williams's "whole actual life"—and the incapacity of the administration to actually redress that loss.[68] The commission's metrics, in its promulgation of the sanctity of the origin that once was but is no longer—its drive to "[put] together the pieces which have been shattered by the forces of war"—identified the prewar period as the model for comprehending the totality of destruction and the charge of rehabilitation.[69] But in his study, Schein recommended that in order for "rehabilitation to be constructive [it] must be along modern designs with a view to improvement rather than restoration of the *status quo ante bellum*. The nipa hut ought to have been replaced by livable dwelling quarters; the outhouse or tree-stump eventually has to give way to plumbing and a septic tank."[70] Noting that the United States "is the repository of a considerable portion of the usable wealth of the world as well as most of the remaining hopes of mankind," Schein positioned postwar rehabilitation as a vehicle for instantiating the new, postcolonial terms of empire. Here rehabilitation is not simply a return to the origin. It is modernization according to the imperial nexus of US expansion.

Johnson's later delineation of the CCP as "postwar rehabilitation" is noteworthy for these reasons. The CCP, funded in part as reparation for war damages, enacted rehabilitation in the face of its earlier failures. The CCP as rehabilitation advanced national culture as the modernization of the nation and the nation as inextricably attached to the terms of US overseas empire. Under this arrangement, postwar redress was no longer impossible but now viable in both the US and Philippine states' nexus of value. That the US administration of postwar rehabilitation facilitated the exchange of the CCP for Philippine military assistance in Vietnam rendered such redress possible only through these imperialist and liberal terms of exchange. To put it differently, national culture is war by other means.[71]

The construction of the CCP required the "reclamation" of Manila Bay, the man-made process of extending the length of the bay to build the complex atop of it.[72] For Imelda Marcos, the choice of location was a matter of practical consideration: it provided an unobstructed view of the Pacific Ocean, an homage to the natural beauty of the archipelago and its position in the middle of the ocean. The First Lady described a conversation she had with John D. Rockefeller about the construction of the CCP:

> You know, it's funny how even [he] was amazed at how I was able to build the CCP. During a visit here right after Ferdinand was elected President, I showed Rockefeller the Manila Bay area where I planned to build the CCP. He said: "But my dear girl, that's all water!' . . . I said, 'No, Mr. Rockefeller, I can do it. . . . On the first year, I'll drive the pile. On the second year, I'll cover the soil. On the third year, the building will rise. On the fourth year, the curtains will rise."[73]

The First Lady's promise to Rockefeller that she would tame Manila Bay wrestled with the contentiousness of the bay's historical significance. As the site of key military struggles during the Spanish-American War (Battle of Manila Bay, 1898), the Seven Years' War (Battle of Manila, 1762), and World War II (Battle of Manila, 1945), the bay has long signified the rise and fall of empires at different historical iterations as well as the global shifts that underline competing Spanish, British, US, and Japanese imperialisms. Marcos's description of the emptiness of Manila Bay narrated the New Society as the point of origin of Philippine modernity. The CCP evidenced the Marcoses' politics of miracle and magic, what Neferti Tadiar has described as a developmental paradigm that appeared to make something of nothing. Atop the Manila Bay and apart from the spatial and sonic disarray of the city, the CCP enjoined the transnational circuits that crossed the Pacific. The complex on the bay was a littoral border between the nation and ocean, aligning national culture with global possibility.

By extending the bay—reconstructing the size and shape of its natural constitution—and building atop it a complex of unprecedented proportion, the reclamation performed a literal and figurative memorialization. At the formal dedication of the CCP in 1969, the First Lady announced: "It is highly symbolic that the Center, whose mission it is to reclaim from the past the things that belong to our present and our future, should stand on land reclaimed from the sea; appropriate that the building should be the realization of the vision of Filipino minds and the work of Filipino hands; appropriate that its first cultural presentation should tell the ancient story of our people through the medium of a newly created Filipino art-form, the 'Dularawan.'"[74] The CCP's task, according to the First Lady, was to "reclaim" what rightfully belongs to the Filipino. She proclaimed the end of racial abjection signified by colonial war and simultaneously announced the arrival of the nation to the world. Yet as both boundary and intersection, the littoral exposes the limits of this sovereignty. The Marcoses' conception of decolonization usurped and foreclosed the revolutionary potential of anticolonial struggle by insisting on forms of national subjectivity bound by the juridical and political possibilities afforded by the regime. The First Lady rooted the CCP in the motto "truth, beauty, and goodness," which she expressed as "katotohanan, kagandahan, at kabaitan." The center's logo is composed of three figures of the *baybayin/alibata* "ka" enjoined to form a circle. This image of the three *k*'s of the "katotohanan, kagandahan, at kabaitan" resuscitated the Katipunan society, whose own three *k*'s stood for its formal name, the "Kataas-taasan, Kagalang-galangan, Katipunan ng mga Anak ng Bayan" (or Supreme Honorable Society of the Children of the Nation).[75] In summoning the anticolonial separatist society that formed in radical opposition to Spanish colonization as a way to situate it within the time and space of the CCP, the CCP resignified anticoloniality as an extension of national culture. As the CCP worked to cohere national culture with national development, it employed the Katipunan to serve the formation of Filipino national identity even as the contestation over the role and importance of the Katipunan has long characterized its disjuncture within the linearity of Philippine history.[76]

The regime's conceptualization of national emergence was tethered to the logics of global capitalism. In the oft-cited case of the Manila Film Center, part of the CCP complex, the First Lady envisioned the film center as the venue for the first Manila International Festival. For Marcos, the festival would both elevate Filipino artistry and attract an array of distinguished guests who might have grown tired of Cannes.[77] In an effort to complete construction of the center in time for the festival's opening, a floor of the center collapsed and buried hundreds of workers alive within the rubble. Rather than pause construction, the First Lady ordered that the crew continue to build atop the workers' bodies.[78] Filipino folklore has it that the film center's untimely demise and its regression into ultimate disuse was a product of the restless spirits of the workers who continue to haunt it well into the present day. Imelda Marcos aligned national culture with the tenets of universalism by divorcing it from the people for whom she said it would serve.[79] Simultaneously heralding Filipino culture while ordering the continuation of construction atop actual Filipino people, the First Lady denoted value according to the promise of international revenue garnered by the future film festival. As the laboring force that constructed the CCP, the workers established the worthiness of national culture. They produced an exportable culture by translating the locality of Filipino experience into capital. This is culture that gains value in its circulation. Literally buried within the walls of the structure but obfuscated by the First Lady's demands, the workers—"the work of Filipino hands," as she described it—remained abstracted from her pronouncement of national culture. It is their continued presence, in the form of a haunting, that emerges in dialectical tension with the regime's production of culture. Made visible and knowable only through such retellings, the hauntings refuse the aim of subjectification, demanding a reckoning with state power that lays bare the state fictions that constitute Philippine sovereignty.

THE NOVELLA, THE JOURNAL, AND THE HISTORICAL ENCOUNTER

Eric Gamalinda offers one such retelling. In *Empire of Memory*, culture is both the accumulation of political violence and the vehicle for alternative forms of people's expression. Gamalinda, like the protagonist in the novel, is a "Marcos baby," a description that names a generation of Filipinos who came of age during the Marcos regime and for whom martial law has been a critical facet of their lives. A poet and novelist, Gamalinda also worked as a journalist during the Marcos years, "which was one way for [him] to find out what was going on under Marcos."[80] The body of writing that has emerged from this generation evidences the ways that authoritarianism continues to shape a group of Filipino cultural producers. Writing about a 2010 collection of martial law writings, editor Rolando Tolentino explains that the volume provides Marcos babies with "the space for articulating their coming-into-being" and that their "already substantiated being becomes the nexus for living and dying in the period's aftermath."[81] Similar to the collection, *Empire of Memory* identifies personal memory not as an individuated recollection of events but as a vehicle for unmaking Filipino subjectivity to highlight the socialities forcibly marginalized by the regime's operations.

At the novel's opening, it is 1966, and the Beatles have arrived, performed, and then been banned from Manila for refusing the First Lady's request to visit Malacañang Palace. The chapter begins with two of the novel's protagonists, Al and Jun, as they, together with Al's sister Delphi, navigate the early years of Marcos's presidency. In the following chapter, it is 1982, and Jun convinces Al to work with him at the regime's censorship office, where supervisor and Marcos crony Max Plata tasks them with the creation of an encyclopedic project of "Philippine prehistory" for the president in celebration of the ten-year anniversary of martial law. While the president planned three volumes ("one on the early Spanish era, another on the beginnings of the American empire, and the third on Marcos' ascent to the presidency"), the first volume must set the tone for the historical legitimization of the regime, martial law, and the New Society. As Al and Jun begin their assignment, Max orders them to travel to the small island of San Miguel to quell a potential "public relations disaster." San Miguel is bisected by the Monte de Oro, with the Villa del Fuego property on the west and Akeldama on the east. The natural divider separates distinct yet interconnected histories—those of war and betrayal that begin with the US war with Spain, move into World War II, and continue into the present day. Colonel Jose and Dolores Zabarte inherited the villa from Dolores's family, an old, land-owning family that accumulated its wealth from the logging industry in the first decade of the US occupation of the country. Akeldama, on the other side of the island, is riddled with poverty and teems with sex "entertainment" that feeds the servicemen of the US La Paz Naval Base. The island gained notoriety for the discovery of the Isnegs, a "Lost Tribe" previously untouched by civilization; it is also the site of a refugee processing center and an ongoing civil war between Colonel Zabarte's military and the insurgents of the New People's Army.[82]

While the novel could be characterized as historical fiction, its conceptualization of memory as "anti-history" challenges the historicism that organizes national culture. Presenting national culture as a configuration of state and colonial power, it unravels obfuscated and foreclosed memories that must be suppressed to maintain the cohesion of national culture.[83] Within the novel, Al describes the Philippines as a "land both fact and fiction, where generations leave no trace of themselves and everything is constantly wiped out, punctually, by clockwork destruction: typhoon, tsunami, earthquake, drought. Because of this we have no memory of ourselves: we remember only the last deluge, the last seismic upheaval."[84] The regime's articulations of national sovereignty hegemonize particular kinds of "remembering and forgetting" while delegitimizing other temporalities. They define historical meaning in an effort to achieve historical permanence. Throughout the text, however, state fictions function not as the absence of truth but, rather, as the discourses, narratives, and performances that legitimize the state, its conceptualizations of history and culture, and the ideologies that determine what counts as a life worth living.[85] The novel challenges the regime's production of national culture by directing attention to both the labor that is required to produce it as such and the marginalized cultural forms that are elided in its formation. It points to "the critical role of narrative and other representational forms in the interplay of the personal and the public, constituting a dialectic that always underlies transactions in collective memory."[86] Written six years after Marcos's fall, the novel itself is memory. It does not argue for the recovery of a more veritable account of Marcosian history; instead it directs attention to the production of the regimes of knowledge that construct the bounds of national culture. It centers these state fictions to uncover the multiple struggles that constitute the regime's presentation of the nation, situating it within the legacy of construction and destruction and war and empire that characterize Philippine historical experience.

Together, Al and Jun constitute the Agency for the Scientific Investigation of the Absurd (ASIA), where they administer censorship for the government, conduct research and writing for the regime's historical and cultural projects, and serve as the president's ghostwriters. Jun, for instance, orchestrates the story of the Isnegs, a "prehistoric" tribe of the Philippines deemed an anthropological marvel and a national treasure worthy of protection by presidential decree. Prehistory denotes a point of origin within empty, homogeneous time that is used for claiming political legitimacy. The proclamation of a "prehistory" generates programs for conservation, where conservation underscores the necessity to preserve a particular historical model of origin and development to legitimize the urgency of the national present. The production of the Isnegs "covered up a lot of things," obfuscating the regime's extrajudicial endeavors, the designation of export processing zones, and efforts to contain leftist insurgencies.[87] In the 1970s, Marcos instituted the Presidential Assistant on National Minorities (PANAMIN) in an effort to recognize and protect "tribal Filipinos," an office I describe in more detail in chapter 4. Such efforts effectively nationalized tribal lands in the name of conservation and then used these lands to intensify production, export, and militarization programs in these regions.[88] These efforts often blocked the struggles of Indigenous and Muslim peoples in the Philippines to attain political legitimacy and power and positioned Filipino national subjectivity as the premier figuration of national belonging.

Al and Jun must complete the First Couple's historical volume—the novel's fictionalized *Tadhana*—and find a way to tie the First Lady's family lineage to the regime's rendition of the national past. In attempting to fabricate this lineage, Al's and Jun's volume not only functions as a legitimization of the Marcoses' authoritarian power but also reflects the regime's use of historical-national time to privilege the discourses of cold war modernity. As part of his research for the text, Jun travels to Villa del Fuego, where he finds a novella about the Suarez family written by Dolores Zabarte's aunt, Amalia Suarez Romaldes. Although Dolores denounces the novella as fiction fabricated by her sick aunt, Jun's exploration of both the novella and the terms of its production trace a genealogy of Spanish, US, and Japanese colonialism alongside Philippine state formation. Jun's relationship to the novella becomes a site of historical encounter, where the purported truths of the regime emerge in dialectical tension with "memory as it flashes up at a moment of danger."[89] Amalia's novella traces the end of the US war with the Philippines and the early beginnings of US colonial governance over the islands, noting the cultural and political changes that emerged in the war's aftermath.

As Jun pores through the novella, he notes discrepancies between Amalia's historical narration and his own knowledge of national history:

> In his notes Jun said the author Amalia Suarez Romaldes must have probably known little of the history of the surrounding islands. The entire novella mentioned the war against the Americans as a tidy little affair that was soon settled and forgotten; but in fact many of the islands around San Miguel had put up a valiant resistance to the American infantries. We knew that in Samar the American army retaliated against a particularly violent insurrection by decimating the population of the island, and male natives above the age of eight were all mercilessly killed.[90]

Even as the regime tasks Jun with tracing the Romualdez family to a noble and heroic national "past," such a past is surely complicated. Jun finds that it is fraught with gaps, fissures, and erasures. Moreover, the task of reading the novella challenges any sense of cohesiveness it may possess as Jun's knowledge of the past brushes up against the novel's presentation of it. Even as the novella form promises a certain historicity, Amalia's novella betrays, instead, the multiplicity of time—where national time, colonial time, and alternative times cohabitate.[91] In other words, time is not empty or linear; it unfolds as a series of colonial and national crises.

Jun's discovery of Amalia's journal disrupts his study of the novella. In her journal, Amalia describes the circumstances of her arrival to San Miguel, her love for Manual Suarez, the ways that World War II ravaged the island, the development of her sickness and eventual hospitalization, and her process of writing the novella. Amalia's writings reveal the ways that the narrative of national history functions through, with, and against the gendered interiority of private memory.[92] Her writings turn to marginalized, disparate, and unrecorded memories, subjugated by the dominance of historical-national time, that reveal the labor required to sustain the Suarez villa in the center of the island. Describing a moment when she walked alone throughout the town at night, Amalia recounts that she walked past "workers there from the plantations, drinking this foul-smelling alcohol they ferment from the heart of palm. They had women with them, ragged and dirty with loud voices and unpainted fingernails."[93] An unknown stranger later approaches her: "He shifted out of the darkness and I saw his face: a most frightful face, pocked and shriveled, dark and grimy, the face of a man long dead."[94] Amalia replaces the solidity and sanctity of the villa here with an illustration of the life that surrounds it. Insofar as the Suarez family continues to make its wealth from its logging mills, workers in the surrounding plantations live in the shadows of transnational capital. Here "[men] long dead" sustain the life of the island. Indeed, the period in which Amalia wrote marked the height of the devastation of Philippine forests due to the logging industry that gained considerable traction during the US colonial period. US colonial administrators, foresters, and entrepreneurs established these logging mills to consistently export rich woods from the Philippines to places such as the United States.[95] These "long dead" figures are those who worked for and were rendered expendable to this industry. While Amalia does not recognize them as living beings, the undead become the residues of a past that might be otherwise interred by the enclosing force of a national history. They "have memories of their own, they are here not whole, complete individuals. They are ancillary forms, relays of a movement of actions and affects that exceeds them but that has no existence outside of them."[96] Offering a different sociality other than subjectivity, they emerge as disruptions to the historical present.

The interior knowledges offered by the journal challenge the versions of subjectivity promised by both the novella and national culture. In Amalia's own narration, neither familial nor national history is the goal of the novella. Motivated not by the truth of the Suarez's family history but by the expression of other knowledges that reside in the gaps and fissures, Amalia's writings seek not the futurity of a modernity based in US industry and imperialist war but, rather, the possibility afforded by the unfamiliar, "so new and so full of light."[97] Rather than exist only in its finished form, the novella becomes a deliberate *practice* of unmaking in the face of aggressive foreclosure. In other words, the novella itself is less important than the act of writing it. As Amalia "recreate[s] these lives," she removes the figures and their historical conditions from the progressive accumulation of events so that they can perhaps reimagine new meanings away from the overdetermination of national history.[98] When discussing her novella, she explains that she "cannot stop" and that she "invent[s] things from a source deeper than memory."[99] Amalia's ambivalent concern about the truthfulness of the narrative and the knowledge that she writes from a source deeper than memory is not the fetishization of a precolonial past. Rather, it exceeds the earthliness of Amalia's lived life. Inventing things from a source deeper than memory, the journal refuses the legitimization of subjectivity directed by national history and instead provokes a different kind of freedom unbound by historical-national time. The labor of writing removes Amalia from the earthly realm and places her into the time-space of other lives that she might not immediately recognize. It is in this "altered world" where she is "at peace."[100] It presents, as Stuart Hall explains, identity not as "a fixed essence at all, lying unchanged outside history and culture" but as "*something* . . . always constructed through memory, fantasy, narrative and myth . . . the unstable points of identification or suture, which are made, within the discourses of history and culture."[101] This "source deeper than memory," this "something," is what Tadiar has discussed as the creative labor required to sustain revolutionary energy beyond the comprehension of both state regimes and leftist ideology. The production of new temporal affiliations not necessarily with the living but with the figures long dead allows the palimpsestic remains embedded within national culture to come undone.

SAL X

Such conceptualizations of history and writing direct attention to the regime's pronouncements of national culture that relied on a linear historicism to trace it to grander visions of international recognition. With her remarks at the dedication of the CCP, Imelda Marcos explained that Filipinos' "greatest strength lies in being truly what we are: by nature and by grace, one people; by fortune and by fate, Filipinos."[102] Indeed, the First Lady was clear to name the CCP as "a treasurehouse of the Filipino soul," one that would house "our works in stone and story, in dance and drama, in music and color."[103] For the Marcoses, culture was born of the nation and served as an instrument of its projects; as such, the regime used culture as an instrument to express racial cohesion within an emerging discourse of global multiculturalism. The regime's treatment of national culture reflected its insistence on defining the bounds of Filipino subjectivity according to its value and mobility within the global market.

Structures like the CCP monumentalized battles against the passage of time by making grand declarations of national sovereignty. The CCP promised a resolution to national trauma by declaring its arrival to modernity. In the novel, the regime's cultural projects validate its state fictions. The narrator explains:

> It was often difficult to understand what obsessions haunted our presidential family: or perhaps every one of us felt we had to monumentalize our small existence. Because no matter how much we cried we were small, our small lives speckled across the South China Sea. Driving past the dingy barrios of Manila, I couldn't help feeling all this jubilation was unreal. All along the South Superhighway, the Department of Public Works set up fences of wooden planks, twice the height of man, to cover the dilapidated warrens from visiting dignitaries. The fences extended northwards to Taft Avenue and onto Espana, all the way to the wattle houses of Tatalon, Quezon City. This was the New Society's 35th parallel, anything below minimum wage had to fall out of view.[104]

The passage highlights the regime's efforts to hide and sanitize the country's unseemly parts from foreign dignitaries, "the feeling all this jubilation was unreal." This sanitation, which mandated the removal of the city's poorest residences in an effort to beautify the city, set the stage for aestheticizing Philippine modernity. During her Manila Summit visit to the Philippines, Lady Bird Johnson wrote that she "noticed bamboo screening— barricades like fences of palm leaves . . . screens [that] were part of the city's cosmetics for the Summit Conference, I suppose."[105] More than simply a screen for hiding Manila's unseemliness, the cosmetic devices that the US First Lady identifies act as a barricade for dividing a modern Philippines from the masses who labor for the materialization of that development and who must be made invisible to maintain the solidity of its coherence.

The passage uncovers a modernity that aligned with the developmentalist paradigms of Cold War politics. Al's description of the "New Society's 35th parallel" supplants Marcos's Manichaean concept of globality (East and West) for a different cartography of modernity duly attentive to the materiality of the aftermath of war, imperialism, and capitalism. It makes visible the production of the North and South as the organizing paradigm of the racial cold war and the political and social inequalities that constitute such a bifurcation. These political divisions, evidenced in the militarized borders that separate Korea and Vietnam, constitute the logics of Cold War security and containment that supported imperialist declarations of a new political order. This narrative division not only uncovers the inconsistencies between the regime's conceptualization of national sovereignty and other articulations of Filipino life but repositions it as a condition of imperialist geopolitics. That "we cried we were small" but "our small lives speckled across the South China Sea" exposes the incommensurability between the regime's declarations of national arrival and greatness, on the one hand, and the masses' lived lives, on the other. The regime's definition of Filipino subjectivity could not fathom the extent of Filipino presence "across the South China Sea" and throughout the world. Divorcing Filipino subjectivity from the schema of national sovereignty, this contrast between big and small reduces the regime's conceptualization of racial becoming as a limited and myopic concern in relation to the afterlives of New Society policies, which forced Filipinos to move outside the Philippines. The New Society did not repair Filipino colonial abjection. Rather, it reorganized Filipino subjectivity as a vehicle for transnational transaction. In decentering the nation as the locus of knowledge in this way and, in turn, pointing to the "small lives speckled across" the ocean, the novel turns to the archipelagic to offer another way of conceiving of time and space unhinged from the hegemony of the continent.[106]

The Marcoses' promotion of a national cultural renaissance called forward the Filipino as the decolonial agent of historical-national time, wherein Filipinoness articulated both the defeat of racial abjection and a new historical agency. Within this paradigm, Filipino raciality is the product of a historical evolution, an amalgamation of East and West. Marcos's turn to Asia as a point of identification and racial referent coincided with his own economic investments in the ascendancy of Asia and the Pacific within the global market. In the novel, the character Sal X complicates national culture and Filipino raciality. While Jun travels to the villa, Al travels to the other side of the island to Akeldama to meet Sal X, a man made famous for his annual performance of the Pasyon, or Christ's suffering on the cross, during Holy Week. The child of a Filipina mother and white American GI father, Sal X's paternity is simultaneously born from the specificity of continued US militarized occupation of the Philippines and rendered illegible within the administration's insistence on a singular national identity. Sal X performs this ambivalence as both a pop singer in an Akeldama bar—a pitstop for US military servicemen stationed on the island—and through the Pasyon. As he performs old American songs at the bar, Sal X becomes popular precisely by activating nostalgia for an American home, one for which he longs yet to which he is a stranger. Such performance focalizes the intimacies of US militarized occupation in the Philippines, intimacies that force Filipinos to bear the memories of US culture—what Lucy Mae San Pablo Burns has theorized as an "episteme ... a way of approaching the Filipino/a body at key moments in US-Philippine imperial relations."[107] Yet Sal X's performance of distinctly non-Filipino songs illuminates an alternative cartography of Filipino raciality.[108] It is the success of Sal X's Pasyon performance that leads to his rise to fame. His eventual tour in Japan and recognition as a star of global popular music traces the routes of Filipino historical experience through transpacific circuits of movement and exchange. Attention to such routes, as Balance notes, "broadens our definition of translocality to include networks of places within a single nation."[109] The novel treats Sal X as a configuration constituted by the tripartite politics of the Philippines, the United States, and Japan.[110] This geopolitics illustrates the various modalities by which he is included, excluded, recognized, and made legible within the politics of raciality that characterizes national citizenship in each of these locations.

Sal X's performance of the Pasyon calls attention to cultural forms that seek not a triumph over a historical past but, rather, a communion with it. As Reynaldo Ileto has discussed, Filipinos in the nineteenth century performed the Pasyon as a way to reconceptualize and transform Catholic teachings into tactics for mobilizing and organizing the masses around a revolutionary consciousness.[111] Sal X was the first repentant who proposed that he be nailed directly to his cross rather than simply tied to it, believing that "enactment was not enough; true sacrifice demanded true blood."[112] Calling into question the regime's own forms of cultural reenactment in the form of Filipino culture, the opposition here between "enactment" and "true blood" challenges the state fiction of "true blood" as racial purity by asking whether or to what extent Filipinoness might cohere only through these eugenic forms.

In his own refusal of his self in exchange for the embodiment of the Pasyon, Sal X seeks integration into and transformation within another time. Here the "historical past" is not a period that has ended in order to make way for another era; instead, the present emerges in the past's wake. In the physical trauma of the crucifixion, Sal's "vision failed him and he turned blind in the heat, passing from oblivion to oblivion like Christ passing from the world."[113] Where the regime's rendition of historical-national time and national culture insisted on a clear recognition of the Filipino within the New Society, oblivion here contests these strictures of visibility. Oblivion speaks, instead, to a convergence between temporalities. These cultural forms are rendered incommensurable with the Marcoses' articulation of Filipino culture. Their excesses make room for otherworldly possibilities, ways to commune with other pasts and futures and construct other subjectivities.[114]

MEMORY AS ANTI-HISTORY

By the end of the novel, the people's revolution ousts Marcoses from the presidency, and Al wonders about the fate of the historical volume that he and Jun created. He muses, "I often wonder if it were indeed the real manuscript Jun handed to the fleeing President. I look back and find memory closing like the end credits of a film: too fast and too full of names. I think of what might have happened to the lives we had crammed in our prank of a book. . . . But as I began, so shall I end: with a story, because there is nothing in this world to keep us going but the retelling of our lives, and of those we love."[115] The novel directs the reader to what Jenny Edkins has described as a kind of "encircling" or an insistence on a "retelling of our lives" that struggles to save the story from historical-national time. It is an effort to uncover the ways that parts of the story emerge in multiple elsewheres.[116]

Empire of Memory presents an island within an archipelago, a novella within a novel, a performance within a show. It is, as Leonard Casper wrote in a 1996 review, "a-story-within-a-story."[117] It effectively brings the period of martial law to contend with the colonial century, bookended by multiple wars. There is no singular history available within the novel. Instead, there are a series of secret routes. At the outset, the novel operates as Al's memoir, a sustained reflection on his time as an agent for the Marcos administration. As Al's work for ASIA requires the reconstruction of historical-national time, it mandates the mitigation and obfuscation of memories rendered inconsequential and dangerous to the regime's conceptualization of national culture. Where the Marcoses' historical volume seeks to define the contours of Filipino subjectivity, the novel's portrayal of the ongoing struggle between Colonel Zabarte's men and the insurgent forces of the New People's Army, the excise of Indigenous peoples from their land, and the marginalization of Amerasians from the rhetoric of national belonging illustrate the ways that the regime's pronouncement of cohesion depends on expunging contesting narratives from the framework of national belonging. In the novel's illumination of the multiplicity of stories that constitute Filipinoness, it points not to the historical coherence of Filipino subjectivity but, rather, to the persistent instability that characterizes its proclamation.

The novel ends with Al as an older man, over a decade after the end of the 1986 people power movement that deposed Marcos from office and the country. If the novel stood only as Al's memoir, it might read as a kind of bildungsroman, a coming-of-age story set to the opulence, contradiction, and violence of the Marcos era. As Al's work for ASIA takes him to other locations, however, his research summons other cultural forms that might be otherwise discounted if *Empire of Memory* were simply a novel about martial law. The story consistently undercuts the novel with alternative narrative forms—Jun's passages for the Marcoses' historical volume; sections of Amalia's novel and journal; Sal X's performances and transpacific travels. These journal writings, oral histories, the Pasyon and its processions, the Beatles, fortunetellers, and popular music illustrate not an individual consciousness but a collectivity of historical experience. This experience is unknowable by the reach of Al's memory alone and exceeds the time and space organized by the singularity of Al's authorship. As Al reminisces on the passage of time, memories other than his own penetrate his recollection so that they become indistinguishable from his thoughts. He prepares John Lennon's jacket—a souvenir from his first interaction with the regime in 1966—as a gift to his dying sister Delphi, a balikbayan or immigrant returnee from the United States, to give to her son, Nico: "I place the box on my lap and open it, and I take out the coat I had kept and had not looked at all these years: except for the painfully mended sleeve, it looks almost new. We shall let Nico wear it, it shall be too tight for him, and we shall remember and have a good laugh."[118] An old relic of Al's past that marked both an end of innocence and the rise of Marcos's power (Al and his schoolmates "were rounded up in a classroom and made to sit on hardboard chairs as directors from the school snipped the mops off our heads"), it reemerges in 1999, looking almost new. The coat's ability to help Al and Delphi remember signals memory's radical potential to dislodge the past from the sanctity of history. That Nico might wear a coat that is too small for him but wear it nonetheless points to the role that remembering can play for repositioning one's self in relation to other people. Unlike Al, Nico is not a Marcos baby; he can reimagine a new subjectivity in relation to histories and places that are not his own.

The coat is the ephemera of the New Society, part of an unlikely archive of power and dissent that the novel reveals by unmaking the configurations of the racial cold war. Strewn across the novel, the objects—the coat, the novella, Sal X's cross—carry with them insight into the state's organization of cultural memory.[119] The fragments bear more significance than their whole. Ephemera invoke a "flashing moment" that belongs to no one person but to the many someones organized by a structure of feeling. Destabilizing the historical archive of fabricated facts and figures as the location of national truth, the novel conceptualizes memory as anti-history, where "the Philippines must be (re)moved and (re)imagined" to make room for the longings and desires of those buried within a perceived past meant to be subsumed by the force of the present.[120] The past does not simply commune with the present to illustrate the continuous nature of time. It challenges the modes of representation that employ the Filipino as the premier figuration of subjectivity. Memory acts not in obverse to historical-national time but as a landscape for convening shared and distinct experiences of authoritarianism, nationalism, colonialism, and imperialism, a collective consciousness of Philippine historical experience, that defamiliarize any one configuration of Filipino America.

TWO. BALIKBAYAN MOVEMENTS

A 1976 special issue of the *Philippine Quarterly*, a short-lived periodical published by the Marcos regime's media office, celebrated the rapid development of Manila under martial law. An article titled "Old and New Manila" surmised: "The modernization of Manila has been going on at such a fast pace that an absentee of only a few years can literally find himself lost on his return. Familiar landmarks no longer stand. New ones have taken their place. A bridge where everybody can still remember was cogon land; a four-leaf clover connects a maze of new roads leading to everywhere."[1] The article underscored the importance of the "absentee," a familiar figure who can only comprehend his time away from Manila on returning to the city. It imagined the absentee traveling through the megacity to find it almost unrecognizable, memories of familiar sites replaced by the impressiveness of a new metropolitan infrastructure: bridges, high-rise buildings, and "new roads leading to everywhere." These new pathways signaled both the innovation of Manila's urbanity and the dexterous movement that it enabled. At the same time that these changes leave the absentee momentarily dazed, the article envisioned, his exploration of the city legitimizes its development. In short, the modernization of Manila requires his movement. The absentee is not an abstraction but refers specifically to the overseas Filipino who left the country for the United States and did not witness the transformation of Manila under Marcos. Three years before the quarterly published the article, Marcos introduced the figure of the balikbayan to the general public to name the increasing number of Filipino immigrants to the United States, a group that he encouraged to return to the Philippines for holiday visits. Marcos's hope was that these absentees would find old problems resolved by new solutions.

Infrastructural reform operated through the regime's fetishization of movement and mobility as the condition for development. More than only the construction of bridges, buildings, and roads, the regime's fixation on mobility within the capital city operated concurrently with its reconceptualization of Filipino subjectivity as a modality for movement within the nation and outside it. As Filipino emigrants fled the economic and political strife of the martial law period, they settled in the United States in response to the liberalization of US immigration law. As part of its Operation Homecoming program for overseas Filipinos, the Marcos administration treated the absentee as the object of many of its reforms. The balikbayan is a configuration that emerged from intersecting Philippine and US governmentalities and prescribed the conditions for a postcolonial raciality that might operate as global recognition within a racial cold war. Throughout this chapter, I analyze Philippine and US periodicals that capitalized on a transnational circulation and readership to argue that mobility undergirded a disciplinary logic that set the contours for the multistate management of the balikbayan configuration as well as for the paradigms of illegality and abjection in the Philippines that criminalized the squatter. This chapter illustrates the multiple, variegated, and sometimes competing state projects that invested in the balikbayan as a Filipino American formation that could legibly traverse the uneven terrain of Cold War modernity.

THE BALIKBAYAN VISITS ESCOLTA

The Marcos administration declared the period from September 1973 to February 1974 "homecoming season" for what it identified as a new group of overseas Filipinos, or balikbayans, which translates literally as "those who return to the homeland."[2] Operation Homecoming was intended to ease the return of nearly 100,000 Filipinos living in the United States back to the Philippines, where they might witness for themselves the "indisputable" success of Marcos's New Society.[3] In Washington and California, the former foreign affairs officer and vice consul of the Philippines, Doroteo V. Vite, delivered a series of lectures in which he described to his audience the necessity of martial law to the realization of a more capable democracy in the Philippines.⁴ According to Philippine state officials, balikbayans from the United States were "desirous to come home but have been deterred by the prohibitive air fares and by tax problems."⁵ As a result, the Marcos administration instituted reduced airfare, airport privileges, and tax holidays for returning Filipinos.⁶ In addition to these travel incentives, the Operation Homecoming campaign initiated a "nationwide hospitality and reception program" that rewarded local provinces and barrios that attracted the highest numbers of returnees to the country.⁷ As part of this local program, state officials established informational sessions in these towns to enforce knowledge about what constituted "traditional Filipino courtesy and hospitality."⁸ In chapter 1, I discuss exhibitions of national culture as avenues through which the regime consolidated Filipino subjectivity into a modality for expressing postcolonial arrival. Local programs marketed "traditional" Filipino culture to overseas Filipinos and other potential visitors in order to generate a curiosity that might translate into tourism.

The regime's invitation to US-based Filipinos to "visit their homeland and see for themselves" the products of martial law aimed to activate Filipinos' affective attachment to the nation that the regime projected would result in capital inflows from the United States to the Philippines.⁹ Throughout the 1970s, the administration ventured to redirect Filipino immigrants' diasporic longing and attendant remittances into a burgeoning tourist program. In 1971, Troadio Quiazon Jr., the secretary of commerce and industry, speculated that "these Filipino tourists and returning residents are expected to bring and spend more than $1 million during their Christmas vacation in their mother country" and placed "special significance on the arrival of the Filipino tourists who would come at a time when the country needs foreign exchange badly."¹⁰ In the mid-1970s alone, Filipino immigrants sent a combined $200 million to the Philippines.¹¹ In 1973, a World Bank committee acknowledged that the "sharp increase" of the country's trade account deficit was stalled, in part, by a "rise in private remittances from $95 million in 1970 to $158 million in 1972," and "as a result, the current account deficit of about $30 million in 1970 was replaced by small surpluses in 1971 and 1972."¹² Throughout the 1970s, the regime relied on these remittances to alleviate a series of economic problems precipitated by the global crises of the period, namely the oil crisis.¹³

Balikbayan Magazine, a Philippine-based "international" publication distributed by the regime's San Francisco office in the early 1980s, targeted as its readership Filipinos living in the United States who sought news from and about the Philippines. It was designed first "for Filipinos and their friends all over the world" and then "for all others who wish to keep in touch with the Philippine scene."[14] The articles often presented the Philippines as a familiar landscape where one might now travel within the country as one never had before. The magazine strove to cultivate a balikbayan readership that could become prospective tourists and serve as a vehicle for tethering the nation to a simpler, bygone time. By featuring familiar places throughout the country alongside new sights to explore, the articles balanced the tone of nostalgia that often characterized the regime's balikbayan recruitment strategies with a feeling of anticipation that outlined a tourist program in the country that had preceded the regime but gained new momentum under the Marcoses. The First Lady's construction of the Cultural Center of the Philippines (CCP) and its adjoining centers paved the way for a revival of the tourist economy. Large-scale events such as the 1974 Miss Universe competition; the 1975 championship boxing match between Muhammad Ali and Joe Frazier, billed as the "Thrilla in Manila"; and the 1976 IMF–World Bank Conference promised to draw new international audiences to the Philippines.

In one *Balikbayan Magazine* feature article, "Escolta Revisited," writer and playwright Floy Quintos spotlighted "La Escolta," a famed street in the historic marketplace town of Binondo in Manila. Beginning the article with a description of the street during the Spanish colonial era (established by settlers in 1594), addressing the arrival of the British, mapping Chinese business in the area, and then moving on to its development during the US colonial period, Quintos positioned Escolta as a hub of transnational trade and movement. In addition to noting the specific sights, sounds, and smells of the marketplace, Quintos profiled notable shops and the routes that led to their arrival on the street.[15] For instance, the article noted that "1899 was the year when *Clarke's*, that 'Mecca for Thirsty Souls' introduced the sweet that continues to tantalize and dominate our summer fantasies: ice cream," along with "one special store with the striking name, *Paris Manila*, [that] dealt in fashionable textiles."[16] He personified the street through the figure of "the fashionable Filipino of early 1900's, weary of revolution and ready to embrace the new order of things."[17] Escolta visualizes a turning point between a past age of "revolution" and the "new order" of twentieth-century modernity, similar to what Benjamin described as the clerk who "measures the century by the yard, serves as mannequin himself to save costs, and manages single-handedly the liquidation that in French is called *revolution*."[18] Yet it is precisely this "fashionable Filipino" who bridges the gap between the revolution and the new order to march toward the latter.

No longer fastened to a waning revolution, his capacity to purchase and consume luxury international goods ushers Manila into the new century.[19]

Indeed, Quintos presents this figure as imperative for materializing Escolta as a critical site of encounter. He notes that shoppers in the 1900s traveled to the famed street to search for

> champagne, tabacco [sic], fine silk chemises, elasticized stockings, Magnani, Stetson, Surefit and buntal hats, diamonds, Omega watches, fine lace, ices, cut crystal paper weights, chandeliers, embroidered piña cloth, satin dress gowns, perfumes, linen, canned Brunn Butter, silverware, Cordovan leather, harnesses, carriages, saddles, phonographs, Tin lizzies, Hanan shoes, Indian textiles, sharkskin for the *Americana Cerrada*, opera glasses, legal advice, trunks and valises, rubber coats, whips, sporting goods, gold embroidery, advertising space and a fine set of teeth from an expensive dentist.[20]

Quintos's extensive list pronounces capital's arrival to the Philippines as horizontal and obscures the colonial hierarchization that managed its movement. Such descriptions present Escolta's rich history through the objectification of transnational capital and the street itself as the location of a bourgeoning twentieth-century cosmopolitanism. One can find the Stetson hat of the American West, tobacco from the plantation fields of the New World, and textiles of British-occupied India as luxury goods next to each other on the same street. With few designations other than its national markers to describe the various objects, the list blurs the circuits of racialized labor and forms of extraction that brought the luxury goods to Manila and removes them from the settler colonial landscape of their production. The fashionable Filipino seeks "all the luxury and finery that Escolta offered, 'all new, all different, all worth having'—as an ad for *Heacock's* went." Fixated on the new and holding little desire for what came before it, he traverses Escolta with little memory of a past life where it operated as a resting place for foreign generals during various colonial occupations. Escolta brings the world to him, and he brings the world to Manila.

The longing is palpable: this portrait of Escolta gestures toward a greatness that had once existed but is currently threatened by the developments of the present. Near the end of the feature, a sudden break forces the narrator to note the "stagnant waters of the Estero Sagado" that "[release] a stench that breaks the mood of nostalgia."[21] At this point, Quintos brings the balikbayan reader to the present-day street. Quintos speaks directly to the balikbayan reader (addressing him as "you"), imploring him to compare the Escolta of the nineteenth century to that of the twentieth. Contemporary Escolta no longer possesses a "snobbish distinction" or "genteel air." Instead, it is "many shades removed from its former self," an outdated alternative to the glistening shopping centers in Cubao, Greenhills, and Makati, "another old street in a struggling Metropolis." Quintos's imagined traveler moves uninhibited by restriction. He boards the bus undisturbed, alone with his thoughts, holding the historical knowledge necessary to comprehend the significant changes that have occurred throughout the city. In her analysis of the US colonial construction of Kennon Road through the Cordillera Mountains, Vernadette Vicuña Gonzalez notes that colonial and imperial infrastructure has depended on "masculinity as tied to the ability to penetrate into previously inaccessible mountain regions and render these regions as sites from which to view scenery."[22] Within colonial travel narratives, the male settler traverses unknown landscapes in order to tame them. Quintos's article positions the balikbayan as a resurrection of the fashionable Filipino man, where both articulate historical and political turning points. The narrative replaces the colonial drive for conquest with a nostalgic presentation of a lost past, where the "previously inaccessible mountain regions" are bygone histories that the modern traveler makes accessible through his voyage. The balikbayan is a masculinized protagonist whose knowledge of both space and time allows him to remember and reclaim the glory of this past through his movement across different planes. Where "the rest of Manila goes by," moving blindly toward modernity, the balikbayan's extended absence from the country removes him from the progression of development and instills within him the capacity to identify the present as a vital political crossroads between the old and the new.[23]

While the article's ambivalence about Marcos-era modernization presented a noteworthy caution about the administration's reforms, it is important to note that its rendition of the balikbayan offers both the promise of tourist capital and a distinct knowledge of the landscape made possible by his departure and absence: "You look around you, at the sea of humanity that has never ceased to cross the Escolta and suddenly you are wary, suddenly you realize that the old Escolta is gone forever."[24] It is the "sudden" consciousness of being both from then and now, from there and here, a unique diasporic awareness, that positions the balikbayan as a configuration of modernity and equips him with a critique of the harmful consequences of uninhibited development.

By the final paragraphs of the article, the balikbayan is interrupted by the new figures that have replaced the "imperious doñas" who used to gallivant across Escolta. These are the "moneychangers" who "[offer] pesos for your dollars," the sidewalk vendors, pet peddlers, and a "beggar with the hideously swollen foot." These people exist in contradistinction to the balikbayan. They are social formations whose stagnancy make them "look strangely incongruous" to the new urban infrastructure. Notably, both the dollar and the fake designer bags "na galing pa sa U.S." (that came from the United States) thread these suspicious figures. Despite their apparent incongruity, the "strangely innocent" balikbayan and the moneychanger both emerge from the long-standing legacies of US occupation.

THE POST-1965 IMMIGRANT

The regime envisaged the balikbayan through a Cold War discourse of postcolonial raciality that transcended the terms of the balikbayan program itself. By the time the administration instituted Operation Homecoming in 1973, the Filipino population in the United States had already risen to unprecedented numbers, due in large part to the instrumental passage of the Hart-Celler Act, otherwise known as the Immigration and Nationality Act of 1965. In a symbolic gesture, Lyndon Johnson signed the act into law on Ellis Island in 1965 to amend the McCarran-Walter Act of 1952 and to signify Washington's apparent commitment to racial pluralism. Although the act removed the national origins quotas that archived the country's legacy of xenophobic immigration policies, Johnson assured the American public that the bill would not drastically alter the demographic makeup of the United States.[25] On the contrary, the law unwittingly catalyzed the mass migration of non-European peoples from Asia and Latin America to the United States.[26] This political inclusion struggled to resolve a discourse in crisis. Amid growing social and political upheaval within the country, the act sought to reframe the United States as a tolerant nation that welcomed peoples from all over the world to its borders. Outside the United States, it aimed to evidence the progressivism of US policy when the deployment of anti-American propaganda around the world showcased the hypocrisy of US democracy.[27]

More significant than the emergence of this new diaspora, however, is the way that the act developed a discourse for delineating the past and future of colonial and immigrant subjectivity. No longer subject to the exclusionary laws that characterized nineteenth-century Asian immigration to the United States, the post-1965 Asian immigrant unwittingly evidenced the possibility of a new multicultural citizenry that could be divorced from the debilitating mandates that had long characterized US immigration law.[28] Studies of Filipino immigration in the United States often distinguish post-1965 Filipino immigrants from earlier groups of migrants who were tied to labor contracts and restricted by national quotas throughout the first half of the twentieth century.[29] The Tydings-McDuffie Act of 1934, for instance, granted US commonwealth status to the Philippines and concurrently transformed the Filipino migrant from US colonial to foreign alien, effectively limiting Filipino movement between the commonwealth and the United States. The liberalization of immigration reform in the second half of the twentieth century directed postcolonial Filipino subjectivity away from the restrictions that characterized it during the period of US tutelage over the Philippines. The Hart-Celler Act established a preference system that granted priority entrance to professionally skilled migrants and those reuniting with spouses or other family members who had already immigrated to and settled in the United States. The right to migration and naturalization afforded to Filipinos and other immigrants, especially in the midst of the resistance movements in the United States throughout the late 1960s and 1970s, reveals state efforts to incorporate them into a model of abstract citizenship that saturates racialized difference within the juridical parameters of national belonging.[30] While such immigration reform strove to reconcile US national policies with its pronounced ideologies, it could not respond to imperatives for self-determination articulated by the complexity of these movements. Rather, the state's cession of individual rights to immigrants established identity, or self-ownership, as the defining characteristic of post-1965 racialization.[31]

This "new" immigrant was differentially incorporated into the United States not as colonial subject but as participatory citizen. The formation of the post-1965 Filipino diaspora into a politically recognizable social formation provided the language for reconceptualizing Filipino subjectivity through the framework of US citizenship. Insofar as this group was unrestrained by the mandate to return to the Philippines, the act effectively integrated Filipinos into a broad paradigm of US national belonging that permitted Filipino recognition, representation, and movement within the liberal and neoliberal discourses that characterized US Cold War politics. The passage of the immigration act reinforced the state as the guarantor of individual rights while it strengthened the framework on which those rights depended—a capitalist structure of white property ownership buttressed by a racialized and gendered laboring class.[32]

At the same time that the act celebrated US racial pluralism, it also heralded the emergence of a new postcolonial world order produced from the legacies of US overseas empire. The Hart-Celler Act is significant not simply for its permission of immigration but especially in the ways that it facilitated the arrival of a distinct type of immigrant—the national subject of a postcolonial nation. This connection between the maturity of the Philippine nation-state and the recognition of its national subject points to the inextricability between sovereignty and migrancy, where the impositions that govern the former structure the possibility of the latter. Structural adjustment policies imposed on the Philippines in the decades following independence, for instance, organized labor around crony capitalism and multinational finance. *Balikbayan Magazine* presented a much more complicated rendition of the post-1965 Filipino immigrant than those espoused by US immigration discourses. In one article about the large number of Filipinos settling in California, journalist Recah Trinidad interviewed Armando Fernandez, the Philippine consul general in Los Angeles. Fernandez described some of the difficulties of painting an adequate portrait of the diasporic community in southern California. The article quotes Fernandez: "'Twice the government count would be a safe estimate of the Filipinos in California,' Fernandez reveals. 'The 300,000 heads should account for metro L.A. alone but if we have to include others in the suburbs, then the count could readily climb to half a million. We can never have an accurate count because there are countless illegal entries, the TNTs—*tago nang tago*—while others couldn't be accounted for as they avoid revenue census.'"[33]

While the article attempted to trace the early formations of Filipino America as a post-1965 political body moving toward increased US visibility, it also named the limitations of this visibility. This recognition depended on the legibility of the Filipino immigrant through the mandates outlined by the Hart-Celler Act: the act privileged professional skill and the reunification of family, and it also established economic productivity and heteronormative affiliation as a prerequisite for proper immigrant subjectivity. Yet *tago nang tago* (TNT), "those who continuously hide," expresses the instability of this immigrant subjectivity insofar as it names another set of migrants who claim presence beyond and despite the recognition structured by US immigration law. Here, while TNT migrants also highlight transnational movement, this movement is rendered illegal within the jurisdiction of proper immigrant mobility. Vernadette Vicuña Gonzalez has aptly noted that the "idealization of mobility as modernization did not merely rely on the exclusion of unfree subjects; it also produced and intensified the very conditions of exclusion and unfreedom."[34] The permission of movement is always already structured by its regulation. Citizenship produces the mechanisms for recognizing and policing immigrant subjectivity within the bounds of national discourses. The liberalization of US immigration law occurred alongside and through the expansion of the mechanisms for adjudicating illegality. For example, while the act unintentionally permitted immigration from Asia to the United States, it also more heavily restricted immigration from Mexico, establishing new punitive definitions of legality.[35] The post-1965 period also saw the rise of aggressive immigration control along the US-Mexico border. In her historicization of the US Border Patrol, Kelly Lytle Hernandez notes that "the number of Mexican nationals apprehended by the U.S. Border Patrol crossed the 100,000 mark in 1968 and inched toward 500,000 in 1973."[36] The concomitant advent of US immigration reform and the fortification of border policing showcase the ways that US liberalism manages the constant interplay between permission and regulation.

US immigration law also helped organize a set of geopolitical practices that constructed the circuits and pathways that connect the Pacific, Asia, and the United States. While the emergence of the post-1965 Filipino immigrant to the United States remains one configuration of Filipino American subjectivity, the influx of multinational capital to the Philippines under international restructuring measures and the continued US occupation of military bases in the country established other forms of subjectivity that materialized through the Philippine-US relation. The forms of political representation and legality that make visible immigrant subjectivity often render the latter illegible as Filipino American social forms. Critical studies of US overseas empire highlight the ways that the US militarization of the Philippines in the postwar, postcolonial period produced sexual economies that served US military servicepeople. Victoria Reyes writes that "sexual relationships between U.S. servicemen and Filipinas ... as necessarily bad and exploitative ... are centered around gendered identities that become symbolic of the nation; that is, Filipina women serves as a representative for the Philippine nation while U.S. servicemen represent the United States."[37] This racialized and gendered conceptualization of both US and Philippine nationalism is one that has characterized the US postwar reconstruction of Asia, wherein US masculinized military power bears the responsibility of rescuing nations from external threats rendered incommensurable with US democracy.[38]

Yet the articulation of Filipina sex workers as the "bad and exploitative" effects of nationalisms inhibits the extent to which one might conceive of these nationalisms not as already established but as forming within the distinct landscape of the racial cold war. This is significant precisely because the framework of nationalism can delimit the extent to which one recognizes a social formation as a legible political category worthy of state protection. In particular, Filipina sex workers become recognizable precisely at the intersections of Cold War Philippine-US militarized collaborations even if they might be strictly categorized only as Filipino nationals by Philippine law. Indeed, their categorization as Filipino nationals obfuscates the specificity of their labor as well as the materiality of the conditions of their lives at the convergence of multistate military operations. For instance, as I discuss in the following chapter, the Marcos regime categorized Filipina sex work as part of a "hospitality" industry, rendering sex work indistinguishable from other forms of service labor and denying sex workers state recognition and protection.[39] On the other hand, the regime often touted the balikbayan as an abstract or masculinized configuration of economic potential. The administration's recognition of the balikbayan afforded him distinct guarantees and privileges. The repudiation and invisibilization of particular kinds of Filipina work advanced the legibility of a distinct Filipino racial subject that might transcend the depravity of the colonial condition.

PHILIPPINE AIRLINES IN THE OPEN SKIES

The formation of the balikbayan illuminates the complexity of transnational Filipino migration, where migration is not defined by a teleological relationship to the United States but is a facet of a broader racial cold war.[40] The regime capitalized on the growing Filipino diaspora in the United States to ensure that the balikbayan's right to stay in the United States also enabled his right to move beyond it.[41] With Operation Homecoming, the balikbayan delineated a Filipino subjectivity that could exist outside the national jurisdiction of the Philippines yet remain tied to and invested in its economic development. Others have already importantly noted that the balikbayan signified the failure of the authoritarian state to maintain its national citizenry.[42] Yet reevaluating the balikbayan as a product of the racial cold war means refusing the assumption of the balikbayan as a predetermined entity and considering it, instead, as a configuration for reorganizing the terms of national sovereignty and for moving capital across national space.

Balikbayan movement illustrates the progression of a Philippine-US alliance that signaled a distinct kind of Philippine postcoloniality. When

Marcos renewed Operation Homecoming for a second term in 1974 after declaring it an "overwhelming success," he also seized control of the Philippine Airlines (PAL) by consolidating the country's remaining airlines into the single company.[43] The concurrent renewal of the balikbayan program and the establishment of PAL as the national flag carrier provided the regime with the authority to establish and regulate airfare for travelers who wished to take advantage of the incentives of the balikbayan program.[44] Marcos ordered that a "homecoming certificate" be issued to any qualifying "Filipino non-resident and/or his family and descendants in the United States and other lands desiring to visit the Philippines."[45] The certificate guaranteed discounted airline tickets to travelers that were paid, in part, by the Department of Tourism to the "national flag carrier."[46] This so-called balikbayan fare offered reduced airfare to Filipinos living in the United States in an effort to encourage them to experience PAL's newest comforts and visit the homeland.[47] Additionally, it mediated aviation negotiations between the Philippines and the United States. This nationalization of PAL reveals the ways that the balikbayan cohered, in part, through Philippine-US geopolitical negotiations. These negotiations showcased contestations between the United States Civil Aeronautics Board (USCAB) and the Philippine Civil Aeronautics Board in ways that defined the movement and reach of the balikbayan.

As the authoritarian administration sought to implement the balikbayan fare, the USCAB noted that such a mandate compromised the maintenance of "fair" competition between PAL and competing US airlines. For the USCAB, the necessity to establish economical commercial policies was critical to securing an "open skies" framework that privileged consistent and dynamic international travel, itself a system for promoting contact between nations and peoples and integrating them within the free-market paradigm of the broader US Cold War program. Of course, what lay beneath such integrationist rhetoric was a US militarized investment in the containment of Asia during a period of perceived communist antagonism. In 1975, the US embassy advised its state department to accede to Marcos's balikbayan fare despite US airliners' contestation, warning that "it is hardly timely to start a spitting match with the Philippines on fare structure when due to developments in Vietnam we may need maximum good will and patience from [the Philippines] for the use of carriers and aviation facilities."[48]

The balikbayan fare was never simply a Marcos formulation alone. It arbitrated the needs and goals of both Philippine development efforts and US military offensives. These telling contradictions expose the tangled collaborations between Marcos's system of crony capitalism and US imperialism. The liberalism that grounded the US open skies policy absorbed the balikbayan fare as a tactic for appeasing Marcos's authoritarian mandates and advancing US military operations in Asia. By 1985, the term *PALakbayan* had entered the repertoire of Philippine tourism to describe tour package deals and other discounts offered by the airline.[49] This portmanteau suggests that the seizure and development of PAL unfolded precisely alongside and, in many instances, through the formation of the balikbayan. Philippine governmental officials' insistence that PAL accommodate the balikbayan, reminiscent here of Quintos's "fashionable Filipino," showcases the ways that they conceived of the balikbayan not merely as the benefactor of Philippine innovation but precisely as the conduit for bringing it to fruition.

PAL identified the precise location of the Filipino diaspora in the United States. Its routes traveled only between Honolulu, San Francisco, and Manila.[50] As important locations for Filipino settlement, these sites became focal points for activating established and emergent social formations for the regime's programs.[51] PAL's focus on Honolulu and San Francisco as important sites for recruiting balikbayans to the Philippines reveals the longue durée of US coloniality.[52] In the first half of the twentieth century, travel routes between the Philippines, Hawai'i, and California facilitated the movement of colonial migrants from the Philippines to sugar plantations in Hawai'i and agricultural fields in California.[53] Insofar as colonial labor functioned as the currency of exchange within US empire, labor migrants traveled within empire's rise and maturation. The regime's focus on these locations as sites of balikbayan recruitment capitalized on the large Filipino populations in these states. More than that, however, it obscured these legacies by transposing the balikbayan onto the specter of the colonial migrant. Where colonial mandates regulated the mobility of the latter, the former moved unhindered by these past restrictions. The detachment of the balikbayan from these earlier formations established him as a configuration of both Philippine and US modernity.

Philippine Airlines advertisements in popular US magazines ensured the brand's circulation to a wide, global readership. Unlike *Balikbayan Magazine*, which catered to a largely diasporic Filipino audience, these advertisements sought to transform the balikbayan into an international discourse, positioning him as a signifier of movement as modernization. PAL advertisements boasted of the airline's technological innovation. They urged potential travelers to indulge in PAL's newest comforts. PAL travelers, for instance, would enjoy the newest in-flight technology, including wider television and movie screens, custom earphones, and Skybeds for its first-class passengers. In addition, advertisements touted in-flight cuisine acclaimed by the French gourmet society.

An advertisement placed in a January 1980 issue of *Reader's Digest Asia* traced PAL to a legacy of progress that dated back to 1946.[54] Referencing the DC-4 airplane that once "taxied out onto a runway at Manila Airport [and] smoothly across the Pacific," the advertisement invoked the post–World War II era of Philippine independence as a period that ignited a new age of aviation in Asia. Following this logic, it was inevitable that PAL would become "the last word in 747's. From the first airline in Asia." Another PAL advertisement placed in a February 1970 issue of the *New Yorker* emblazoned the declaration "Philippine Airlines is bigger than you thought" above an image of a globe that centered the archipelago confidently emanating international routes from its capital center (figure 2.1). Its claim that PAL is bigger than one thinks boastfully heralded a new era of Philippine technology characterized by modern amenities and new routes that moved its passengers throughout the world. This claim to immensity was made possible precisely by PAL's capacity to illustrate for the potential traveler just how *small* the world actually is—that is, PAL's ability to compress the geographic divide between Manila and the United States and to decrease the amount of time it takes to travel to each. PAL's progression reflected a worldwide insistence on technology as a means for national development. At the 1970 United Nations General Assembly, delegates advocated for "the interest of all countries in benefitting from the achievements of modern science and technology for the acceleration of their economic and social development" and called on governments "to give due attention to the promotion of science and technology in their national policies and to encourage increased international technical and scientific co-operation."[55] These advertisements in widely circulated periodicals invoked global imperatives for technological and scientific innovation. Marcos's consolidation of PAL worked to integrate the Philippines within this schema of global development.

MANILA'S ENTRY FACILITY

While the airline imagined the trajectory of balikbayan movement around the world, the Philippines' international airport also strove to express this transnational mobility within Manila. The reconceptualization and reconstruction of the Manila International Airport helped to facilitate the

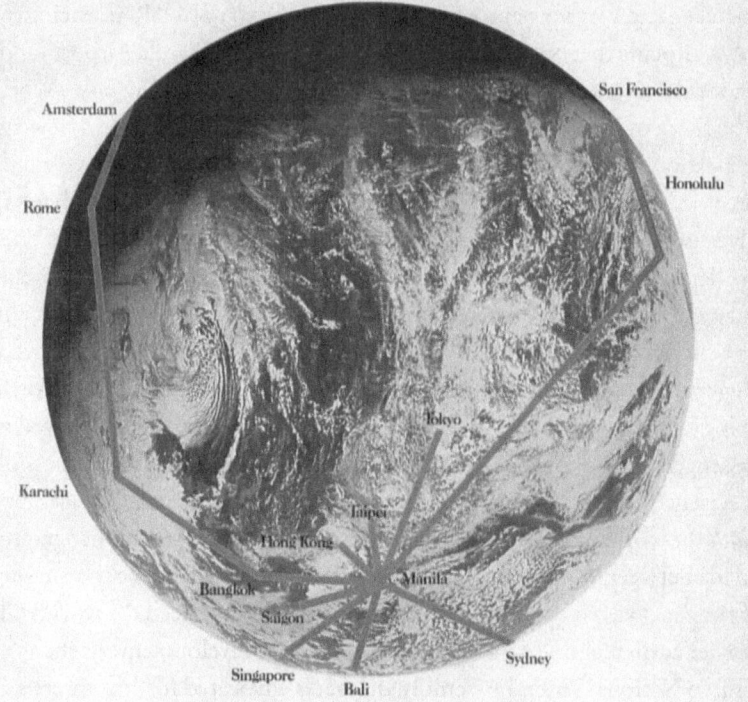

FIGURE 2.1 Philippine Airlines advertisement in a February 1970 issue of the *New Yorker*.

incorporation of the balikbayan into Marcos's agenda for national development. In his 1972 State of the Nation address, Marcos outlined a broad vision for the expansion of the Manila International Airport:

> The DCI [Department of Commerce and Industry] is perfecting a plan which would promote tourism in other countries with the help of foreign-based marketing organizations. The target includes the estimated 400,000 Filipino nationals in the United States. This program also calls for the improvement and modernization of entry facilities into our country, at air and major seaports, tourist plans, amusement centers, and recreational parks, and the removal of tax problems that deter Filipinos from coming to their own country either as tourists, investors, returning residents, or plain visitors. With the tragic fire that caught the Manila International Airport last weekend, the rehabilitation of tourism facilities requires high priority for airport development.[56]

Marcos's description of the airport as "entry facility" reimagined the structure beyond its mere functionality as a transportation hub and more as an avenue for processing the movement of the "estimated 400,000 Filipino nationals in the United States." At airports, officials assess the traveler's legal documentation, verify national citizenship, determine one's right to move, and concretize the traveler's position in the world as belonging to one place, promised to another, or somewhere in between the two. These processes determine a traveler's status—as citizen or visitor—and consequently dictate the extent of movement within the country. However, as entry facility, Marcos proposed, the airport would serve as the initial site of contact between the Filipino traveler and the Philippines, marking the moment that the balikbayan moved from in *transit* to in *place*.[57] At Manila International Airport, officials processed the balikbayan as a returnee. Neither only citizen nor simply visitor, the balikbayan occupied a new category of inclusion and belonging within the nation. With the institutionalization of the balikbayan program, officials gave these Filipino nationals "priority immigration and customs service upon arrival."[58] While Marcos claimed these Filipino nationals for the Philippines (he was, after all, concerned that they are "deter[red] from ... coming to their own country"), he forecasted their reentry as their transformation from only Filipino nationals into "tourists, investors, returning residents, or plain visitors." In naming and concretizing these travelers as nationals-turned–tourist investors, the airport made clear meaning of their return and movement as opportunities for circulating transnational capital within the national economy.

In 1972, Marcos ordered the formation of a committee charged with creating a plan for the "rehabilitation" and "improvement" of the Manila International Airport.[59] In addition to vesting the committee with the authority to outline a plan for the airport's expansion, Executive Order No. 381 (EO No. 381) required that it also address the "further need to establish a trading center in the context of a foreign trade zone within the MIA complex."[60] The rehabilitation of the airport helped materialize balikbayan return into economic advantage. "Differentiated traveling" produces mobilities based on nationalized, racialized, classed, and gendered divisions. Insofar as it produces a "corporeality of mobility," in which the capacity for movement is generated at the "scale of the body," the airport complex transferred hundreds of thousands of overseas Filipinos from the United States into the political system of the Marcoses' expansive urbanity.[61] The flow of foreign movement, made possible by a reconstructed airport, would prepare Manila to become the "center of Far East commerce."[62] While this foreign trade zone sought to centralize Manila as a center for international exchange, it also envisioned the airport as a mediator between the expansive circuits of global movement. The modern airport concretizes the logic of the global market economy insofar as it acts as a vessel for gaining access to a particular form of transnational capital.[63] The spatial system of the airport replicates and advances social hierarchies shaped by national anxieties.

Such lofty visions of the airport preceded, of course, the physical construction of the international terminal itself, which was not completed until nearly a decade after Marcos's 1972 speech. Leandro Locsin, the architect of the CCP complex, also designed the international terminal of the airport.[64] Locsin's design privileged the very type of movement that Marcos described in his speech. Virgilio Maguigad has described the design as reminiscent of the cultural center complex, because it too has "the feeling of a 'massive overhang waiting to collapse' but somehow defies gravity by way of cantilevering at the departure level" and "evokes less of the expectation of flight and seems to content on hugging the ground."[65] Maguigad's description aptly captures the contradiction inherent in the design, the simultaneity of movement and stagnancy. The use of concrete to "hug the ground" insisted on an overwhelming permanence that rendered offensive the ephemerality of the shantytowns that the Marcoses attempted to eradicate in preparation for the airport's construction. Describing the airport as counterintuitive to the "hatid-sundo" (pick up and drop off) character of Filipino transport culture,

Maguigad posits that the design was incommensurate with the realities of everyday movement for Filipinos living in the metropolis. Indeed, Locsin's brutalist design, where "function follows form," severed the airport from the time and space of the city's cacophonic sound and haphazard rhythm. It created a structure that not only adamantly rejected the disarray of Metro Manila but also ignored its seething palpability. The modern minimalism arranged by Locsin sought to tame the chaos of the city's urban jungle. It insisted on a free flow of movement promised by the impermanence of tourists and travelers and the consistency of their capital. It was this movement that the regime understood as both a solution to the disarray of Manila's squalor and an expectation mandated by the country's renewed collaboration with burgeoning Asian economies.

The actual construction of the new airport proved to be a far more difficult endeavor for the regime, as it was forced to contend with the masses of "squatters" living on the land and its surrounding areas.[66] In 1971, airport official Salvador Mascardo "directed his men to give the vacationing Filipinos port entry and instructions to avoid falling prey to crooks outside the airport terminal buildings." In doing so, he advocated for the facilitation of the movement of "vacationing Filipinos" that cautiously sidestepped potentially discomfiting encounters between Filipino visitors and "crooks."[67] Mascardo's instruction tellingly positioned the balikbayan as an exceptional figure that both stood outside the juridical governance of the nation yet still necessitated national protection. Mascardo's directive heeded the president's mandate. By guiding their movement, Mascardo sought to not only direct Filipino nationals away from any risks that might inhibit their capacity to move freely but also return them to a new nation that was different from the one that they had left. The imperative that the balikbayan be afforded the capacity to move uninhibited both through and outside the airport, not to mention the differentiation made between "vacationing Filipinos" and denationalized "crooks," established the balikbayan as the recipient of state protection and rendered the crook outside the recognition of national citizenship.

THE SQUATTER PROBLEM

The "crook" came to embody multiple forms of abjection, many of which signified an immobility rendered oppositional to the movement enabled by the New Society. Specifically, squatters—a designation given to displaced populations and informal urban settlers in Metro Manila—gave tourists and other visitors arriving to the airport and traveling through city streets negative impressions of Manila and the country as a whole. Officials marked them for relocation and eradication. Seven months after Marcos ordered the expansion of the airport with EO No. 381, he issued Letter of Instruction No. 19 (LO No. 19) to make squatting an illegal act. The letter ordered the removal of all "illegal constructions including buildings on and along esteros and river banks, those along railroad tracks and those built without permits on public or private property." The administrative body charged with its enforcement, including the secretaries of national defense, public works and communications, and social welfare, could determine which segments of the city were to be marked as "public and private property" that needed to be protected from squatter encroachment. The mandate also established proper movement as a condition of belonging within the New Society. It intensified the precarity that characterized squatters' lives.

While squatters were, by definition, constituted by a continuous movement, they also, according to officials, inhibited the distinct movement of capital. In his discussion of travel, James Clifford explains that travel, more than simply the assumption of mobility, uncovers a relation between those whose movement is designated as travel and those who have not been or cannot be constituted as travelers. He describes "'travel' as a term of cultural comparison precisely because of its historical taintedness, its associations with gendered, racial bodies, class privilege, specific means of conveyance, beaten paths, agents, frontiers, documents, and the like."[68] LO No. 19 reconceptualized travel not as an act but as a relation; it was not simply a mandate against "illegal constructions" but a rearticulation of subjectivity in relation to the New Society. LO No. 19 defined illegality not simply as *the act* of constructing impermanent homes along riverbanks and railroads but *as those* who obstructed the pathways that enabled the city's movement.[69] It made squatters' personhood illegal within the jurisdiction of the state's articulation of national citizenry.

In the years that followed the end of World War II, squatters epitomized the limitations of postwar reconstruction in the Philippines. A 1972 study found that the movement of poor migrants from rural provinces to port towns followed the transformation of industries throughout the country. In Iloilo City, the "shifting locus of the sugar industry" resulted in "practically no industries, low agricultural productivity, and declining governmental income relative to growth of service needs."[70] In Baguio, squatters both sought and stalled "the presence of government services, tourism, gold mining, and trade and commerce."[71] As Philippine, US, and international entities sought to rehabilitate the country in the decades after the war, these efforts also consolidated resources and capital within the urban centers. Poor, rural migrants who fled the devastated economic conditions of the countryside flooded a city already struggling to rebuild itself after the war. One report estimates that nearly 280,000 squatters occupied areas in Metro Manila in 1963, just two years before Marcos took office. The number rose to 1.6 million by 1981.[72] Marcos's engineering of new transportation infrastructure and social welfare projects throughout Metro Manila privileged progress rather than mere rehabilitation. His intent was not to simply reconstruct Spanish and US colonial architectures razed during the war but, rather, to produce an altogether different Philippine political and cultural identity that radically departed from the agendas of previous presidential administrations.[73] The proliferation of squatters in the urban metropolis posed significant roadblocks to these aspirations, and Marcos's administration devoted considerable attention to addressing these remnants of mendicant and outdated Philippine policies.[74]

Even as the presence of squatter communities in Iloilo City, Baguio, and Metro Manila evidenced the movement and consolidation of transnational capital within these places, the regime presented squatters as obstructions to development. Living on desirable land along rivers and other waterways, squatters stalled the construction of airports, highways, and other public pathways.[75] In 1976, a US newspaper reported that "Mrs. Marcos outlined plans for cleaning up the city's 400 miles of clogged drainage canals—now covered with squatters—filling in 12,000 acres of Manila Bay for a new city and airport, and building nuclear and thermal power plants to make Manila self-sufficient in energy."[76] For Imelda Marcos, the appointed Governor of Metro Manila and Minister of Human Settlements, squatters presented an irreconcilable conflict for the "truth, beauty, and goodness" campaign that she used to justify the transformation of Manila into a new City of Man. In a speech that she delivered to the Rotary Club of Manila, she explained:

> When I took office, we felt three priority problems of Metropolitan Manila to be "a matter of survival." These were floods, which can lead to the city's decay and death; public transport and traffic, for productive movement and circulation; and garbage collection, for sanitation and beautification. It was our immediate view that other problems were secondary until we could relieve these three problems to insure the city's physical survival.... We had to move some of the squatters, which to some quarters is not a very popular

decision but then, is it fair that a few thousand should be privileged to usurp the esteros and inconvenience the lives of millions?[77]

While many have pointedly discussed the First Lady's investment in the transformation of Manila into a city of grand art and enterprise, this passage demonstrates that such a reconstruction significantly rests on an ideation of proper movement within the city itself.[78] By distinguishing the three most pressing problems plaguing Manila, she organized her agenda around a reimagination of the city's transit system, the modality by which people and things moved from one point to another. In doing so, she maintained the idea that squatters stood in direct contrast to such a plan and that the very act of squatting defined efforts to "usurp" and seize these important pathways from the general public. According to the First Lady, these shantytowns were breeding grounds for disease and crime and threatened the social order of the country. Their containment, in turn, would bring Manila closer to its realization as the City of Man to become, once again, "the crown of a *moving* country" (emphasis added). Imploring the Rotary Club to consider the imperativeness of her campaign, she warned that "your city . . . is your image." Marcos's attempt to revitalize movement within the city not only reframed squatters in opposition to her beautification program but also delimited mobility as a privilege afforded to those who worked on behalf of the nation—not against it. This mobility, organized by infrastructural reform and sanctioned by legal restrictions on the utilization of space, drew from a temporal-spatial model of interconnectedness that synchronized the city with the circulation and movement of global capital.

In another instance, writer Francisco Robles published an article titled "Manila without Madness" in a 1972 issue of *Focus Magazine*, another regime-mediated publication, in which he surmised:

> What is perhaps one of the biggest improvements in the physical aspect of the city under martial law is the uprooting of the squatter areas. Within one month after the President declared martial law throughout the country, practically all the squatter colonies in the city had been cleared away and their inhabitants relocated elsewhere. . . . Many of the squatter colonies thrived along the esteros of the city, which factor aggravated the flood problem in Manila. Now that these obstructions had been removed, the dredging and clearing of the esteros have picked up pace and it will not be long before these esteros are again useful adjuncts of the city, not only as a drainage system, but also as a commercial waterway.[79]

Robles celebrated the removal of squatters from along the estuaries of Manila as the solution for reinvigorating the ebb and flow of the city's transit and exchange system. Underlying this assumption was a projected cartography for mediating the movement of goods and people and the demarcation of the population that needed to be removed from this terrain. Against the squatter's supposed parasitic dependence on public land and proclivity for hindering the path of transit, the implementation of EO No. 381 and LO No. 19 epitomized the rhetoric with which the airport not only crafted a distinct kind of mobility based on productive movement but also rendered squatter life practices incommensurable with Philippine modernization.

Modernization under Marcos was outlined by efforts to resolve these contradictions, especially by framing the ubiquity of squatter camps as detrimental to Philippine modernity—not its effect. With LO No. 19, the squatter was subject to immediate removal based on the authority's designation of property for the purpose of airport construction and the presumption of the rightful ownership of that property. As legality depended on this claim to property, ownership also determined the right to count and be counted as a legitimate member of the political body within the juridical framework of the state. Where LO No. 19 positioned the state as the rightful owner of the land, EO No. 381 marked it for the rehabilitation, improvement, and expansion of the airport. These mandates prefigured the path and trajectory of movement as a method for affording to those not living within the nation the opportunities to lay claim to it.

The mandates that governed both the balikbayan and the squatter used transnational mobility to define the structure of the Filipino polity. As the regime relocated squatter encampments throughout Metro Manila, they also designated the proper usage of space as that which encouraged transnational investment. A 1981 *Balikbayan Magazine* article reported that "President Marcos pledged to overseas Filipinos that he will personally see to it that changes in the Constitution would be made to accommodate the Pinoys' desire to once more enjoy the right to own real estate in the country of their birth."[80] The following year, Ferdinand Marcos signed into law a measure that allowed balikbayans to own land in the Philippines for "residential purposes."[81] The Marcoses' promulgation of "home" treated Filipino transmigrants of the 1970s and 1980s as actors who played a critical role in the affairs of the country they had physically left but to which they remained tied. Filipino "transmigrants" were encouraged to invest in "development-type projects at 'home.'" These mandates "defin[ed] migrants as legally and ideologically an important part of the nation-state."[82] The balikbayan right to return was organized by his access both to real estate and special privileges in the Philippines and to the permanence of citizenship, all of which facilitated his ability to traverse the boundaries of the nation. These definitions of belonging provided the language with which to articulate squatters in opposition to the Marcoses' political agenda even as they resided within the nation. The regime's declarations of squatters as the literal and figurative clogs to the cultivation of Metro Manila as a global center for trade and culture invested not only in the promise of consistent movement within the Philippine metropolis but especially in the mandate that the Filipino be consistently moving outside it, a directive that has continued to shape the Filipino condition within national and international politics.

Statements like those of the First Lady and Robles—especially that your city is your image—demonstrate the inseparability of Manila from a reconstitution of the shape of Filipino subjectivity during martial law. As she encouraged the members of the Rotary Club to equate the productiveness of Manila with the condition of their subjectivities, she articulated Filipinoness as always already transnational. The elimination of squatter colonies was never only a matter of their removal from the property of the state alone but a strategy for determining the contours of Filipino subjectivity within a new Philippine nationalism shaped by a racial cold war. Imelda Marcos's and Fernando Robles's articulation of the squatter meets Mascardo's conceptualization of the airport crook and Quintos's description of the peddlers and beggars here to frame them all as taking from the nation rather than contributing to it. Squatters' insistence, according to both officials, on stalling movement—whether this was the movement of vacationing Filipinos or that directed by public waterways—attempted to steal from the nation by inhibiting its capacity to facilitate financial transactions and participate fully within the international and multinational market.

When Imelda Marcos, in her speech to the Rotary Club, argued that squatter colonies needed to be eradicated from the city as a way to reinvigorate its productivity, she ultimately argued that the vulgarity of squatter life lay in its tenacity to remain stubbornly embedded to the crevices of the abstracted structures of Manila's imagined future. And when Francisco Robles argued that squatters must be removed to an unnamed elsewhere, he spoke precisely to the force of squatter resistance to spur the authoritarian government to contend with the irresolvable elements of Manila in the face of worldwide modernization—that is, the incommensurability of Philippine life to global integration. This logic legitimized the exclusion of squatters from the national imaginary and, more importantly, defined progress as the cultivation of private ownership and the reproduction of capital.

Squatter life practices—the work to make home of nothing and everything, the necessity to stop anywhere and everywhere, the imperative to scavenge and steal—were characterized by a precarity produced by the contradictory logic of development within the New Society, between the promise of progress, on the one hand, and the materiality of racialized and classed disavowal and dispossession, on the other. Alberto Languido, discussing the reasons he migrated with his family from Cebu to Metro Manila, explained that "here, at least, he is able to scavange [sic] when he cannot find work on the docks."[83] Squatters used their exclusion from the New Society to generate nondevelopmental models for land reallocation and self-determination. Michael Pante notes that "the regime's 'strong arm and inhuman tactics' produced the opposite effect: urban poor communities organized themselves and created alliances with the religious, student, and other sectors to defend their rights."[84] Marcos's housing policies "gradually created the conditions for the emergence of a landless urban class whose social identity became increasingly tied to the land issue."[85] In 1982, "residents of Freedom Village in Libus [sic], just outside Manila, set up barricades and threatened to fight Government men carrying out orders to demolish their homes on land near the Capitol Golf Course and Country Club. To guard their compound, squads of men built a five-foot-deep trap filled with sharpened bamboo sticks and barbed wire. Negotiations postposed the demolition."[86]

Organizations like Ugnayan, which formed to resist state encroachment on squatter communities, described the Marcos administration's program for development as "'diametrically opposed to ours.'"[87] In this way, squatters enacted other forms of relation that tied their subjectivity to the redistribution of land rather than to abstracted notions of citizenship that deliberately excluded them. Holding their ground next to the Philippine country club, squatter communities actively resisted demolition by stalling capital's overgrowth, as Imelda Marcos had warned in her 1976 speech. By creating traps constructed of scavenged material, squatters not only sought to stop the demolition of their homes and their eventual dislocation but also to aggressively resist the reallocation of urban space for the purposes of egregious development, what Tadiar has described as the "solid, cleaned-up, timeless social edifice of the New Society."[88] In doing so, they arranged formations of personhood and well-being that resisted the mandates for private ownership bolstered by the Marcoses' narrow propagations of subjectivity.

Unlike Quintos's singular balikbayan traveler who navigated and lamented the modernization of Escolta against what it once was, squatters emerged and resisted according to the materiality of the space itself.

Without any claim to property, squatters' elision from state recognition inspired the formation of collectivities that could be positioned against governmental reforms. Fearing that squatter encampments served as hotbeds for leftist insurgents with ties to the Communist Party of the Philippines, the Marcos administration moved to quell any instances of resistance. In 1985, US newspapers reported that demolition crews backed by Philippine marines killed Segundino Sanchez, the teenage son of a squatter couple, along with an unnamed twelve-year-old girl. The funeral procession turned into a protest march.[89] Blurring the lines between a ceremony for the dead and a fight for the living, the marchers illuminated the ways that state policies rendered squatter lives meaningless against development. Simultaneously absented by the New Society and existing everywhere throughout the City of Man, the protest constructed an alternative rendition of life rooted in the conditions of the present rather than in the projection of future possibility. In doing so, it rejected the enunciations of subjectivity advocated by the Marcoses within the New Society. This conceptualization of self-determination took shape outside the modes of identification named by state nationalism: it stood against the first couple's projection of self-autonomy as an abstract condition and moved toward a project of solidarity against the authoritarian regime. Squatter resistance illustrated a type of lifemaking that centered practices for survival and self-articulation conceived against liberal definitions of personhood that cohered around ownership and transnational mobility.[90]

Squatter resistance articulated a disinvestment in state recognition within civil society. Squatters—often a catchall category that encompassed informal settlers and "day laborers, the unemployed, ex-convicts, alcoholics ... in the grim huddle of gray one-room hovels made of scrap"—engendered affinities based not on a New Society yet to come but on the immediacy and the materiality of daily survival.[91] Squatter protests, which wielded wooden stakes and barbed wire to fend off officials and used the dead to highlight the conditions of the living, constructed lifeworlds outside the modalities of belonging spearheaded by the regime's constricting articulations of humanity. In other words, squatters expressed forms of subjectivity that were incommensurable with authoritarian valuations.

Aurora Labasbas asked of the government as it threatened to remove her from her home: "'Why are we Filipinos out here, way out here, when those foreigners are in Manila in those big new hotels, in those big new buildings?'"[92] In doing so, Labasbas offered a different version of Filipino subjectivity not merely separate from but antagonistic to the Marcoses' animation of national identity. Labasbas named Filipinoness as the informal settlements themselves: the impoverished, the nameless, the evicted, and the uncontainable. Weaving Filipino subjectivity away from individualized forms of recognition and toward collective articulations of illegality and poverty, Labasbas identified Filipinoness less as national identity and more as a politics of condition.

Squatters do not name the balikbayan's obverse but, rather, point to the historical and political circumstances that had to exist in order to make legible the configuration of the balikbayan. For the regime, the balikbayan embodied the promise of transforming diasporic longing and unceasing transnational ties into capital. The administration invested in the construction of the balikbayan as an indisputable member of the nation and a critical agent in the success of the New Society. As such, the balikbayan could be incorporated into the imagined community of a new Philippines while remaining independent of its resources. The fulfillment of the balikbayan as a new mode of identification reveals the Philippine state's investment in the production of a subjectivity that cohered around the terms of the racial cold war. The interrogation of the formation of the balikbayan as a form of modernized subjectivity *in relation* to the squatter of Metro Manila is an exploration of this subjectivity as having enabled (and doing so still) a set of relationships and practices that created political frameworks for displacement and dispossession. The conditions that made recognizable post-1965 Filipino immigrants in the United States as balikbayans not only affirmed the state as the guarantor of political legibility but also cited national recognition itself as a rightful end in the journey toward global modernization.

The balikbayan illuminates the kinds of Filipino American configurations that materialized at the intersections of a racial cold war, where immigration reform and urban development functioned as means for consolidating transnational investments in movement and modernization. The advent of immigration reform realized with the passage of the Hart-Cellar Act in 1965 provided the narrative for acknowledging immigrants from formerly colonized nations as important contributors to upholding US versions of racial pluralism. For the Philippines under Marcos, the advent of the New Society was a medium for reclaiming Filipino subjectivity as the locus of a new politics of modernization, a response to continuous efforts to cultivate a decolonial nationalism that could outgrow its neocolonial reliance on the United States during a period that promoted the materialization of new forms of national sovereignty. The balikbayan became a receptacle of transnational anxieties, his mobility serving as testament to the possibilities that reform and development afforded. At the same time, ongoing political and social turmoil in both the United States and the Philippines spoke to the incapacity of this type of subjectivity to address the multiple forms of marginalization and subjugation enabled by Cold War conflict and its attendant transnational alliances. The Marcos regime's celebration of mobility as fundamental to development set the groundwork for a labor export system—one that would gain strength after Marcos's exile—that would systematically move Filipino labor migrants outside the nation as it solidified their economic ties to the nation itself. The interrogation of the balikbayan as a modernized subjectivity that I present here not only cautions against the lure of representative national politics that leads to state recognition; it also speaks to the kinds of politics that subjectivity forecloses and the types of historical forgetting that it enables.

THREE. THE NEW FILIPINA MELODRAMA

In February 1969, the Philippine Women's University (PWU) conferred onto First Lady Imelda Marcos an honorary doctorate. In her acceptance speech, Marcos introduced to the audience the figure of the New Filipina, whom she lauded as a "new ideal of Filipina womanhood."[1] According to Marcos, the New Filipina constituted both a modern sensibility and a penchant for tradition. She was, in other words, a "woman of the times, equipped intellectually and culturally to meet its challenges" as well as "the daughter of those ancient Filipino women who long before the strangers came to these shores worked side by side with their husbands... the kind of woman Rizal eulogized in his letter to the women of Malolos."[2] This feminine ideal, argued the First Lady, heralded an important compromise between a Western feminism that haughtily proposed independence from men and a Filipino feminism that acknowledged women as natural "mother[s] and housekeeper[s]." With this pronouncement of the New Filipina, Marcos encouraged women to invest in national development alongside men and take seriously their irreplaceable role in sustaining the Filipino family and home.

Among her multiple roles during her husband's presidential administration, Imelda Marcos served as the first chair of the National Commission on the Role of Filipino Women (NCRFW), a committee tasked with identifying and addressing the barriers to women's full participation in national affairs. By the late 1970s the NCRFW functioned as a political body that promoted the full integration of Filipina women into programs for development and modernization. The New Filipina emerged as a configuration that held historical and political tensions about women's place within discourses of national modernization and whose recognition revealed international concerns about women's subordination and gender inequality. Distinguishing the New Filipina as a non-Western formation, the First Lady assigned to the feminine the work of "life giving." Life giving articulated the reproductive labor of care, and it functioned as a point of access for sanctioning UN and US development projects within the Philippines. Engaging emerging discourses of women's empowerment, the New Filipina offered a new subjectivity that simultaneously bore the investments of national sovereignty while encouraging women's differential and often violent inclusion into the global economy.[3] The configuration of the New Filipina by the regime during the period buttressed a nascent labor export program that even in its early iterations would shape state labor programs for decades to follow.[4]

In the latter portion of the chapter, I read celebrated Philippine filmmaker Lino Brocka's 1976 film *Insiang* against the administration's framework of women's rights. Positioning family not as the location of belonging but as a site of multistate power, the film unmakes the New Filipina configuration by tracing the transformation of family drama into family dissolution, directing attention to the life conditions of poor Filipina women under martial law and regimes of global development. Placing Manila's slums in contrast to Insiang's beauty, the film treats beauty not as a universal fact but as an analytic for outlining the intimacies of racialized and gendered violence. In contradistinction to the Marcoses' use of a heterosexual romance narrative to pronounce proper articulations of gender and sexuality, Brocka's use of social realism and melodrama offers a language for imagining alternative lifeways beyond the regime's configurations of Filipino subjectivity.

THE ROMANCE OF "MALAKAS AT MAGANDA"

The Marcoses' public romance narrated a tale of national unification, wherein the president and First Lady played distinct roles within a gendered division of labor that provided a didacticism for advancing the regime's objectives for modernization. If Ferdinand Marcos was rational, virile, and heroic, Imelda Marcos was his perfect counterpart, the "Archetypal Woman," graceful, charming, and undeniably feminine.[5] The president's version of masculinity reinforced his strongman persona and justified his rule: he circulated tales of his bravery during World War II and evidenced his virility with stories of his many women admirers.⁶ The First Lady displayed her beauty as public spectacle, employing what Christine Bacareza Balance describes as *palabas* (the theatrics of song and affect) in her quest to illustrate both her provincial roots, connection to the masses, and her complementariness to Marcos's capable leadership.⁷ As the country's "Adam and Eve," the pair symbolized the coupling of different regions of the archipelago (the president was from Ilocos Norte and the First Lady from Leyte), the resolution of political conflict, and the realization of national unity.⁸ Through their heterosexual romance, the Marcoses staged a singularity and wholeness that emblematized a racial and sexual purity through which a new Filipino nation might emerge. Such articulations of raciality, as I describe in the previous chapters, promised to overcome notions of Filipino abjection, the "defeatism, sloth, and self-deprecation" Marcos cautioned was often ascribed to Filipinos.⁹ The two referred to themselves as "Malakas at Maganda"—the Strong and the Beautiful—the human embodiment of these virtues sprung from a bamboo tree and divinely chosen to usher the country into a new era of national greatness. Romance structured the fantasy of national unity, and the Marcoses' performance of it offered a vehicle through which a public audience might engage its fictions. As Malakas at Maganda positioned the Marcoses as father and mother of the nation, they demanded the cohesion of a national family comprising an extended kinship of citizens that would be beholden to the administration.

Such articulations of kinship positioned the nation as the familial body to which Filipinos were required to offer their loyalties. Widening the bounds of family in this way, the Marcoses' public image attempted to permeate the divide between the public and private dimensions of Filipinos' lives. Their presentation of themselves as such strove to access and activate Filipino preconceptions and familiarities with the family as the basic unit of political organization.¹⁰ At the same time, the Marcoses practiced this kinship through a cronyism that consolidated capital and power in the hands of a select few. Mina Roces describes this inextricable dynamic between family and nation as "not fixed, immutable laws" but one that operates through "symbolic messages, discourses used by individuals in the ideological context of political relations and political actions."¹¹

Throughout the Cold War period, US narratives about family often reflected cultural anxieties about race, sexuality, and reproduction. Daniel Patrick Moynihan's 1965 treatise, *The Negro Family: The Case for National Action*, attempted to situate African American families within an objective empiricism that pathologized Black genders and sexualities. Framing the

Black family as innately dysfunctional, the report vilified Black life and reaffirmed white heterosexuality as the model of heteronormative kinship. Crystal Mun-hye Baik, moreover, has studied the ways that the Korean War and the continuity of militarization on the peninsula continued to shape the formation of the Korean diaspora in the United States. Baik's notion of chrononormativity describes the "migrant subject's wholesale assimilation into the American(ized) heterosexual family and multiracial national citizenry."[12] These narratives about family and reproduction reveal the contradictions that outlined the moral liberalism that guided US Cold War discourses.[13] New narratives of rectification and inclusion, while seeking to address perceived wrongs, maintained, if not strengthened, the rigidity of normative categories of race and sexuality by permitting the nation's racialized and sexualized others to enter its rhetoric of belonging. As a US framework of inclusion, family served as a mode of governance for redrawing once again the stakes of citizenship around American exceptionalism and heterosexual reproduction.[14]

Yet family also served as a transnational Cold War mode of organization that disciplined gender and sexuality outside the United States. With the story of Malakas at Maganda, the First Lady's beauty emerged as her most striking characteristic and defined the role of the feminine within the authoritarian regime. Unlike past First Ladies, Imelda Marcos "came across as a striking presence—tall and youthful in her formal gowns, generously granting requests for songs."[15] The young Ferdinand Marcos was instantly captivated by the former beauty queen, and the gravitas of her presence became his "secret weapon" on his presidential campaign, holding the attention of distinguished statesmen from around the world.[16] Beauty often marks women as sites of national signification. Denise Cruz has discussed the importance of the figure of the beautiful mestiza Maria Clara as an instantiation of an emerging Filipino national identity near the end of the Spanish colonial period. On the other hand, Roces points to the importance of the beauty queen during the US colonial period for expressing both patriarchal control over women and also the rise of new roles of national service for Filipina women. She writes that the beauty queen "typif[ied] the ambivalent modern woman of the times."[17] In such instances, Filipina womanhood did not merely symbolize Philippine nationalism; beauty as a virtue *communicated* the promise of the nation. The difference here between the stagnancy of the symbol and the fluidity of communication underscores beauty as the gendered labor of expression for articulating universalist ideals of fraternity and sovereignty in the service of emergent nationalisms.

Writer Quijano de Manila, reporting on the Marcoses' political career in campaign years and early years of the administration, observed that while "not so long ago all [Imelda Marcos] was noted for was her beauty," "the awe is [now] armored with a hard qualifier, like the *iron* to *butterfly*."[18] The shift that Quijano de Manila describes marks a certain end of political innocence and points to the transformation of "beautiful" as mere marker of the First Lady's aesthetic appeal to her *use* of beauty as a political tool. Even as the First Lady articulated beauty as an abstraction, she often weaponized it as the force behind development programs. As Governor of Metro Manila, Minister of Human Settlements, and Patroness of the Arts, Marcos used beauty to guide her speculation and investment. In the previous chapter, I discussed her attempt to transform Manila into a new "City of Man": she directed massive sanitation programs and construction projects to rid the city of its "human garbage," its refuse and waste, and its general unseemliness.[19] Marcos's identification of Manila's squalor as inherently ugly mandated its eradication in the name of beauty and modernization. As these measures aimed to increase productivity by targeting its most unproductive and nonproductive parts for expulsion to make room for multinational finance, Marcos made beauty inextricable from the accumulation of capital.[20]

In 1974, the Marcoses hosted the Miss Universe contest in the newly constructed Folk Arts Theater in the CCP complex.[21] While the event itself aimed to garner corporate and tourist capital by bringing the international event to the archipelago, its celebration of beauty employed normative ideas about gender and sexuality in the service of Manila's modernization. Three months before the pageant, the *New York Times* spotlighted Manila's tourist scene, describing the city as "hold[ing] the largest concentration of beautiful women in the world," indeed, Manila's "natural resource" and "capital asset."[22] Just as enticing as its beauty queens, the author surmises, are the "water fountains and flower beds" of the old walled city of Intramuros, the reproductions housed in the Nayong Filipino museum, the "Manila Hilton ... an elegant blend of Philippine marble, woodcarvings, shell-inlaid furniture and Western hotel expertise," the restaurants "as diverse as the city," the nightclubs filled with "sultry singing and the rhythmic dance music," and shopping that caters specifically to tourists. As far as beauty is a consumable feminized object, the article claims, it is also an instrument for articulating value.[23] It was not only that the pageant offered a cultural and performative spectacle of the First Lady's ideologies. The event signaled a refinement of such ideology as a mechanism for organizing race, gender, space, and money.

Beauty marked the division of labor that assembled what Primitivo Mijares has described as the Marcoses' "conjugal dictatorship," wherein the First Lady performed the immaterial labor of activating and operating beauty.[24] In other words, beauty no longer only signified a set of inherent qualities; rather, it functioned as an instrument for transforming aestheticism into the *feel* of modernity. Vernadette Vicuña Gonzalez has described this as a "social feeling or 'setting the mood' for and of domination."[25] Moreover, in her theorization of beauty as biopower for maximizing life during times of war, Mimi Thi Nguyen describes beauty as "an important site of signification, power, and knowledge about how to live."[26] The feeling of modernity articulates the underlying sentiments attached to US Cold War discourses about international cooperation, the important cultural strain that was imperative for imaging and capitalizing on the saturation of Asia within the US imagination. Marcos often used beauty as a method of instruction for training the masses to develop what they did not have or had little opportunity to exercise.

In her speech at the Philippine Women's University, Imelda Marcos explained that the New Filipina will, "because she is a woman, find time, even if it is her leisure time, to be concerned with what is beautiful. She will encourage it in every form.... She will see that beauty is necessary for the soul of the nation, that it is not by bread alone that man lives."[27] Marcos advised that it was not enough for the New Filipina to be beautiful; she must also employ her beauty as a service. She must be "down to earth, practical, and industrious."[28] As Marcos equated womanhood with beauty and beauty with productivity, she distinguished women's work as the nourishment of the Filipino soul, the other half of the work of national development. This New Filipina was responsible for communicating the ideals of "sympathy, tenderness, compassion and love."[29] Marcos implored women to lay claim to the affective work of nurturing the human spirit, the labor necessary for spurring national progress, and assigned the feminine to serve as the guiding force for distinguishing the beautiful from the repulsive, the true from the deceptive, and the good from the evil. The feminine bridged the divide between the antiquated and the modern, the past and the present, and underlined the living labor necessary for generating value from the previously invaluable. As Marcos identified the true, good, and beautiful as intrinsic to an uncorrupted humanity, the production and practice of such ideals within the Philippines became imperative for instilling within Filipinos the sensibilities of modernity.

Referring to the Filipina woman as "the eternal mother to man," Marcos identified "life giving" as the work of beauty, the reproductive labor that sutured women's intrinsic roles as mothers and caretakers to the materialization of national development. Within this reorganization of familial kinship, care operated as the affective register for rearticulating women's relationship to the New Society. Womanhood, according to the First Lady, was rooted in "that tiny word, that slender syllable, *help*" and is "of its very nature ... a giving." While Marcos's pronouncement of the "new" Filipina promised an unprecedented role for women, similar past declarations heralded critical political shifts in Philippine nationalist politics. Marcos's New Filipina speech drew from past constructions of Filipina femininity that often advanced discourses about women's place in the nation as ways to mediate national anxieties. The changing formations of Filipina subjectivity articulated the upheavals and movements of colonialism, war, nation-building, state formation, and migration. For the regime, the New Filipina became a mechanism for translating the shift from the postwar economy of reconstruction and isolation to that of export-oriented neoliberalism. The work of the New Filipina was not simply to serve or to be in the service of others but also to generate economic possibility for the nation. The sophistication of the regime's efforts to construct the New Filipina lay in its articulation of Filipina women's subjectivity as inextricably tied to the labor of care and especially in the configuration of her subjectivity as exhaustively generative for the nation. As the regime aimed to define women's role within the international economic order, the logic of modernization reset the shape of women's empowerment through an expansiveness the size of the globe.

    Feminist scholars of labor and migration have pointed to the institutionalization of labor export from the Philippines as the force behind the fragmentation of the traditional family unit. Within the multitiered structure of global domesticity, Filipina women serve as domestic laborers for women from the United States, western Europe, and West, East, and Southeast Asia while poor Filipina women in the Philippines sustain the households of overseas Filipina workers while they work as nannies and maids abroad. Rhacel Salazar Parreñas has written that "the international transfer of caretaking is a distinct form of the international division of labor in which Filipina domestic workers perform the reproductive labor or the 'private sphere' responsibilities of class-privileged women in industrialized countries as they leave other women in the Philippines to perform their own."[30] Yet such conceptualization of fragmentation as an effect of Filipina women's reproductive labor redeploys family as an uncontested mode of organization rather than its ongoing use as a mechanism for the extraction of women's care work well before the Marcos era.[31] Such understandings of gendered work assume the disruption of an otherwise properly functioning civil society. Instead, it is important to note that the cohesion and coherence of new subjectivities like the overseas Filipina domestic worker were themselves a consequence of the development of labor export policies under the regime's cronyism and politics of beauty. The recognition of the Filipina as such articulated modernity through the expansive possibilities precipitated by gendered labor and tied the Philippines to the multidirectional circuits of the transnational economy.

"Life giving" labor not only symptomizes the "subjugated" Philippine position within modern circuits of globalization. More significantly, it pinpoints the regime's calculated arrangement of a gendered subjectivity that guaranteed the transformation of Filipina women's position within a new postcolonial international order increasingly defined by neoliberal dictums. Life giving denotes a liberal feminist "agency" with which the regime repositioned Filipina women as the subject of Philippine sovereignty and away from the object of colonial domesticity. In his postulations on affective labor, Michael Hardt makes the distinction between Michel Foucault's theory of biopower as sovereign power from above to create life and the immaterial gendered labor as power from below to create forms of subjectivity, society, and sociality.[32] Hardt's delineation between "affective labor, the production and reproduction of life" and "the production of affects, subjectivities, and terms of life" identifies possible modes of liberation inherent in this distinction.[33] Life giving addresses the gap that Hardt identifies, making indistinguishable immaterial labor from the terms of women's belonging within the New Society, where value is extracted precisely in the recognition of this subjectivity within the global market. Parreñas notes that Filipino women constituted 75 percent of the labor force in export processing zones by the early 1980s and more than half of international migrants by the 1990s.[34] The statistics are staggering; and the issue here is not only that Filipina women have performed an unequal proportion of the world's reproductive labor but also that the immaterial labor of life giving structured Filipina women's global recognition according to its potential value. That is, "Filipina domestic workers" must be contextualized as a social formation that emerged precisely alongside the regime's articulations of sovereignty and the broader mechanisms of multistate liberalism that defined the economic mandates for postcolonial modernization.

What does recognition, in other words, obscure in its insistence on acknowledgment? Outside these terms, who and what is forgotten? Writing in the context of Taiwan's state feminism and sexual politics, Naifei Ding has theorized that state feminism's denouncement of sex workers strives "to outcast 'unrecognizable' forms of parasitic lives and operations—such as those of the prostitutes movement, and those of feminists who do not primarily align or work with housewives, but rather with marginal sexual and other inferior class/caste positions."[35] Ding's postulations here call into question the dualistic framework that structures Taiwan's state feminism's conceptualization of a women's movement only through the political possibility of state power. Ding's challenge to the "imaginary boundaries of 'the' women's movement and issues" contests the epistemological and political investment in the frame that delineates a singular women's movement. It insists that any invocation of women as such yield more critical analyses of the "asymmetry" that constitutes its pronouncement.

In the context of Filipina domestic workers, a singular focus on the determination of the processes that have facilitated massive outward migration risks foreclosing an interrogation of the terms of recognition that structure political possibility within state power and the global economy. While the pronouncement of the Filipina domestic worker betrays its own intellectual and political imperatives, its coherence already connotes a set of temporalities, locations, and other assumptions that themselves must be constantly unmade. The regular deployment of the Filipina domestic worker emerges from the Marcos regime's capitalization on the global recognition of Filipina women's subjectivity. The regime's recognition of women through the work of life giving justified women's inclusion into the global economy as service workers while eliding other forms of feminized labor structured by imperialist investments in the US militarization of the Philippines. Alongside the steady rise of Filipina domestic workers outside the Philippines, new sexual economies proliferated through transpacific military collaborations. Jin-kyung Lee has outlined the trajectory of South Korean development as inextricable to the import of sexualized labor, writing that "the import of military sex workers, mostly Filipina and Russian women, into South Korea began in the mid-1990s, in many ways following the precedent of Okinawa, where the demand for sex and sexualized labor had begun to be met by Filipinas since the mid-1970s. The South Korean state assisted in importing women by making legal provisions available."[36] The transpacific trajectory that Lee names here charts the development of US Cold War military occupation not only through strategic military offensives but also as the shifts from colonial to postcolonial policies that materialized through women's sexual labor. From Okinawa to South Korea, Lee identifies Filipina women's sexual labor as the currency for political exchange between Asian nations under modernity. Further, while the regime celebrated the role of Filipina women within the New Society, officials in Olongapo, Subic Bay, made women's sexual labor invisible by insisting on recording their professions as "hostesses" rather than as "prostitutes."[37] The term designated women's sex work as imperative for facilitating congenial transactions between the US military and the Philippine state. It also imposed a tenor of individual will onto Filipinas' sexual labor even as ongoing military partnerships helped to create Olongapo's infrastructure. Such euphemistic language rearticulated the continuity of US occupation through a paradigm of women's self-determination. An interrogation of life giving not only betrays the expansive circuits of Filipina labor but also reframes the recognition of Filipina domestic and sex workers as configurations of the racial cold war.

"WOMEN'S RIGHTS" AS GENDER EQUALITY

In the summer of 1975, Imelda Marcos and twelve other delegates from the Philippines attended the International Women's Year (IWY) conference in Mexico City, heralded as the first meeting of its kind. The Philippine delegation, composed largely of women holding administrative positions in politics, law, and education, joined thousands of representatives from around the world to address the most urgent issues facing women.[38] In an opening plenary speech at the conference, the First Lady relayed to her audience the story of Malakas at Maganda. Similar to yet departing from the biblical story of Adam and Eve, Marcos explained, the Philippines has "another story of the genesis." She advised: "It is said that the birth of humanity came about when a divine intent split a single bamboo and from it sprang forth simultaneously a man and a woman. The woman was called Maganda, meaning beautiful, and the man was called Malakas, meaning strong. They were equal in their own way, the strong and the beautiful, and they have been equal ever since."[39] In the Report of the World Conference of the International Women's Year, published the following year, IWY officials reflected on the program as an extension of the broader United Nations mission for global justice.[40] Framing the absence of "women's rights" around the world as "incompatible with human dignity," the report explained that gender *equality* was inextricably tied to human rights. Here the report defined human rights through accords such as the "Universal Declaration of Human Rights, the Declaration on the Granting of Independence to Colonial Countries and

Peoples, the International Development Strategy for the Second United Nations Development Decade, and the Declaration and Programme of Action for the Establishment of a New International Economic Order based on the Charter of Economic Rights and Duties of States."[41] The report stated:

> Since the integral development of the personality of the woman as a human being is directly connected with her participation in the development process as mother, worker and citizen, policies should be developed to promote the co-ordination of these different roles of the woman so as to give the most favourable conditions for the harmonious development of her personality—an air which is equally relevant to the development of man.[42]

Human rights established international cooperation as the telos of decolonization. Declaring women's rights human rights, the report identified gendered difference only to submerge it within an articulation of a universalist humanity.[43] The report reified a definition of humanity that relied on Western conceptions of the human grounded on the colonial and imperialist logic of post–World War II liberalism.[44] Randall Williams, writing of the critique of international human rights organizations propounded by the Ejército Zapatista de Liberación Nacional (Zapatista Army of National Liberation) in Mexico, explains that human rights as such underscores a "violence ... figured through the ideological-material practices of elimination whose logic emanates from the privileging of economic productivity."[45] The report articulated difference through a dualistic conception of gender that reaffirmed the position of Western humankind as the ideal form of political subjectivity against which women's rights must be evaluated, extolling Western humankind as the origin of being rather than as the vehicle of colonial violence.[46] As the report pointed to the Declaration as the primordial figuration of postwar justice, it also used the ideological boundaries of the Universal Declaration as the realm of possibility for imagining the scope of women's rights. The postwar pronouncements of modernity that outlined these decrees of postwar reconstruction shaped the scope of "women's equality."

As the report expressed equality as the capacity of women to fully participate in the development of their respective societies—and the absence of equality as their inability to do so—it defined women's self-determination through the rationality of production. In this sense, women's rights adjudicated progress by relying on a schema of productivity outlined by the mandates of global capital. Even as the report sought to rectify the "problem" of difference, it positioned women's political representation squarely within the framework of intelligibility afforded by these instantiations of national sovereignty, international cooperation, and global finance. Connecting the advancement of "equality between the sexes" to a more sustained quest for worldwide collaboration, the report addressed not the history and political intricacy of gendered subordination but, instead, generated the strictures for the liberal governance of "women" within the UN-led paradigms of international integration.

"Women's rights" produced a category of women that provided the instruction for including gender within the schema of international reorganization. Jocelyn Olcott has detailed the ways that the IWY meeting expressed a culmination of US-Soviet struggles over the attention of the Third World, especially through the contention over the theme of the conference—between development and peace, on the one hand, and racism and self-determination, on the other.[47] The report's promulgation of an uncontested enunciation of who and what constituted *women* obfuscated the consistent tensions that underscored the meeting, advancing, instead, a universalist conception of women that ordered a distinct set of mandates for her protection and inclusion into national frameworks. Indeed, women as a universalist category articulated gendered difference as a matter of exclusion and gender equality as one of inclusion. Such notions set the bounds of self-determination as women's participation in international programs for development. In her study of the intersections between women's rights and human rights, Julietta Hua has aptly articulated the contradictions of the "women's rights" paradigm:

> The trouble with categories like *human* and *woman* is that despite (or because of) their ambiguity, they nonetheless need to gesture to a particular way of being—a way of being that is always already prescribed at the conceptual moment of knowledge. At once referring to universality, concepts like *woman* convey a sameness and sharedness even while the category is itself defined through a particularity and difference from what it is not (man). This is the central paradox of human rights and global feminisms: such terms necessarily convey a particular set of definitions (sometimes multiple definitions) even while they imply nonparticularity and universality.[48]

As Hua argues, the report's attempt to universalize "women's issues" advanced a broad pronunciation of womanhood that made invisible the political maneuvers by which the category of woman functioned in specific postwar, postcolonial contexts.

The uncomplicated rendition of "women's issues" betrays both the histories of competing empires and, more importantly, the reimagination of empire within a new world order. A transpacific feminist analysis interrogates the proposed universality of "women's issues" during the period. As Denise Cruz explains, the critical attention paid to the transpacific constitutes an admission "that U.S. and European management of Asia and the Pacific Islands depended upon a constellation of intersecting strategies: military encroachment . . . epistemological endeavors . . . discursive representations in varied cultural forms . . . and geopolitical and economic measures that formalized European and U.S. power in the region."[49] This racial cold war—constituted by authoritarian governments and imperialist policies—often shaped localized articulations of women's empowerment.

Imperialist and masculinist aspirations for postwar sovereignty defined the terms of women's inclusion within postcolonial contexts. The recognition of women as such points to the construction of a new imperial benevolence whereby the postimperial society is reorganized for a new era of gender and sexual politics. The liberation of Japanese women from their patriarchal male counterparts, as Lisa Yoneyama has written, both evidenced the capacity of the United States to serve as the bearer of egalitarianism and legitimized the postwar demilitarization and reconstruction of Japan.[50] The US reconstruction of Japan into a demilitarized capitalist economy illuminates the overlapping arrangement of US hegemony, Japanese nationalism, and East Asian decolonization propelled by efforts to reclaim wounded Asian masculinities.[51] In the case of former "comfort women" forced into sexual slavery by the Japanese imperial army during World War II, the South Korean political struggle over the recognition of Japanese war crimes positioned women as a site of national reckoning. Grace Cho has discussed the *yanggongju* as both the object of South Korea's loathing and a figuration of its shame over centuries of Japanese and US colonialism. Cho thus points to the Korean sex worker as a configuration of both the colonial legacies of sexual violence and South Korea's postwar nationalism, a "figure that takes center stage in national and transnational scenes as she moves in and out of visibility."[52] The US drive to modernize South Korea in the wake of World War II in order to redirect it away from the remnants of Japanese colonialism and the perceived threat of North Korea organized a system of rapid industrialization within the country. Jin-kyung Lee's study of the gendered and sexualized labor that buttressed South Korean modernization reveals that the development of the country occurred simultaneously with the production of new sexual economies through military camp towns.

The "woman question" has long served as a critical site for staging the trajectory of national progress. The achievement of Filipino women's suffrage in 1937, for instance, articulated women's subjectivity through the ideals of republicanism proffered by US coloniality.[53] The advent of women's enfranchisement evidenced the success of the United States to materialize liberal democracy within Asia. Imelda Marcos's conception of women's empowerment rearticulated the historicity of gendered violence in the Philippines by propounding a singularized version of this empowerment. She relied on earlier liberal models of women's subjectivity even as she claimed to offer something new. For the Philippine delegation to the IWY conference, women's rights provided an avenue for negotiating the meanings of national sovereignty in the postwar, postcolonial period. Marcos used the IWY platform to advance a brand of Filipino feminism that sought to depart from what she described as a framework for women's rights that advocated a separation from men and relied on a Western ideology of individualism. In Marcos's estimation, the paradigm of equality propounded by the conference was inadequate for identifying the distinct struggles of Filipina women, whose lives were structured by the realities of a poverty unknown to most of the women of Western nations. She argued that "equality of status has no connection with reality. [Filipino women's] status is one [of] equal degradation with their men; theirs is an equal share in the struggle for bare survival."[54] Estafania Aldaba-Lim, head of the Philippine delegation, lauded the First Lady's opening plenary speech at the conference and described it as a "significant contribution to the ideology behind women's liberation which contrasts sharply with the issues which concern the feminist movement in highly developed countries."[55] Aldaba-Lim explained that Marcos's central argument that a "pro women" approach is not an "anti male" mandate "was repeated by the other Asian speakers like Prime Minister [of Sri Lanka] Banderanarke [sic] and Mrs. J Sadat of Egypt."[56] Delineating the specificity of the "Oriental woman and her mystique," Marcos believed that the Asian woman's "concept of equality transcends the individual and her personal prerogatives, ambitions and achievements" to share the national aims of her male counterparts to build a New Society.[57]

Cruz's study of Cold War Filipino literature showcases the ways that Filipinos presented the nation through and in opposition to the "unruly" Filipina, made modern by transpacific routes. She has noted that "one might recast patterns of patriarchal nationalism versus feminism . . . as discursively connected to the twofold oppositions that determined Cold War ideologies."[58] In the case of the New Filipina, the binary is not so stark: Marcos's feminist ideals advanced the patriarchal nationalism of the nation's Cold War agendas. Yet rather than presenting Filipina women as different from "Oriental" women and more allied with US women, as Cruz describes in her analysis of Filipina feminist writings in the earlier decades of the Cold War, Marcos's feminism strategically aligned itself as a racialized Asian feminism. Criticizing equality as an out-of-touch Western imposition and counterproductive to the realization of Philippine decolonization and modernization, Marcos advanced a cultural relativist feminism that identified the particularity of the Filipina woman's condition and rooted Filipina women's subjectivity within the investments of postcolonial sovereignty. Refusing equality as an end in itself, Marcos identified national development as the aim for which women's rights functioned. For Marcos, women's empowerment required a conceptualization of the distinct contributions that women must give to the national project, and these distinctions did not outline any deterministic articulation of gender but, rather, delineated the specificity of women's labor. Marcos's feminism attempted to iron out any contentions over the position of women in relation to Philippine modernity.

Citing the UN mandate to participate in international efforts for women's empowerment, Ferdinand Marcos issued Presidential Decree No. 633 six months before the IWY conference to create the National Commission on the Role of Filipino Women (NCRFW) as an "international action-program including short and long term measures aimed at achieving the integration of women as full and equal partners with men in the total development effort."[59] By 1975, the NCRFW listed as its major accomplishments the completion of drafts of presidential decrees ordering the deletion of discriminatory provisions in legal statutes and the amendment of labor provisions to include the fair treatment of women; the revision of sexist educational curricula; and the establishment of "more dynamic involvement" of rural women.[60] With regard to the latter, the First Lady's paradigm of women's empowerment centered on the "rural Filipina" as both the quintessential figure of Filipina femininity and a definitive example of gendered subjugation.

Indeed, the NCRFW focused its attention on the critical importance of the rural Filipina to the New Society. Imelda Marcos's 1975 UNESCO speech proclaimed that the rural Filipina is the "archetypal Filipina, with all her virtues of modesty, fidelity, fortitude and industry" and that a national plan needed to "[eradicate] the anachronistic demarcation line between city and country, *poblacion* and barrio."[61] Marcos identified the rural Filipina as the dividing line between the past and the present, an emblem of Philippine reality as well as its future, the perplexing figure of Philippine modernity. This divide calls attention to the postwar processes that centralized capital within Manila, effectively investing in its radical transformation as the country's urban center while intensifying the feudal political landscape of its countryside. Marcos's ahistorical rendition of such a divide not only facilitated a historical forgetting of the strategic positioning of the colonial Philippines within the United States' war of imperial expansion. It also positioned the rural Filipina as a medium for resolving the country's bifurcation. In many ways, the NCRFW orchestrated her reclamation in order to produce a victory over a historical past and herald a New Society.

In 1977, the NCRFW launched the Balikatan sa Kaunlaran program for the "more effective integration of women through coordination of government and organized private sector efforts to accelerate national development and maximize its benefits for all the people."[62] The project took special interest in the rural Filipina in the provinces outside urban Manila in regions such as Ifugao, Zambales, and Davao. The regime's interest in these locations was a deliberate and calculated attempt to recognize the "national minorities" and political dissidents they held, so that their saturation within modernization programs might also reorganize land for the purpose of strengthening export-oriented industries.[63] Balikatan sa Kaunlaran programs functioned as a biopolitics for producing life through the management of gendered work. "Knitting machines," guides for nutrition and conservation, and instruction for "effective motherhood" attempted to institute caretaking as the specialized work of rural Filipinas within the broader production of the Philippine national citizenry.[64] Marcos isolated the rural Filipina as a configuration of potential, a medium for bridging a gap between underdevelopment and modernization, and the regime imbued her subjectivity with possibility by consistently speculating on her value. Imelda Marcos's articulation of particularity is embodied here: as the premier figure of Filipina femininity, the rural Filipina as nourisher and caretaker operated as a vehicle for national productivity.

NCRFW programs managed the gender and sexuality of Filipino women—and rural Filipinas, in particular—through multistate collaborations in the racial cold war. "Family planning" programs underscored transnational measures for population control. The First Lady herself was a tireless advocate of family planning, describing it as "one of the pillars of the New Society, undertaken not because we want to protect the wealth of the few against the explosion of the poor, but undertaken because we do not want to condemn unborn generations to misery and servitude."[65] The NCRFW praised efforts in Bataan to officiate the "mass wedding of unmarried couples" and those in Cavite to organize programs for "effective motherhood."[66] In a 1978 meeting between US officials and the leaders of the Catholic Church in the Philippines, the Church accused US officials of forcibly sterilizing poor Filipina women. One bishop described population control measures as "a new form of colonialism."[67] While US officials declined the accusation, a report published by the Rand Corporation, a US-based research group, that detailed the findings of a Southeast Asia Development Advisory Group seminar identified family planning as an important tool for managing the rapid increase of the Filipino population and one that must work in tandem with agrarian reform to "assist the Philippine government in improving the well-being of its citizens."[68]

For the United States Agency for International Development (USAID), the urgency of population control was propelled by racialized discourses about the profligacy of colonial sexualities and guided by efforts to maintain the governability of the country.[69] As an arm of US foreign policy and its strategies of anticommunist containment and counterinsurgency in the Asia and the Pacific, USAID worked with national governments to manage international populations in areas of US interest as a way to maintain the political stability of those areas against threats deemed antithetical to US political and economic interests.[70] Thus deploying family planning pilot programs in the 1970s, USAID alongside the Philippines' Population Commission "construct[ed] population control ... as a solution to economic instability and geo-strategic threats to US hegemony."[71] Population control involved "incentive schemes" that included "leave with pay for sterilizations [and] cash incentives."[72] Along with land reform policies, these population control programs sought to quell rural unrest, thwart communist influence, and acquire the stability necessary to keep "Marcos ... in power more easily and to attract large foreign investments."[73]

The Rand report advised that USAID work in strategic cooperation with the US military to leverage military base renewal negotiations between the Philippine and US governments in an effort to persuade Marcos to abide by US recommendations for population control and agrarian reform.[74] While the report ultimately illuminated the inefficacy of the Marcos regime and its lack of "political will" to produce lasting positive change in the country, its affirmation of such schemas of modernization betrayed the imperialist logic of US expansion. Its indictment of the Marcos administration relied less on an acknowledgment of corruption and more on its incapacity to abide by the strategic terms of US foreign policy. The NCRFW's paradigm of "effective motherhood," which strove to inculcate "efficiency" within the rural Filipina, underlines the regime's work to cultivate women's subjectivity along these strictures of the Philippine-US alliance. While the discourses that structured the discussion of the New Filipina often touted her life giving work and the arrival of the modern Filipina in the world, it also operated as a mode of containment and control. Programs geared toward the uplift of the Filipina consolidated national and imperialist concerns about population and land management into racialized and gendered configurations.

THE NEW FILIPINA IN LINO BROCKA'S *INSIANG* (1976)

Lino Brocka's 1976 film *Insiang* offers a critical portrait of these configurations. Brocka, often regarded as a leading filmmaker in the New Cinema Movement that captivated the Philippines in the 1970s, rose to prominence during the Marcos years as a young, talented artist whose films used social realism to portray the tragedy of the Filipino condition amid the poverty and political corruption that defined the era.[75] *Maynila sa mga Kuko ng Liwanag* (1975), arguably his most celebrated film, portrays a young man forced to move from a rural province to Manila to rescue his lover from the city's illicit sex industry. The regime heavily censored Brocka's films, along with works by many other artists of the period. In one instance, the First Lady almost prevented *Insiang* from traveling to the Cannes film festival due to its negative depiction of Manila. Brocka's use of social realism in his films, however, allowed him to illuminate the realities of Filipino life through seemingly universalist ideals that could bypass the regime's censorship bureau. José B. Capino incisively discusses the effectiveness of Brocka's cinematic technique as a method of imagination: "While the authoritarian state anxiously holds vigil over insurgency, it often lacks the power and imagination to deal with peculiar forms of resistance."[76] Brocka's negotiations with such constraints, his "peculiar forms of resistance," evidence a significant characteristic of Marcos-era cultural production: that cultural producers deployed innovative methods for navigating the restrictions of the regime while also presenting the violent intricacies of its governmentality.[77] Analyzing Brocka's films, Jonathan Beller argues that "'the individual'—a concept somewhat removed from bourgeois individualism—emerges dialectically in the passing of the particular through the universal that raises it to the individual. Such a progression—particular-universal-individual—better describes the dialectical aspirations of Brocka's work."[78] Organized around themes of "love versus revenge" and "good versus evil," for instance,

Insiang relies on a certain level of universalist abstraction to circumvent—perhaps even to assuage—the eyes of the regime. Where the regime itself deployed the universal as a modality for accessing global capital, Brocka also theorized the universal as a method for enlivening the political consciousness of the Filipino masses.

Brocka committed his films to the edification of the Filipino audience.[79] In an interview with film scholar Hamid Naficy, Brocka postulated that "cinema can be used to make people think, to make people remember and remind themselves that all is not rosy, that all is not just.... While you make people escape into the never never fantasyland... let us also make films that make people not forget but remember."[80] Speaking with Naficy about escapist cinema that had saturated the film culture in the Philippines and removed the Filipino audience from its own reality, Brocka described his artistry as the effort to remember—not as a recollection of past events but as a field of recognition for reimaging one's self within the world. As Brocka expounded on "Filipino imitation" not simply as mindless reproduction but as the re-creation of cinematic formulas in excess, he theorized "third world cinema" as film that deconstructs the ideologies of colonial knowledge production that consolidate agency and possibility within the individual human subject. Brocka's engagement with universalism interrogated the discourses that structured the regime's claim to and deployment of authoritarian power. By employing melodrama—especially through tropes of passion, obsession, betrayal, and revenge—Brocka strove not for a simple connection between character and audience or a unidirectional transmission of sentimentalist affect. Instead, he employed it as an analytic for contending with the force of authoritarian ideologies to shape articulations of personhood.

Insiang portrays the harshness of life in a Philippine slum. Set in an unnamed area of Metro Manila, it follows the titular character as she undergoes a cycle of abuse at the hands of her mother, boyfriend, and mother's lover.[81] Raped by her mother's lover, Dado, and abandoned by her boyfriend, Bebot, Insiang spirals into emotional disarray by the end of the film, taking revenge on her abusers by manipulating them into fighting and killing each other. The film begins with a pig slaughter, where butchers kill and prepare swine for distribution, and then turns to the cacophony of the town marketplace. The disarray of the first scenes is followed by a slow introduction of Insiang, who walks from her job as a laundress to the crowded home she shares with her mother, Tonya, and the extended family of her father, who left the family before the start of the film. Despite the denseness of Insiang's surroundings, she remains apart from its chaos. Throughout the film, she acts as a model of morality, attracting attention not only for her outward beauty but also for her goodness. In this way, she is an aberration, rendered distinct from the slum despite its capacity to swallow other characters whole. When her cousin Edong confesses to her that the desperation of his poverty often goads him into committing malicious acts, Insiang urges him to resist such temptations and to strive to maintain his goodness. When Tonya chastises Insiang's relatives for failing to add to the household income and forces them from the home that they inhabit together, Insiang outwardly expresses sympathy toward them. Moreover, she maintains her chastity in the face of her boyfriend's persistent sexual advances. At each social interaction, she evidences a moral strength that opposes the failings of the people around her. Insiang's goodness is made more apparent by her filial duty and labor. Not only does she work as a laundress; she also serves as her family's primary housekeeper. She "sustain[s] the productive labor force" of her town by washing the clothes of other people and families and then returns home to perform the domestic labor needed to sustain her own home.[82] Insiang is the New Filipina, the ideal instantiation of Filipino womanhood and the paradigmatic figure of life-giving reproductive labor.

Yet it is precisely Insiang's beauty and goodness that make her susceptible to the slum's violence. Tonya steals Insiang's income to sustain her gambling addiction and berates her daughter for provoking the lust of the neighborhood men. In the film's climactic moment, Dado rapes Insiang. Dado convinces Tonya that his sexual urges were simply a natural response to living within the same quarters with her daughter, a young woman who continuously tempts him. With no allies, Insiang turns to her boyfriend, Bebot, to marry her and take her away from the slum. Bebot agrees to this plan only as a way to manipulate her into having sex with him before he abandons her in a motel. The first scenes of the film find narrative cohesion with Insiang's rape to illustrate sexual violence as intimately linked to the management of women's labor. The film parallels the harshness of Dado's work as a butcher to systematically prepare swine for mass consumption with the violence of sexual assault as a way of describing the mechanics of the political economy as largely dependent on the feminization of labor in the era of late capitalism. Rolando Tolentino describes this as the Philippines' "vaginal economy," or its reliance on both the export of feminized domestic labor abroad and sexual labor at home to sustain its political economy. Tolentino points to women's bodies as the terrain on which Philippine administrations enact national aspirations.[83] Indeed, feminist scholars of globalization have long pointed to structural adjustment policies as facilitating the production of informal economies that render poor women especially vulnerable to exploitation. Within the film, such violence illustrates the failures of the First Lady's political discourses to account for the distinct positionality of Filipina women. On the contrary, the cinematic juxtaposition between beauty and violence in the film illustrates the extent to which the First Lady's discourse of beauty structured Filipina women's suitability for transnational circulation and labor.

Returning home as a broken woman, Insiang transforms from a figure of morality into its obverse (figure 3.1). With this fall from grace, she abandons her resolve to practice the goodness with which she had earlier instructed Edong and instead undertakes a plan of revenge against Bebot, Dado, and Tonya. Dado continues to rape her, but Insiang leads him to believe that she loves him. Armed with Insiang's "love," Dado beats Bebot to a bloody pulp at her request. Leading Dado to confess his plans to remove her from the slum within earshot of Tonya, Insiang's orchestration provokes Tonya to stab and murder Dado while Insiang watches the scene with satisfaction. Wielding "love" as an instrument of revenge rather than goodness, Insiang deploys it not as romantic affect but as living labor for enacting a practice of survival and justice.[84] This is what Tadiar has described as Filipina women's attempt "to free themselves from family, from poverty, and in general from their socially prescribed gendered and sexual functions and measures used to enforce them ... the acts of defiance and violence for the sake of living."[85] Martin Manalansan, analyzing the cinematic portrayal of transgender Filipina care workers in Israel in *Paper Dolls*, has also written that "disaffection ... is not about a privileged insouciance but is about survival—about being able to live and bear the almost maddening regimen of domestic routines and tasks."[86] Where Insiang's submission to Tonya confines her to a life of impossibility, the revenge that she enacts on Bebot, Dado, and Tonya, a type of disaffection, is shocking, in part, because it challenges the rigidity of filial piety that structures Insiang's life.

Against New Filipina parameters that mandated a renewed commitment to the national family, Insiang's deliberate act of disloyalty to her family enables, instead, an allegiance to other forms of kinship and collectivity that seek different forms of relation. No longer bound to her abusers, Insiang is moved, instead, by *tsismis*, or gossip, which circulates throughout the neighborhood as alternative public knowledge. Tolentino has explained that "gossiping is another way of 'talking back' to the dictatorship [and] allow[s] people

FIGURE 3.1 Scene from Lino Brocka's 1976 film *Insiang*.

to listen attentively to the dictatorship while at the same time undermining from behind what the regime has said."[87] As the administration's fictions sought to produce the New Filipina, tsismis invests not in the production of subjectivities that are identifiable to the regime but in the construction of different formations that emerge from public, shared knowledges. For instance, while town tsismis indicts Insiang as a whore, it is precisely this abjection that facilitates her conceptualization of the dangers of love and duty that Bebot, Dado, and Tonya present to her and encourages her to act against that danger.[88] Family, in other words, is the location of violence, not the source of empowerment.

Insiang's becoming is not a movement from false consciousness to liberation; rather, it signifies the transferal of labor as discipline to labor as refusal. Where Insiang's domestic work once sustained the home, she rejects the demands for her loyalty through a rage that removes her from the hold of her family. As she enacts her revenge through her sexuality, she activates another kind of work that provides energy not to her betrayers but to the slum itself. Insiang is now not rendered apart from the slum but woven into its very fabric, much like the squatter protests that contested the regime's urban development projects. By the end of the film, the slum absorbs each of the characters into its grasp. The slum is not the abject place of immorality; it offers reprieve from the intimate violence that Insiang bears under the sexual regimes of the New Society. Insiang's devolvement is a refusal to succumb to the regime's instruction for womanhood, which provides the discourse for the extraction of women's labor in the service of national modernization. She is not moved by pronouncements of life proposed by the regime's investment in a new society but is instead motivated by other iterations of being that lie outside the state's mandates.

Insiang's relationship to the slum presents beauty and ugliness not as oppositional ideals but as a dialectic for destabilizing any notion about beauty as women's virtue.[89] Beauty does not reveal women's innate goodness nor her inherent proclivity for care. Rather, it operates as a mode of governance for upholding a paradigm of development that organizes subjectivity along the terms of productivity and value. As Imelda Marcos defined beauty through the language of feminized reproductive labor, global capital, and liberal progress, Brocka's recalculation of beauty here identifies, by contrast, a politics of development, sovereignty, and imperialism. Describing her as his muse, as the story goes, Brocka plucked Hilda Koronel, the actress who plays Insiang, from the slums of Pasay to star in his films. For Brocka, Koronel symbolized the beauty that might emerge from squalor. Born of a Filipina mother and a white American GI father, Koronel's beauty is less a marker of inherent aesthetic qualities than it is an illustration of the specificity of the Filipino condition born of a racial cold war that brings US militarization and Philippine state development together in unending collaboration. Brocka's artistry in addition to Koronel's own creative work on screen rearticulates beauty against both the regime's dismissal and eradication of the slum's unseemliness and imperialist devaluations of Filipino life. Rendered as part of the slum and emerging from its very lifeworlds, beauty uncovers another field of intelligibility that locates the contradictions that are fundamental to the formation of postcolonial subjectivity.

Insiang was the first Philippine film set in Tondo, which at the time was Manila's largest slum.[90] Before World War II ravaged Manila, Tondo served as a critical port town. The destruction of the war, however, left it in ruins. In the decades after the war, the growing urban poor—many either displaced from the war or migrating from the rural areas of the country into Manila—constructed informal encampments in the area.[91] Tondo was later "branded as Southeast Asia's largest squatter slum colony where all-out unemployment, poverty and malnutrition bred crime, violence, disease and death, and moral and spiritual decay."[92] The Manila Urban Development Project, a program created by USAID in 1976 to transform the city's transportation, housing, and sanitation infrastructure, focused on resolving Tondo's "high population density, inadequate water and sewerage facilities and very poor drainage."[93] At one time celebrated for its economic potential,

Tondo emerged from the detritus of war to become the object of the regime's reconstruction efforts and political posturing. Tondo's devolvement into an ugly and worthless slum paralleled the Marcos regime's transformation of Manila into a cosmopolitan center. At the same time that the slum was made to evidence impoverishment and destitution, it also, as I chart in the previous chapter, served as a site of critical resistance against state-sponsored imperialism. The Zone One Tondo Organization (ZOTO) emerged from earlier organizing efforts shaped by the radical National Democratic Front during the martial law period to wage an "intractable urban poor struggle" against development programs, which were responsible for simultaneously aggravating poverty while employing the poor to bolster its political campaigns.[94] ZOTO and its offshoots successfully fought for basic services for the poor, halted demolition and relocation plans at various points of construction, and became a bloc with which developers were forced to negotiate.[95] The ZOTO movement reconstructed this paradigm of value to deploy an anti-state politics that relied on the collective consciousness of poor people's resistance.

In his discussion of the role of the "artist as citizen," Brocka explained that although "it is the duty of the artist to work for what is true, good, and beautiful, first we have to expose and fight for what is wrong."[96] Framing the First Lady's mantra of the "true, good, and beautiful" as legitimate yet unattainable without the struggle to "expose and fight for what is wrong," Brocka presented the contradiction between the First Lady's promulgation of truth, goodness, and beauty and the political suppression on which this mandate rested. Indeed, Brocka's reflections on the divide that separated the good from the bad and the right from the wrong illuminated such Manichean logic as fundamental to Marcosian politics. The regime not only delineated the beautiful from the ugly but also used that bifurcation to command violence by presenting a clear dividing line between the republic and everything that acted to threaten its solidity. Brocka, however, explains that "my stories are not painted in that stark black and white way. What [the audience] see[s] is a situation and the fact is that people are products of particular situations and are trapped in a particular system."[97] Brocka's conception of subjectivity not as always already constituted but as a configuration shaped in relation and opposition to the state guided his cinematic portrayal of the Filipino condition under martial law. For Brocka, the struggle to "remember" is not necessarily the task of recalling the past in order to contextualize the present. Rather, it is the work of unmaking, the effort to situate the present as a battle over cultural memory.

By engaging questions about universality and citizenship, Brocka's cultural politics contested state articulations of personhood to engage Filipino subjectivity as an arena of contestation and a site for political becoming. Brocka's films possess, as Jose Gutierrez III writes, a "resonance with experience—what we discover in natural cognition as the 'world,' that is, the totality of individual objects that could possibly be experienced."[98] As Brocka's films navigated the tension between film as escape and film as return, they presented the space in between as a place of possibility for reimagining otherworldly sites rooted in "justice and freedom."[99] While the Marcoses mandated public participation in their fictions through erasure, censorship, and the totalizing command over the use of culture, Brocka's attention to the Filipino audience motivated participation, confrontation, and creation.

As the Marcoses' "National Family melodrama" positioned Malakas at Maganda as origin and ideal, *Insiang* rendered another performance of melodrama that ended not in a celebration of heteronormative romance nor in the justification of the Filipina woman as life giver but in the evacuation of these ideals. Melodrama expresses, as Tolentino posits, an "affinity with the feminine and the popular" and makes "connections between the female subject and the nation."[100] Whereas the Marcoses' organized their romantic melodrama around the couple's perfect union of strength and beauty and communion with the nation, *Insiang* unhinged the feminine from the nation to present it as a political force in continuous struggle with the nation. By the end of the film, Insiang explains to Tonya the rationale behind her revenge. With no conclusive resolution following this confession, the two women leave each other—Tonya goes back to her prison cell and Insiang back to the slum. Carcerality provides no meaningful or just solution here, and the film ends in a palpable tension between the state's proposal of justice and an urgent insistence on other conceptualizations of self-determination. For Tonya and Insiang, mother and daughter for whom life giving has offered little restitution for the difficulties of their lives, the New Filipina is not a promise of empowerment but an overdetermination of Filipina women's being.

The rise of the NCRFW occurred alongside and often in conflict with the ascent of various feminist movements in the country committed both to articulating the intricacy of women's subjectivity in the 1970s and 1980s and to challenging the administration's prescriptions for liberation. A new women's organization, MAKIBAKA (Malayang Kilusan ng Bagong Kababaihan, or Free Movement of New Women), emerged during the martial law period in response to pronouncements of national liberation by anti-Marcos activists.[101] Jurgette Honculada has outlined three women's organizations that formed during the period:

> Many groups within the second wave of the women's movement which emerged at the height of the Marcos dictatorship sought to balance class and gender issues, exemplified by two autonomous women's organizations, PILIPINA and KALYAAN, founded in 1981 and 1982, respectively. PILIPINA affirmed that "the struggle for social transformation would have to be waged along gender lines" and not just in terms of "class and property relations." KALYAAN viewed itself as "autonomous but not separate [from]" and "distinct but not integrated [with]" the national democratic movement, refusing to sacrifice women's liberation for some "higher goal" of national liberation, according to former NCRFW Commissioner Fe Mangahas.
>
> A third organization, GABRIELA, was founded in 1984 as a broad coalition to rally various women's groups against the Marcos dictatorship. Part of a larger political formation, GABRIELA has disavowed working directly with government, and that includes the NCRFW. Organized in 1975, the KaBaPa (Katipunan ng Bagong Pilipina or Association of the New Filipina) also belongs to a larger political group and has roots in the peasant movement. Infusion of gender concerns came in the 1980s.[102]

I do not point to these organizations as an antidote to the First Lady's feminism nor as exceptional cases of feminist empowerment. Indeed, as Roces describes, "Women activists, with the exception of militant nuns, have enjoyed less power in post-war Philippines than their sisters who exerted unofficial power."[103] Rather, the rise of many of these organizations during the Marcos period illustrates the extent to which an anti–martial law politics identified the distinctly gendered structure of authoritarian power. These organizations reveal the emergence of an array of theorizing and organizing that worked to articulate the composition of gendered subjectivity during the Marcos era. They analyzed, as Honculada writes, the multiplicity of experience that constituted women's lives amid the inchoate neoliberalism of the period.

In one specific case, a women's anti–nuclear power march in Manila in 1984 protested the regime's construction of the Bataan Nuclear Power Plant.[104] For these marchers, the urgency of their protest emerged not through an admonishment of the ways the plant affected Filipina women specifically but through an articulation of the mechanics by which development and modernization programs produce new instantiations of gendered violence. In 1976, Marcos awarded to the Westinghouse Corporation a multimillion-dollar contract for the construction of the plant. In collaboration with Westinghouse, both Philippine and US officials orchestrated a series of partnerships that brought new technologies to the Philippines while enhancing the wealth of the regime and its cronies.[105] As I describe in the following chapter, the development of the plan was part of the Marcos administration's broader scheme to transform the Bataan peninsula into an export processing zone that would function as a major site of multinational investment outside the Manila metropolis. In addition to the tremendous cost of the plant during a period of economic crisis, critics pointed to the accident at the Three Mile Island plant in Pennsylvania in 1979 as a cautionary tale about nuclear power.[106] Undercutting the regime's New Filipina proclamations, the marchers wore death masks, and spectators held signs denouncing the regime's neocolonial order of death and contesting the conceptualizations of life defined by the terms of global capital (figure 3.2). They

FIGURE 3.2 Kim Komenich's 1984 photograph of anti–nuclear power plant demonstrators in Manila. Antinuclear protesters, all women, marched from Plaza Miranda to Mendiola Gate, where they confronted riot police. Fang family *San Francisco Examiner* photograph archive negative files, BANC PIC 2006.029:KKI984-09-13D.07—NEG, box 3177, © Regents of the University of California, Bancroft Library, University of California, Berkeley.

articulated power as the force of multistate collaborations and transpacific actors to determine the conditions of their lives. Framing their claims against this violence through death and for the dying, the marchers called for alternative instantiations of life. The coalition "signalled the arrival on the national scene of a powerful, militant and progressive women's voice that would articulate and act on demands across the political spectrum, from stopping nuclear power plants, ousting United States . . . bases and ending dictatorship, to recognizing and fairly renumerating women's labour, acting against institutionalised prostitution, and ending all forms of discrimination against women."[107] Such examples point to the ways organizations in the Philippines "became alert to the possibilities of women's empowerment as a group," individually and collectively charting a cartography of the landscape of Filipina women's lives under state violence, US militarized occupation, and global capitalism.[108] The "peak of women's protest politics" coalesced not through the emergence of the New Filipina but as a broad, shifting, and multivalent coalition of factions.[109] Describing gendered violence at the intersection of the regime's mandates and US and international policies, they offered a distinct kind of unmaking that challenged the model of recognition proposed by the configurations of the racial cold war.

FOUR. THE FILIPINO HUMANITARIAN

On January 21, 1980, President Ferdinand Marcos addressed the residents of Morong, Bataan, at the inauguration ceremony of the Philippine Refugee Processing Center (PRPC). Nearly five years after the fall of Saigon, Marcos encouraged these residents to extend compassionate service to their "siblings from Vietnam."[1] The PRPC saw thousands of Southeast Asian refugees pass through its doors from its first day of operation in 1980 to its eventual closure in 1995. As the final stop in Asia for refugees of the US war in Vietnam, the PRPC arbitrated their departure and resettlement. Like its counterparts in Thailand and Indonesia, the center intended to relieve "first-asylum" nations with the burden of housing and rehabilitating thousands of refugees. Answering the call from the United Nations High Commissioner for Refugees to find a "humanitarian solution to the Indochinese refugee problem," the Philippine government, along with the support of the International Catholic Migration Commission (ICMC) and the US government, constructed the PRPC to provide refugees with basic shelter and services, vocational skills training, and cultural orientation programs to prepare them for their new lives in their countries of final destination.[2] In his speech, Marcos reassured the people of Morong that construction and operation would not threaten their farms; on the contrary, their livelihoods could only stand to benefit from a new opportunity to "sell [their] produce to the processing center [and] have a market for [their] products."[3] The Marcos administration established Task Force Morong "to benefit the peripheral community of Morong [and] to assist the Morong residents in furthering their socioeconomic development."[4] The central task of the PRPC, however, remained "the rehabilitation of the refugee; that is, his transformation from a displaced individual into a person equipped for a productive and meaningful life in his country of final destination."[5] What might we make of these parameters for operation? How is the economic self-determinism of Morong residents congruent with refugee rehabilitation? How does the PRPC encourage us to reimagine the place of the Philippines within the cartography of the racial cold war?

The primary focus of this chapter is to interrogate the Marcos regime's construction of Filipino raciality around the paradigm of international humanitarianism and a key tenet of US Cold War discourse, the guardianship over freedom and liberation. Of course, "freedom and liberation" were made possible by the protracted occupation of independent postcolonial nations, the militarization of national borders, the consolidation of the security state, and the ongoing disenfranchisement of racial, gender, sexual, and religious minorities. The Marcos administration cultivated a discourse of race and gender grounded in the "ultimate ideology" of humanism. Its so-called humanist revolution armed the regime's state of exception, providing the discursive justification for Marcos's rule by martial law and authoritarian governance. The regime's apparent commitment to humanism and its deployment of the gendered labor of moral care guided its participation in international humanitarian efforts for refugee rehabilitation.

The configuration of the Filipino humanitarian evidences the Philippine state's collusion with US imperialist operations in the racial cold war. Such a configuration authorized the saturation of an affable and translatable Filipino subjectivity within the global market. I chart a genealogy of the PRPC through an interrogation of Marcosian ideology and US-led guidelines for refugee rehabilitation. The chapter ends with my reading of "Teacher, It's Nice to Meet You, Too," a 1985 text written by PRPC instructor Ruby Ibañez and published in a journal of refugee education, to discuss Filipino teachers' racialized and gendered humanitarian work as subscribing to yet also confounding the overdetermined discourses of refugee rehabilitation.

RESIGNIFYING BATAAN

Marcos introduced the PRPC through the language of postwar possibility and pronounced its significance as the rise of a new Philippine-US partnership that cohered not through the misery of defeat but as the optimism of peace and prosperity. In his opening speech, Marcos assured Morong residents that the center's location in Bataan would help reposition Bataan away from the memorialization of loss and toward the commemoration of modernization. In the process, he rehearsed some well-worn narratives about Bataan's historical importance: "You know, Morong and Bagac was the Western terminal of the last line of defense of the United States Armed Forces in the Far East in the fighting in 1942.... Here in Morong were many battles, and we lost many brothers here.... We know misery, deprivation and death because we lost about one million people in the last war."[6] As the stage of US-Philippine military surrender at the hands of the Japanese armed forces during World War II—what is commonly known as the Bataan Death March—Bataan has long represented one of the most devastating US conquests of the Pacific Theater. Often remembered as a shared loss between the United States and the Philippines, military narratives of Bataan also laud it as a symbol of a burgeoning US-Philippine alliance in which the fledgling Philippine republic valiantly struggled alongside its former colonizer to wage a war against fascism and safeguard global freedom. The memory of Bataan underscores the "special relationship" between the United States and the Philippines. Bataan has legitimized the continuation of US imperialism in the Philippines and throughout Asia and the Pacific. Vernadette Vicuña Gonzalez writes that the memorialization of Bataan and Corregidor as struggles of liberation—rather than as the locations for the extension of empires—foregrounds ongoing military partnerships between the United States and its former colony.[7] Indeed, the Marcos administration's deployment of the Philippine Civic Action Group to Vietnam in 1966, the US military support for Philippine counterinsurgency programs, and the renewal of the US lease on military bases in the Philippines reveal the incompleteness of Philippine liberation even as the story of Bataan invokes its arrival.

The memory of Bataan remains a site of contention, and its remembering and forgetting structure the shape of its invocation in the present.[8] When Marcos declared the opening of the PRPC the "beginning of a new spirit," he resignified Bataan not only as the location of past war but also as the place of modernization. He explained:

> Today, however, we come to open a center in an effort to recover what has been partially lost of man's humanity and integrity. Today, you see the very same nations who fought against each other on this soil—Japan against the United States and against the Philippines—coming together to establish a refugee center, which shall reaffirm once again man's humanity for his fellow

human, and perhaps, give us fresh hope that no matter how delicate the fabric of the international community, that fabric will not be torn apart because the great majority of men do believe in the maintenance of harmonious international relations and peace.[9]

According to Marcos, the specificity of "this soil" of Bataan is the primordial place of profound national loss, and the only remedy for that loss is Bataan's reclamation. Reynaldo Ileto has argued that the United States and the Philippines have long been immersed in a "past memory war" that structures the justification of US imperialism in the present.[10] At the PRPC, the Philippines joined both Japan and the United States to form an alliance of nations committed to "harmonious international relations and peace." With the invocation of the "international," Marcos purported a lateral political arrangement that rearticulated the conditions of Manila's destruction and Japan's reconstruction. Several years earlier, in 1973, Marcos signed the Treaty of Amity between the Philippines and Japan, originally drafted in 1960 but not formally ratified due to the pervasiveness of anti-Japan sentiment in the Philippines.[11] This laterality, preceded by the normalization of Philippine-Japanese relations in 1973, "forgets" the Philippines' position as the staging ground for imperialist war as well as the conditions of war's aftermath that reorganized US dominance through militarization and reconstruction.

This narration of Bataan as the site of new partnership also recuperated the injured masculinities of earlier war through a narrative of transpacific brotherhood that elided both the gendered violence of war and the ways that such violence continued to shape development in the aftermath of war.[12] With the formal opening of the PRPC, Marcos reorganized the defining hostilities of the Pacific Theater into a performance of reconciliation, where conflicts between empires and nations could be resolved by a transpacific commitment to humanity. Such proclamations of Bataan as the setting of both national and international possibility, in fact, authorized the aggressive pursuit of Philippine development to translate Bataan's gravity into the language of financial exchange. Before the construction of the PRPC, Marcos commissioned the development of Mariveles, Bataan, into an export processing zone (EPZ) that would house the country's manufacturing plants and serve as the "Philippines' first industrial estate."[13] Relocating industry outside Manila, Marcos used the Bataan EPZ to transform the port towns of the region into a system of manufacture and export. In an effort to lure foreign capital into the country and cultivate the nation's global flexibility, Marcos's Foreign Trade Zone Authority incentivized multinational investment by offering to industries numerous trade exemptions and lucrative labor agreements.[14] As a facet of this broader program for redevelopment, the PRPC and its facilitation of foreign capital aligned Bataan with the dictums of free trade, structural adjustment, and counterinsurgency. A critical facet of the regime's recuperation strategy was the management of largely women workers at EPZs.[15] As Marcos romanticized the fraternity of the Philippines' military partnerships as key to its maturation, it was women's labor that was central to the nation's modernization.

Marcos's reference to the "fellow human" "remembers" humanity as a rubric for organizing the terms of international integration and situates refugee subjectivity as the object of reconciliation for past wars in a way that establishes the terms of new war, what Mimi Thi Nguyen has articulated as "the calculation of freedom's continuation."[16] Where Marcos described war as epitomizing the original degradation of human life, the PRPC and its affirmation of the life of the refugee—indeed, the refugee's potential—sought to rectify the inhumanity of war. The regime's historical revisionism also located the Philippines as the ideal site for refugee rehabilitation. Sylvia P. Montes, deputy minister of the Ministry of Social Services and Development for the Philippines, delivered an address to the Congress of the International Movement of Catholic Jurists, in which she claimed that the Philippines had historically served as a place of refuge for the persecuted:

> It has been a place of refuge for many people. After World War I, refugees from Russia, who escaped and did not want to live under the communist government, arrived in the Philippines. When Hitler came into power in Germany in 1933, a good number of refugees of Jewish origin came to Manila and some of them are still with us, having adjusted themselves to the conditions of the country, and have prospered materially and professionally. The victory of the communists in mainland China in 1949 brought about the influx into the Philippines of thousands of Chinese, who were able to acquire permanent resident status as naturalized citizens, and who are integrated and participating actively in community affairs.
>
> These previous experiences influenced the Philippine government under the able leadership of President Ferdinand E. Marcos in the handling of the biggest refugee problem in Southeast Asia—the Vietnamese Refugees—particularly the Boat People.[17]

For Montes, the claim that the Philippines "has been a place of refuge for many people" attaches the "refugee problem in Southeast Asia" to a long tradition of state humanitarianism, through which the Philippine government had long extended its concern and goodwill to the persecuted. Marcos's "handling of the biggest refugee problem in Southeast Asia" justified current rehabilitation efforts and declared Marcos's role as a humanitarian leader, especially important in the face of mounting charges of human rights abuse against the regime. However, Montes's assertion that the Philippines offered Jewish refugees a safe haven against Hitler's power obscures the colonial conditions that facilitated Jewish refugee migration to the Philippines. The contentious terms of the Philippines' US commonwealth status complicates the claim that "a good number of refugees of Jewish origin came to Manila" in the 1930s.[18] By 1924, US immigration restrictions prohibited the entrance of Jewish refugees into the United States. The admission of Jewish refugees into the Philippines did not emblematize the Philippine government's humanitarianism but, rather, exemplified its status as a frontier of US overseas empire.[19] Subsumed within the geopolitical declaration of the US nation yet excluded from the bounds of the national polity, the Philippines functioned as US empire's exception as well as a fundamental component of its articulation as the location of freedom. The simultaneous exclusion and allowance of Jewish refugees into the United States allowed the US government to negotiate the contradictions of its own political ideologies and racism against its adjudication. Its ability to concurrently close its borders and grant entrance to Jewish refugees into its colonial protectorate named the Philippines as the condition of possibility for American exceptionalism's pronouncement of freedom for all. In other words, the US claim of liberty depended precisely on the colonial occupation of the Philippines, Puerto Rico, Hawai'i, and Guam and the utility of these protectorates as US outposts; yet the obfuscation of this coloniality was the necessary condition for the US expression of freedom.

Montes's narration positioned the Philippine nation as arriving precisely at the intersections of these historical events. In 1933, when, according to Montes, Jewish refugees arrived to the Philippines, the Philippines was one year away from becoming a commonwealth. In 1949, when Chinese refugees arrived in the Philippines, the commonwealth had only been independent for three years. Montes's attachment of Marcos's decision to assist with the "biggest refugee problem" to these earlier historical moments presented the contemporary period as another moment of national cohesion, where the response to international crisis became the galvanizing point for reasserting political sovereignty.

The Marcos administration's invocation of the history of state humanitarianism redeployed this colonial liberalism to better position itself within the demands of Cold War geopolitics. Montes's summoning of Jewish refugees fleeing the Nazi Party and Russian and Chinese refugees fleeing communist governments illuminated an apparent Philippine commitment to preserve global democracy against its various antagonists. More specifically, the invoking of Jewish refugees to contextualize the importance of the PRPC positioned the Marcos regime squarely against National Socialism and framed Marcosian authoritarianism in contradistinction to the malignancy of totalitarianism. Such an opposition declared an uncomplicated political conflict solely between republicanism and totalitarianism. This bifurcation obfuscated the specificity of Marcos's authoritarianism as well as the regime's rapprochement with China through the revitalization of more flexible trade policies during the Cold War period. It also occluded the conditions of the state's emergence: namely, the ways it formed from the landscape of postwar reconstruction in Asia. Montes's account overdetermined Philippine sovereignty through the pronouncement of liberalism's dominance.

The opening of the PRPC in the Philippines coincided with the passage of the US Refugee Act of 1980, which aimed to "serve the country's humanitarian traditions well" by "meet[ing] the needs of the homeless around the world." The act amended the immigration legislation of 1952 and 1965, signaling a more liberal US immigration policy toward refugees. While the 1965 immigration act had permitted refugee relocation to the United States based on a seventh criterion of special immigration status, the passage of the new Refugee Act subscribed to the principles outlined by the United Nations Convention and Protocol on Refugees to address the specificity of political persecution and "legitimate fear."[20] The act's delineation of the refugee from the immigrant established a new protected category that ordered a revised process for adjudicating freedom.[21] Situated in between persecution and liberation, the refugee circulated within legal discourse as a "transitional" figure whose conditionality was premised on the urgency of rehabilitation. Rehabilitation necessitated a governmentality whose purpose was to transform the refugee from the victim of persecution into the proper subject of freedom.[22] The act did not simply afford protection to the refugee, for, as Wendy Brown has written, "rights are not just defenses against social and political power but are, as an aspect of governmentality, a crucial aspect of power's aperture."[23] This rights-based paradigm functioned through and in tandem with military support promised by other nations to the United

States. As Marcos had described it, rehabilitation was an international affair that necessitated the concerted participation of several nations.

The Philippine government had already agreed to build a refugee processing center in the Philippines before the act's passage, with the US government contributing the largest portion of the funds for its establishment and Japan and South Korea also supplying financial support. As I discussed in earlier chapters, the enlistment of Japan and South Korea, along with the Philippines, in the program of postwar reconstruction signaled the ways that an emergent transpacific alliance organized a Cold War logic of integration that buttressed US imperialism and the new world order of international cooperation and global capitalism.[24] Yến Lê Espiritu has argued that such a project evidenced not only the lasting effects of US overseas empire but also the dissolution and varied reemergence of its force. Espiritu contends that "the material and ideological conversion of US military bases into places of refuge—places that were meant to resolve the refugee crisis, promising peace and protection—discursively transformed the United States from violent aggressor in Vietnam to benevolent rescuer of its people."[25] Refugee rehabilitation emerged within a sustained transpacific project that facilitated the reconstitution of US military programs into other institutions for determining the lives of people dispossessed by the effects of these programs. The afterlives of empire cohered through varying circuits of connection and collaboration between former colonial sites.[26] Rehabilitation legitimized the aims of US overseas empire by illuminating the success of past imperialist wars to construct proper nation-states that worked in the service of global freedom. The rehabilitation of the refugee mitigated the defeat of the Vietnam War by centering the refugee as the battleground for US liberalism and its antagonisms.

THE FILIPINO AS HUMAN

Rehabilitation required a system of transpacific labor to liberate the refugee, and this labor congealed as new configurations.[27] Ferdinand and Imelda Marcos tasked themselves with the paternalistic project of encouraging the formation of a Filipino subjectivity that might cohere as this labor of rehabilitation. According to the Marcoses, as I have noted in the previous chapters, the country's participation in the modern world of nations and the attendant reconstruction of the good image of the Philippine nation depended first on the cultivation of a distinct Filipino consciousness—that is, the Filipino's awareness of history and self. The regime's articulations of historicism and globality were instrumental for communicating modern Filipino subjectivity as the possession of historical knowledge and the didacticism necessary for transmitting this knowledge to others.

In his "New Filipinism" speech, Marcos announced his philosophy for "spiritual and intellectual transformation," a complete "metamorphosis." He proclaimed a historical continuity between his political vision and that of national hero Jose Rizal, claiming that in "the 1890s Rizal saw the rise of 'new men' and 'a new social order' within a century" and that Marcos delivered "in 1968 . . . the New Filipino and the New Filipinism."[28] Framing Rizal's conceptualization of "new men" as the origin of modern Filipino subjectivity, Marcos reasserted the issue of "race" as the most urgent quandary of his governance. Marcos's pronouncement of Rizal here "ma[de] possible a field of knowledge whose function is to recover it."[29] John D. Blanco's discussion of "race as praxis" is instructive for understanding Marcos's conception of raciality. Blanco writes that "colonialism does not simply reproduce an already existing difference or set of differences anchored in science and awaiting future discovery. Rather, colonial rule *creates and ramifies differences that do not preexist the historical event of conquest and domination*, and sets in motion identities that become tied to historical themes of fall and redemption."[30] Race is not the colonial exploitation of a predetermined difference; rather, race is the emergent political consciousness produced from an ongoing struggle between the concepts of "fall and redemption." Marcos promised that, under his guidance, the New Filipino would not only serve as a fulfillment of Rizal's vision of "new men" but would also "[symbolize] the extinction of Juan Tamad as the underserved archetype of the Filipino race and the emergence of a new type of Filipino more competent, more confident, more eager for challenge and achievement than all his ancestors before him."[31] Race marks the postcolonial location of the Filipino in the world. The New Filipino as a racial category, similar to the First Lady's New Filipina, attempted to establish a relation with a broad range of humanity tied to the ebbs and flows of global capital. Marcos's configuration of this subjectivity in historical relation articulated a Filipino depravity against the positive, complete figure of human potential.

Filipino depravity was, in Marcos's estimation, the result of centuries of self-definition structured by colonial subjectivity. Marcos attributed the fragmentation of the nation to a tenacious adherence to colonial historiography, which was the sole frame of human reference; true national sovereignty, in his estimation, required the reclamation and possession of Philippine history. At the Eighty-Fourth Anniversary of the Ministry of Foreign Affairs, the president described the importance of what he termed the "Philippine historical point of view." The Philippine historical point of view rejected an "almost exclusively western and American" education and called for an "indigenous" history that centered the barangay as the locus of Philippine governing power, insisting on the reclamation of a Filipino primordialism as the framework for Filipino subjectivity.[32] He instructed that "what we must always keep in mind is that sovereignty from the Philippine historical point of view or from the story of the Philippines is never won once and for all; rather it must always be fought for, guarded and promoted with care. In our daily work to keep it intact and to enjoy its application in the widest sense possible, we are limited only by our own free and enlightened will, and by no other interest than our own."[33] Explaining that the Philippine historical point of view requires no other work than "our own free and enlightened will," he described historical knowledge as critical to Filipino self-definition, which, in turn, facilitated the reunion between the Filipino and himself.[34] This possession of historical knowledge was key to the "completion of the development of our nation-State" and the "full withdrawal of the curtain of seclusion which our colonial confinement placed around our relations with the rest of the world."[35] Insofar as Marcos advised that knowledge of this history was at the core of "national unity," Marcosian historiography undercut and delegitimized any conflict that undermined this conceptualization of Filipinoness.

This veneration of a "national story" rooted Filipinoness in a singular humanity that predated national conflict. It justified the state's ongoing attempts to stifle struggles for land within the country by superseding other claims of subjectivity formed from the exigencies of self-determination. The regime's establishment of the Presidential Assistant on National Minorities (PANAMIN), for instance, instituted a system for testing the "loyalty of national minorities."[36] Established as a measure of "security" against perceived national threats, PANAMIN enforced the removal of Indigenous people from their lands. By ordering the removal of those people whose charges against the nation were deemed inconsistent with national unity, PANAMIN operated through the regime's cultivation of a singular, homogeneous Filipino identity that subsumed within its logics any difference understood as antagonistic to the Marcoses' ambitions.[37]

If the Filipino's disassociation from his history defined his depravity and deepened the divide between the Filipino and his self, the Filipino's possession of this history, by contrast—that is, his adoption of the Philippine historical point of view—facilitated the "return" of the Filipino to his essential humanity.[38] Heralding the Filipino as Human, Marcos argued that the "humanistic thrust of our ideology precisely takes into account the fact that apart from being rational, in the Cartesian sense of the term, man has a gift of creativity that expresses itself not only in his art but also in his science and social institutions. This creativity is what makes man truly man."[39] Further, the president asserted that "to change others, we must first change ourselves. The transformation of the world begins with the transformation of the individual. Society and, I dare say, political authority do not exist simply to be targets of one's frustrations; they are more than that. They are the focus of one's compassionate concern for one's fellow men."[40] Decentering civil society as the most important realm for expressing political agency, Marcos pointed to each individual's humanist responsibility to his fellow man as an equally—if not more—appropriate avenue for political empowerment. He explained that this "moral" revolution was instrumental for repositioning Filipino subjectivity not as beholden to the state but as indebted to something far more significant—humanity.[41]

The First Lady also employed the human as the central figure of her political vision. Addressing the United Nations General Assembly in 1976, she cautioned, "We have too often fallen back on the old selfish concept of the *raison d'etat*, the reason of state, to justify whatever ends we seek, and have forgotten *l'etre humain*, the simple being, the common man, for whom the state exists, and in whose interests all states must, in the last and most valid analysis, interact with one another."[42] In another address, she contended that "it is in the very nature of human beings to be aware of the rightness or wrongness of their actions, to pass judgment on their own acts and those of others, and to make the decisions which we call ethical. For indeed what we know or have learned to call ethics is nothing more than our consciousness of human values; it is nothing more than a sense of our *humanitas*, our own humanity. For to be human is to be moral."[43] Gayatri Chakravorty Spivak has argued that "to rationalize the question of ethics fully . . . is to transgress the intuition that ethics are a problem of relation before they are a task of knowledge."[44] For the regime, morality underscored, as Spivak notes, a human response to the call of the other. Following Spivak's lead to reconsider morality not (only) as a problem of relation but as one of knowledge, however, is to understand that the discourse of morality assembled Filipino subjectivity through the language of global responsibility and human rights, where human rights, in this instance, operated as a vehicle for international organization and neocolonial governance. The regime's articulation of morality necessitated an other to whom the Filipino was called, and this call distinguished a Filipino capacity to assume another subjectivity aside from depravity. As morality concerned itself with the ethical framework that defined the human condition—the capacity and imperative to distinguish right from wrong—it structured the Filipino's capacity to transmit the lessons of Philippine history into the labor of moral action.

The labor of moral action has defined a distinct Filipino relation to the world even after the fall of the Marcoses. In her theorization of the gift of freedom, Nguyen posits that "to be gifted freedom, which is also the demand of time, is to be beholden to an unfolding of human sovereignty *that has already happened elsewhere*, that has yet to happen here, and, crucially, *that may yet fail to do so*."[45] It is precisely this anachronism that structures refugee subjectivity as a configuration of liberal transition that "proposes to hasten the termination of its mandate."[46] The regime subscribed to such paradigms of a human sovereignty yet to come in order to maintain global legitimacy and, more importantly, configured Filipino subjectivity into a modality by which to express the successful transition of that freedom elsewhere.

The regime theorized humanism as the framework of modern sociality and the Filipino as Human as its basic unit; in doing so, it determined the prerequisites by which one could *count* as human within the New Society. Insofar as humanism celebrated the extension of compassion onto others and moral goodness in general, it also justified extrajudicial violence against dissidents in its legitimization of this mission. Humanism extended the contours of Marcosian power by justifying the urgency of authoritarianism. Declaring that it was Filipinos' "primordial concern . . . to survive with dignity," Marcos contended that the aim of his governance was not the guarantee of "political rights," which he denigrated as the consequence of personal, selfish desire, but, rather, the protection of postcolonial self-definition and actualization. Marcos pointed to the international human rights regime as a hegemony of Western imperialist politics that was fundamentally at odds with the social realities of countries such as the Philippines. Asserting that Filipino depravity was a by-product of the imposition of Western ideologies in the country, he insisted that the push for "civil rights" was a colonial paradigm that would do little to address the grave problems of Filipino depravity.

Marcos's conceptualization of humanism yielded an alternative conceptualization of human rights that located "freedom" somewhere between the "anarchy of desires" and the "tyranny of the State." Marcos's discourse of freedom is one that is, as Wendy Brown has argued, "arrayed against a particular image of unfreedom [that] sustains that image, which dominates political life with its specter long after it has been vanquished."⁴⁷ He presented freedom as a decolonial response to Western imperialism. Marcos attempted to apprehend the terms of that freedom so that he might legitimize his own political power in the progressive march toward its materialization. While Brown's discussion centers on the ways that liberal societies rectify "states of injury," this theorization of freedom as "a project suffused not just with ambivalence but with anxiety" helps delineate the methods by which the authoritarian regime wielded the language of liberalism in the manifestation of its own power.⁴⁸ This so-called Marcosian revolution from the center focused not on the right to civic participation but on the state's cultivation of human potential as a seemingly nonaligned solution to political sovereignty.

It is this turn to human potential that remains most interesting to me. Emerging from the Marcoses' theorizations of humanism and morality—and distinctly not human *rights*—human potential identified Filipino subjectivity as a vehicle of labor that could reorganize political power around the demands of the global market. In his critique of human rights, Marcos argued that the regime's commitment to humanism manifested itself as a "deep involvement in all efforts to right the wrongs that have arisen from an inequitable world-order in the lives of nations, a condition that parallels and extends injustice to the individual, with a corresponding deprivation of economic and civil rights."⁴⁹ Marcos placed the onus of "righting wrongs" onto the "inequitable world-order." He insisted on a shift from the supremacy of human rights as a singular framework for political responsibility to human potential as a method for rectifying global injustice. Marcos admitted that "what the developing countries have to do is clearly to interfere in the play of market forces. This, however, is to strike at the control and dominance of international finance and trade by the developed countries. And this is the heart of the matter."⁵⁰ Indeed, his commitment to the "doctrine of maximum self-help" argued that it was the state's responsibility to "speed up our economic and social progress."⁵¹ Marcos's citation of both Frantz Fanon and Henry Kissinger in his lament against world powers' disregard for the plight of the Third World reveals the striking contradictions of his argumentation. Arguing that decolonization requires an "interfere[nce] in the play of market forces," Marcos's political logic reconciled the persistence of decolonial movements with the aims of neocolonial restructuring. It also betrayed the important point that Marcos's conception of the Filipino as Human, as a decolonized, Third World subjectivity, subscribed to a self-determinism bound to the demands of national security and capitalist accumulation. Marcos's promise to extinguish the languid, apathetic figure of

"Juan Tamad" declared the end of Filipino indolence by setting the limits of racial possibility through the terms of economic self-sufficiency. In Sylvia Wynter's acute theorization of humanism as a planetary philosophy that abrogated the terms of theological absolutism, she writes that "in order to be unified in *economic* terms we have to first produce an *economic* conception of being human." Wynter's theorization is particularly incisive here, for it interrogates the terms of humanity's coherence as imperative for organizing the very logics of colonialism and capitalism. By responding to critics and delineating sovereignty beyond the sphere of the political alone—that is, in the realm of human potential—Marcos endeavored to contextualize his rule as a commitment to the specificities and intricacies of the Filipino condition. This approach sought to attribute a counterbalanced, humanist character to the violence of the regime's political program.

THE EFFICACY OF FILIPINO ENGLISH TEACHERS

The treatment of Filipino subjectivity as a configuration of human potential was instrumental for organizing Filipino labor at the PRPC. As Marcos rehearsed the magnitude of Bataan's historical weight, imploring listeners to acknowledge the momentousness of the occasion, he further explained that Filipinos hailed from a long refugee tradition and should, in fact, try to see themselves in the refugee other. Encouraging Filipinos to extend their service to their Vietnamese "neighbors," whose "hardship is our hardship," he admitted: "Today, I should be in Pangasinan or in Baguio. But when I was told that I needed to come [to Morong] with the First Lady to see something, to witness the compassion of the reformed Filipino and their leaders toward our siblings from Vietnam, I did not hesitate to come here."[52] Marcos described compassion as the capacity to both recognize one's self in the other and to extend care in the service of that other. His recognition of the "reformed Filipino," in other words, depended precisely on the Filipino's practice of compassion. Throughout their tenure, the Marcoses' reiterated the importance of compassion, which they described as empathy, creativity, and love. Imelda Marcos explained, "We find love not in ourselves but in others. This is so obvious yet so often forgotten. One will find it among our people, in their poverty and misery. . . . During our travels to seek out people, I always tried to absorb every little thing that could be of value for our fellow men, for it is by knowing others that we can gain more self-knowledge. And I have one conclusion: that for many of us, the beginning of hope, the keystone of progress, is a Compassionate Society."[53] While it may be tempting to dismiss the First Lady's philosophy as political farce, her call for a "compassionate society" that one finds "among our own people" usefully illustrates the extent to which the Marcoses' articulation of humanism relied on a conceptualization of Filipino raciality. This raciality was tied to prescriptions of life-giving labor that functioned as a framework for conceptualizing women's work and articulating the utility of Filipino affect. Describing compassion as a natural human proclivity for goodness, the First Lady rehearsed its significance as value, a medium for enabling transaction between the Filipino and the rest of the world.

The extension of compassion onto the other structured the shape of Filipino humanitarian work. When Marcos declared that "this project will only succeed if all of you and your leaders in Morong, Bataan are patrons and helpers of this project," he declared that the success of refugee rehabilitation, that is, the "transformation [of the refugee] from a displaced individual into a person equipped for a productive and meaningful life in his country of final destination," rested on the work of the Filipino people. In his speech, Marcos instructed that humanitarianism provided Filipinos with a measure of their abilities and talents ("sukatan n[g] gating kagalingan, katangian"). Whereas humanism required that "the urgent demands of the body" be reconciled with "the imperious needs of the spirit," the regime defined humanitarianism as humanism's expression, which required the two-pronged work of self-recognition—knowledge of the self according to the possession of historical knowledge and the extension of the self for the reconciliation of the other's body and spirit with humanity. Humanitarianism, the use of Filipino "abilities and talents" in the service of the other, provided Filipinos with an opportunity to measure themselves in contradistinction to the refugee, presenting the refugee as a yardstick for expressing Filipino humanity. Humanitarianism rested on a conception of humanity that proclaimed an ontological sameness while humanitarian work structured the divide between the refugee to whom service would be rendered and the Filipino who would extend that service.[54]

Meanwhile, the transpacific governmentality of humanitarianism was astute in its speculation of Filipino humanitarian work. A report published by the US General Accounting Office (GAO) stated that the PRPC would serve as more than a "holding center," that it would operate as the site of "presettlement training." The summary reported that "100 percent [of] U.S. funds" were "exclusively ... contracted with ICMC for a $1.3 million ESL/ CO program for August 1980 through July 1981." The program at the PRPC sought to establish a training program that could address the "morale problems" of refugees in the United States. The report further explained that the use of "local, national teachers" would result in considerable financial savings:

> The ICMC budget provides that 188 Filipino teachers will teach English at an annual salary of $3,376; U.N. volunteers, U.S. citizens, or university exchange students will teach cultural orientation. The ICMC program manager has no reservation about using Filipinos as teachers. He is confident of their ability because the Philippines has an excellent English as a Second Language program, which is given early in childhood education. In touring the RPC, we visited several refugee English classes, ranging from initial pre-literates to advanced English speakers. Our impression is that the Filipino teachers are quite effective.[55]

Filipino teachers were known to "establish rapport with their students, an atmosphere of mutual respect, admiration, and friendliness in the classroom, and a no-nonsense professional attitude toward work . . . because of personality traits that are typical of Filipinos."[56] Filipino teachers—many of them students from Ateneo de Manila University and the Philippine Normal School who had visited the United States—comprised a majority of the center's teaching force.[57] The regime's humanist discourse and the narratives offered by the US logic of rehabilitation structured humanitarian work not through any abstract notion of morality but through racialized and gendered articulations of Filipino efficacy and affability.[58]

As "mutual respect, admiration, and friendliness" characterized Filipino subjectivity, it also charted the affective register of US Cold War propaganda for diffusing the politics of global integration and containment into a program of cooperation. The report's cultural essentialism translated Filipino affability through the terms of rehabilitation. The division of labor ordered by the PRPC functioned in tandem with the Marcos regime's investment in human potential. The efficacy of Filipino English teachers was, on the one hand, articulated as the fruition of historical possession ordered by the Philippine historical point of view. The Filipino command over English reflected the saturation of colonial history into a modern instantiation of Filipino subjectivity. Capitalizing on this legacy of English instruction, in 1974 Marcos established a bilingual education program, which mandated that mathematics and science courses be taught in English in Philippine schools.[59]

Filipino teachers' apparent fit for refugee instruction was also a testament to the legacy of colonial English instruction in the archipelago since the early twentieth century, which solidified English as a lingua franca in the Philippines. US officials selected English as the language of instruction, according to a 1908 US Report of the Philippine Commission, because "it is the language of business in the Orient, because it is the language of free institutions, and because it is the language which the Filipino children who do not know Spanish are able more easily to learn than they are to learn Spanish, and it is the language of the present sovereign of the Islands." The commission report continued to explain that English instruction in the Philippines "began with the soldiers of the American Army, one of whom was detailed from each company to teach schools in the villages which had become peaceful."[60] While English instruction was an essential feature of the US mission of "benevolent assimilation," through which officials touted self-rule as the end result of colonial governance, such a notable description of English presented language as the operative link between Western liberalism and the expansion of global capital. The language of "the present sovereign," of "free institutions," is the one equipped to operate as the language of "business in the Orient." As a matter of linguistic practicality, English was well suited for establishing a clear delineation between the Spanish of a past empire and the language of a modernity guided by the United States. Moreover, that US soldiers were the first English teachers in the colony reveals the role of English for obscuring a central contradiction of modernity—that war and militarized occupation are the precursors of "peace."

The ubiquity of English in the Philippines was a testament to the tenaciousness of US colonial education in the archipelago, and the success of Filipino English teachers evidenced the efficacy of US models of "cultural orientation" for addressing the "morale problems" of colonial and imperial dispossession. In other words, Filipinos' expertise in English not only testified to the utility of US benevolent assimilation but also articulated Filipino subjectivity as the capaciousness of liberal humanity to reassert and reproduce itself elsewhere and in a variety of forms. Cristina Evangelista Torres has described the development of English language instruction in the first decades of US colonial rule as producing the perplexing problem of cultivating ill-mannered schoolchildren who learned some of the language from US soldiers stationed in the islands. As a result, teachers taught English alongside proper etiquette under the mandate of the "Good Manners and Right Conduct" bulletin. Colonial language instruction has often carried with it the framework for colonial discipline.[61] The role of the Filipino as

English teacher materialized the didacticism necessary for translating the lessons of such history into the labor of rehabilitation, and this efficacy coalesced as a calculus for determining the logistical and financial arrangement of the PRPC.

TEACHER-AS-SOMBATH

In 1959, under the guidance of the Modern Language Association, US officials instituted the Center for Applied Linguistics (CAL) as an instrument of US Cold War knowledge production. Its aim to facilitate English language training in the United States and around the world reflected the development of English as a medium for facilitating international cooperation and global finance in the period of global decolonization.[62] The rise and development of CAL as a premier body of US linguistic and language research not only intersected with the work of other US agencies outside the United States, particularly in decolonizing nations, but also strove to establish a "clearinghouse" for resolving any tensions between these agencies. In 1962, in an effort to connect the shared work between the Bureau of Indian Affairs, the Department of Defense, and the Peace Corps, all of which incorporated English language learning and training as part of their broader goals, CAL formed the National Advisory Council on the Teaching of English as a Second Language, asserting that the "teaching of English as a second language is a problem of such critical international importance that it calls for a sustained national effort, governmental and nongovernmental on a greatly increased scale."[63] In the midst of US political upheavals of the 1960s and early 1970s, CAL presented English as a modality for imagining historical continuity between the US settler project and postwar global modernization. The narrative of national cohesion advanced by CAL and other US international development agencies strove to manage persistent racial crises that consistently threatened to undo it.[64]

Linguistic research conducted throughout the 1960s on behalf of the Bureau of Indian Affairs described the need for more effective and innovative English language instruction that would better manage "cultural differences" as well as provide data for the production of English language learning "for other non-English speaking groups and disadvantaged groups in the United States."[65] At the twentieth anniversary of its founding, CAL officials in 1979 gathered for the Georgetown University Round Table on Languages and Linguistics to discuss the role of "language in public life." In his progress report on the President's Commission on Foreign Languages and International Studies, Georgetown University president Timothy Healy advised that language research centers should function as national resources to "help render impossible an American military approach to anybody known as 'slopes' or 'gooks'" and admonished "our blindness to [East Asian] people and our misreading of their history, their politics, and their very souls."[66] While Healy's remarks proffered a policy of tolerance, his articulation of "cultural" understanding especially in contradistinction to "slopes" and "gooks" conceptualized the severity of racial difference not simply as difference in and of itself but as the threat of an always-present decolonial insurgent war within which such terms provided a language of colonial humanity.

In 1985, CAL published its inaugural issue of *Passage: A Journal of Refugee Education*. Sponsored by the US Department of State, CAL published eleven issues of *Passage* dedicated to English language and cultural orientation instruction for refugees. In the final issue, a US State Department official lauded the journal as an "effective forum for information exchange."[67] With the journal, refugee center administrators, instructors, and staff from the different centers in Southeast Asia shared strategies for teaching, highlighted the work of their students, and provided readers with general updates about refugee education in the various processing centers. Other issues included reader letters from English teachers in the United States, for whom the lessons of the journal provided pedagogical instruction. The journal also included pages filled with classroom plans for integrating science and math into course curriculum, addressing different teaching strategies for elementary and secondary school students, and utilizing technology as a teaching tool. These articles modeled for readers the methods by which refugee responses to instruction could be studied, assessed, and addressed. As the journal sought to analyze student responses to English in relation to the centers' humanitarian goals, teachers and administrators often adopted ethnographic approaches to investigate the efficacy of their methods. The journal's accumulation of data and empirical approach to instruction sustained the teacher's authority as an important vessel of humanitarian aid. Indeed, one article described English training as "language as a form of knowledge."[68] Language training strengthened the production of Cold War knowledge about US imperialist projects.

The journal also reflected the divisions of the center, distinguishing the difference between those who were responsible for the distribution of aid from those to whom aid must be given. While the journal, for instance, identified critical figures of the center as its administrators, teachers, and students, the center conceptualized such configurations within the hierarchization of a colonial humanism. The journal positioned the refugee, belonging elsewhere but needing to be incorporated into the present time and space of the Western world, as the object of aid. The methods of incorporation attempted to instill within the refugee student an appreciation for the liberal principles of individualized responsibility and productivity. The journal measured student gains through promises of self-sufficiency and economic potential. In a 1985 article that discussed "pre-employment training," the author explained that the goal of instruction was to assist "students to hear the steady ticking of the internal clock that Americans hear throughout the day and which has been missing in the lives of most of our students most of their lives. It is in the measuring of the minutes of their lives against the idea that time has monetary or personal value. It is knowing that time is tangible, can be managed, and can be either saved or lost."[69] "Pre-employment training" defined refugee subjectivity as fundamentally lacking a necessary form of knowledge critical to a productive life. It was the goal of cultural orientation to align students with the notion of time as inherently valuable, that is, time as adhering to the mandates of capitalist accumulation.

The task of cultural orientation was not to simply instill within refugees the basics of the English language. Instead, its goal was to teach refugees how to *properly* communicate. Program directors encouraged teachers to move away from facilitating repetitive language exercises to cultivating "natural communication."[70] This type of instruction—what the journal deemed a "revolution" in English language training—sought to change the student-teacher relationship from the notion of the instructor as the mere transmitter of information to the idea of the instructor as a participant in the student's everyday world. Such a move reimagined the classroom as a place of dialogue rather than as a site of mere information accumulation. It emphasized the teacher's responsibility to cultivate the student's whole person, wherein English acted as the medium for expressing the student's life experiences. As refugee training thus focused on the expression of "experience," the cultivation of this experience became a pedagogical imperative that advanced a biopolitical project for measuring life. Experience was already overdetermined through a calculable set of standards that marked a measurable life—a name that delineated individuality; the linear trajectory of one's personhood from birth to death; the person's past, present, and future.

By encouraging the adoption of English as the medium for translating the refugee experience, the program for cultural orientation predetermined the shape of acceptable refugee expression. A supervisor's instruction to teachers advised: "Do everything you can to help students relax and gain self-confidence."[71] In another instance, two instructors advocated for the use of "Indochinese proverbs" for translating American ideologies to students, imploring teachers to ask themselves, "How do we reduce the strangeness of [English]?"[72] Teachers' work to reduce English's "strangeness" labored to mask the sharpness of refugee dislocation by making English inseparable from the communication of their subjectivities. In essence, directors' encouragement to teachers to help their students relax aimed to iron out the contradictions between freedom, on the one hand, and the imperialized warfare that produced that freedom, on the other. The journal upheld the goals of CAL, cultivating, rehearsing, and sustaining the linguistic-anthropological divide between the teacher and the student to uphold English as the language of freedom. The journal treated English, as Vicente Rafael has written, as "the language of 'political harmony' and democratic civility [which] requires as its condition of possibility the violent reworking of differences into sameness."[73]

Filipino English teachers' humanitarian work exemplified Filipino humanity through its efforts to facilitate the refugee's transition into modernity. In its inaugural issue, *Passage* published a letter titled "Teacher, It's Nice to Meet You, Too," written by Ruby Ibañez, a Filipino English teacher who worked at the PRPC. The journal identifies Ibañez as a former ESL teacher at the PRPC and Tagalog teacher to American Peace Corps volunteers in the Philippines. At the time of her writing, she was a teacher trainer for the center's training department. The letter adopts the perspective of a refugee student named Sombath and addresses the teacher to describe the student's frustrations with being unable to adequately articulate in his new language the full scope of his life and the range of his emotions and experiences. Assuming the epistolary format, Sombath urges his teacher to practice patience and compassion with her students. The text reveals the importance of the teacher's life-giving work to rehabilitate the refugee, illuminating the ways that refugee subjectivity was overdetermined by the rigid confines of US liberalism. At the same time, it also illustrates the ways that the classroom generated alternative relationalities that confounded these colonial divisions of humanity.

In many ways, the text illuminates the unspeakability of the refugee condition and the ways that US rehabilitation programs wielded English as an instrument of liberation from abjection. With the letter, Sombath (or, more accurately, the teacher-as-Sombath) lists the harrowing struggles that he endured in order to reach the teacher's classroom. He explains that he is "old, older than all the dying faces I have left behind, older than the hungry hands I have pushed aside, older than the shouts of fear and terror I have closed my ears to, older than the world, maybe." Sombath's claim that the horrors that he experienced made him "older than the world" suggest that there may be no adequate language with which to make them known. Within the structure of the PRPC, however, this unspeakability cannot be inconclusive. The unspeakable must be made to speak. Sombath insists that his classroom learning will be able to give name to the magnitude of his experience. As he describes his life as one of unspeakable suffering, he presents the classroom as a space of healing and eventual transformation. Sombath implores the teacher to "help me . . . know the days of the week or the twelve months of the year," that is, to guide him to find the right words to speak the unspeakable. Moreover, Sombath explains, "When I say my name is Sombath I want to tell you also that back in my village, I had a mind of my own. I could reason. I could argue. I could lead. My neighbors respected me." Sombath's incapacity to tell his story—his inability to reconcile his story with his self, to make himself whole again—stands as the emblem of injustice. Postwar justice materializes through Sombath's ownership over his story and over his self. Sombath's insistence that the teacher conduct her work in order to provide him with the language to tell his story not only marks English as the language of global reconciliation but the teacher herself as the medium for his rehabilitation. The text presents this instruction as the avenue by which the inconclusiveness of war's end might be mitigated to reveal the validity of the imperial project. By bridging the disconnect between who Sombath *was* and who Sombath *is* within the center, the letter lauds English as the medium of proper transition. Cultural orientation and English language training construct subjectivity in relation to history and as a mechanism for establishing the parameters of inclusion into global humanity. Despite the US military defeat in Vietnam, this training sought to extend the literal and figurative site of war to the realm of language and the classroom. In making the unspeakable speak, the narrative resolves the irresolution of the US wars in Southeast Asia and legitimizes humanitarianism as the arbiter of justice.

Still, the very coherence of Sombath's story depends precisely on the teacher's humanitarian work. She both extends her compassion in the service of rehabilitation and assumes the role of translator, taking ownership over the narration of Sombath's story. In his theorization of the work of translation, Rafael discusses translation as labor that serves as a prerequisite for the immigrant or terrorist other who must eventually assimilate into the US nation. Rafael writes that "a broad range of Americans . . . in their mania for monolingualism see translation as a kind of labor that only non-Anglophones should have to do. Since it is 'they' who must assimilate, it is therefore 'they,' not 'us,' who must translate their native tongue into English."[74] Within the transnational space of the PRPC, the work of the Filipino teacher is not only the labor of facilitating assimilation. The labor of translation is the work entrusted to the people of formerly colonized nations to transmit the lessons of democracy onto new colonial others.

This life-giving labor is the racialized and gendered work of translating care into the paradigms of international refugee rehabilitation. The text's epistolary format necessitates the direct address between the "I" of the writer and the "you" of the recipient. Given that Ibañez is the writer of the text, the relationship between the "I" and "you" is complicated, signaling the writer's performance as her own student for an audience of readers. In this performative interplay between subjectivities, the text becomes a testimony of the teacher's work. Sombath, for instance, makes declarative statements about the teacher's role in the classroom, describing her responses to his fumbles: "Now I see you smiling" and "Now you laugh." These statements relegate the teacher to a list of sentimentalist and affective responses that make possible the expression of Sombath's humanity. Sombath's narrative renders the teacher a vessel of humanitarian work for the ultimate goal of his rehabilitation. Throughout the text, moreover, Sombath insists that the teacher practice patience in order to reap the ultimate rewards of his learning. He articulates the necessary work: "Keep that smile," "give me a gentle voice," and "continue to reward me." Focusing on the affective work of care that came to structure Filipina women's transnational work especially in the later years of Marcos's presidency, Sombath presents this work not only as fundamental to his rehabilitation but also as instrumental to the formation of refugee subjectivity produced by such program. It is, as Purnima Mankekar and Akhil Gupta write of call center labor, a type of "intimate encounter" that "generat[es] . . . particular kinds of laboring subjects, thus blurring the boundaries between 'pre-alienated' and alienated selfhood." This labor buttresses the masculinized subject of rehabilitation who is already overdetermined by an internationalist humanism.[75] Indeed, the configurations of the Filipino humanitarian and the refugee subjects are intertwined in the structures of the PRPC. However, insofar as the text's inclusion within the journal makes the letter function as an instruction to English language teachers, the letter also catalogues the materiality of gendered humanitarian work. Both in the teacher's work and in Sombath's narrative of her work, the teacher makes visible her labor, which the journal obfuscates in its primary focus on the rehabilitation of the refugee student. In this way, the testimony illustrates no conclusive truth about the efficacy of English language learning; instead, it interrupts the solidity of US and Philippine humanitarian narratives. In its very disloyalty to the telos and singularity of an individualized story, the letter's multiple—and often competing—narrative strains showcase the ways that the letter exceeds the very subjectivities that it initially proposes.

The text frames the subjectivities of Sombath and the teacher as singular conceptions of liberal possibility, where productivity lines the contours of recognition within the framework of humanitarianism. Yet even as the text promises the refugee's transformation, it confounds the center's divides between the teacher and student to insist instead that the specificity of these configurations be unhinged from the overdetermination of liberal rehabilitation and postcolonial subjectivity pronounced by the PRPC. The text's multiplicity provides the discursive location for reimagining affinities between different people at the PRPC. Although the text's dominant narrative suggests that the teacher's work will allow Sombath to rectify the effects of war's destruction by reconciling his past with his present, the trouble that Sombath encounters with English speaks to the very incapacity of such models to account for life defined by the terms of war and empire. Sombath's inability, for instance, to correctly pronounce "'refrigerator,' 'emergency,' or 'appointment'" is not simply a source of disappointment but, rather, an illustration of the failure of such models of humanitarianism to "complete" the project of rehabilitation.

When Sombath explains to his teacher that his utterance of "Cambodia" and "Khmer" has supplanted "a land of fields and rivers and hills where people lived in a rich tradition of life and oneness," these disjunctures become sites where the teacher can bear witness to the untranslatability of dispossession. Sombath declares to the teacher, "I want to tell you though that I, too, am a person of the past"; the "too" charts an interconnected imperialist history between the refugee and the teacher that uncovers the continuity of war to structure the PRPC and its articulation of the present conditions. Rather than declaring a shared humanity through the logic of humanitarianism, this adverbial addition delineates the differentiated experiences that constitute the "past" for both the student and the teacher. Here English does not communicate universality but identifies its precise limitations. Under colonial and imperial war, the hierarchy of the classroom, materialized as the teacher and the student, is the effect of US overseas empire both at the turn of the twentieth century and near its end.

This difference, signaled by this "too," is a mode of affiliation. By making inextricable Sombath's capacity to speak with the teacher's labor, the text challenges the promise of liberation proffered by English instruction and cultural orientation to imagine other solidarities inside and outside empire. It reveals that any invocation of the "I" inevitably depends on the "you." Such relation makes visible the shape of the teacher's labor. Humanitarianism necessitates the production of refugee alterity to render it viable as a discourse of international exchange. Rafael inquires: "What happens to the I that says 'I' across languages? How does it manage to reach a *you*, and can it always count on a response? What risks does it run, what debts does it incur?"[76] Rafael's query turns to the work and process of translation to uncover the intertwining politics of colonialism, nationalism, and state power that are inherent in the very utterance of language. It helpfully articulates the ways that the invocation of "I" and "you" is always a question of subjectivity, where each points to "one who is always already in transition, on the way to being other than who I am."[77] The "too," in other words, locates the configuration: it challenges the solidity of subjectivity by calling into the student's frame not only the teacher but also other experiences and relations that are called forth by the project of humanitarianism.

To return to the questions that I posed at the beginning of the chapter, the PRPC provides critical ground on which to rethink the landscapes and discourses of the racial cold war. Where dominant narratives of humanitarianism and rehabilitation focus on the refugee as the object of US liberalism, the multilayered relations of the PRPC present the ways that authoritarian governance, US imperialist war, and global capital functioned in tandem to structure the very conditions of humanitarianism and rehabilitation. In this way, the configuration of the teacher as the Filipino humanitarian offers a way to both interrogate the affective labor by which the refugee is rehabilitated and highlight the importance of authoritarianism for conditioning that labor. Ibañez's text, however, unmakes these politics by imagining affinities both within and outside the strictures of the PRPC, challenging the regimes of humanitarianism, in search of new humanities.

CONCLUSION

Reckoning with the Body

In the summer of 2015, I spent a few weeks in Manila to continue research on the Marcos regime. I had planned to end my trip with a visit to the Marcos museum and mausoleum in Batac, Ilocos Norte, to get a look at the preserved body of the late dictator. Never mind the rumors that the corpse on display was a wax statue, a mere replica of a man whose body did not reflect the grand and vicious stories that encircled it.

I am still not sure what I expected to find during my visit, but I was fixated on his body as a lasting physical remnant of the regime. Sometime before my trip, I came across the name of Frank Malabed, Marcos's embalmer, who had, since Marcos's death, made a name for himself as a "mortician to the stars."[1] Beyond the fascinating morbidity that surrounded the body, I was struck by the ways that the dictator's mythology, the pageantry that surrounded his fictions, continued well after his life. I also discovered that Malabed's business was a family one, a trade that he inherited from his father and that he passed down to his own children. He told the story of helping his father prepare and dress the bodies of thousands of dead US soldiers during the Vietnam War in a hangar at Clark Air Base before they were shipped to their families, the "art of caring for the dead."[2] Malabed's story, both connected to and apart from the dictatorship, made the body feel like a single point in an expansive web of transpacific connection.

FIGURE C.1 Anti-Marcos graffiti in Quezon City, Philippines, in June 2018.

I never made it to Batac. The last few days of my trip fell on Philippine Independence Day weekend. I was depleted by the number of hours it took me, with my limited knowledge of Manila transportation and traffic, to get to any given library or museum and by the number of times I was turned away from places because they were closed for construction, repair, or holiday. That winter, I traveled to Hawaiʻi to find other ways to access information about his exile, his body, his death, his initial interment. More than any rich archival find, I noted the tangled means by which people with whom I spoke remembered the contentiousness of Marcoses' residence in Honolulu; the sightings, both bizarre and banal; and the ways that the lines between the true and tall tales of the couple's time on the island blurred into memories.

By the time I returned to Manila three years later, the Marcos family, with the permission of president Rodrigo Duterte, had already buried its patriarch (figure C.1). Before this point, I thought I wanted to study the regime itself, the intricacies of the dictatorship. Yet while I lamented the lost opportunity to see the body for myself, to witness it, to castigate it, it was also clear to me that the body was less important than the act of looking, the routes that led me from California to it as a point of interest, and the circuits that made themselves available to me on the way there.

* * *

After Ferdinand Marcos declared himself the victor of a snap election in February 1986, reaffirming the continuity of his twenty-one-year reign, the Filipino people responded by occupying Epifanio de los Santos Avenue (EDSA) for four days. The People Power Revolution (or EDSA Revolution), as it came to be named, was celebrated around the world as a bloodless revolt, an inspiring display of people's resistance against the Marcos dictatorship that brought together an unlikely coalition—rebel nuns, military generals gone rogue, and a mass of citizens—all committed to toppling the despot. In the center of the storm, Corazon Aquino, widow of Marcos's vociferous political opponent Benigno "Ninoy" Aquino Jr. (whose assassination, in some ways, catalyzed the revolt), took her seat as the first post-Marcos president. In the years following Aquino's assumption of office, critics, denouncing the efficacy of the Aquino administration to restore democracy in the country, lamented the "unfinished" quality of the revolution. Others, more sympathetic to the difficulty of Aquino's task, described the challenge of rectifying the corruption of Marcos's cronyism when many of the regime's key officials continued to hold on to office well after Marcos's exile.[3] In the decades that followed Marcos's removal, the memory of the Marcos regime itself continued to operate as a site of struggle, and the task of remembering became an increasingly grave act.

On September 20, 1999, hundreds of people gathered at the Ateneo de Manila University to participate in the Conference on the Legacies of the Marcos Dictatorship. Spanning three days, the conference convened to deliberate on the continued importance of the dictatorship to the political formation of the country. Organized around the theme of "memory, truth-telling, and the pursuit of justice," conveners pronounced the urgency of remembering the lessons spurred by the Marcos past in the face of a forgetting that structured the cultural milieu of the present. Delivering the opening remarks, Ateneo administrator Alfredo R. A. Bengzon offered the following message: "I feel that the overriding question that faces us is this: How do we make incarnate our memory of the years of dictatorship? How can the truth about the past be made so palpable and so present in our people's lives that revisionists will never be able to rewrite it?" Speaking as foreshadowing only two years before another people power movement removed president Joseph Estrada from office for rampant corruption, Bengzon declared with urgency that Filipinos' "coming of age as free and democratic people" depended first on "forg[ing] among ourselves a collective and inviolable memory of the injustice and outrage of the years 1972–1986."[4] Presenters insisted on the need to assess and redraw the shape of cultural memory around martial law and dictatorship in the Philippines. They recounted in detail their experiences under martial law, outlined the depth of the regime's corruption, and celebrated the various modes of resistance that materialized during and continued well beyond the period. Several participants reflected on martial law as having disturbed, interrupted, or destroyed something that had once existed but that no longer remained. Others demanded that the survivors of the regime's program of torture and salvaging be allowed to testify against the Marcos family and its collaborators, articulating a shared understanding of justice that depended on the unfailing pursuit of truth against the onslaught of post-Marcos historical revisionism.[5]

The conference expressed a kind of national emergence that coalesced around this commitment. The "collective and inviolable memory" on which Bengzon insisted did not belong to an already constituted national culture; rather, it described the work of an imagined one whose materialization relied on these theorizations of memory, rectification, and justice. As presenters expressed their dismay over the shape of cultural memory, the conference troubled the framework of restitution and reconciliation that often arbitrates the aftermath of dictatorship. Declaring forgetting not as the result of neglect or the mere passage of time but as an acute crisis, the conference insisted on an unceasing deliberation with the regime that called forth what Jean Franco has described as "the magnitude and the incalculability of loss."[6] The multifariousness that constituted the conference demanded not a remembering but a reckoning.

GOTERA AND LINMARK ON THE BODY

When Ferdinand Marcos died in Honolulu in 1989, Imelda Marcos declared it her life's mission to contest the Aquino administration's decision to refuse the return of Marcos's body to the Philippines and reject the family's request for a hero's burial in the national cemetery.[7] When succeeding president Fidel Ramos permitted the eventual return of Marcos's remains in 1993 but once again denied the family's burial request, the former First Lady ordered that her husband's body be displayed in the family mausoleum in Batac, where it remained until 2016. Since then, Marcos's body has become the object of national controversy and public debate, illuminating the dynamism of public sentiment around martial law and the Marcoses' legacy. For the Marcos family and its loyalists, the public display of the body empowered a crusade of historical revisionism, igniting a rebroadcast of Marcos's brilliance, heroism, service, and unparalleled leadership. For Aquino and subsequent presidents, their refusal to bury Marcos reasserted a commitment to the new republic promised by the 1986 revolution. And for others still, the body remained an emblem of excess, absurdity, and intrigue.

Imelda Marcos explained that she intended the display of the body to be "not only... a political statement [but] a spectacle—an international spectacle."[8] Malabed, Marcos's embalmer, noted that "Ma'am did not care for [the shriveled skin of Marcos's dead body]" and that "she wanted Filipinos to see President Marcos [the way] he looked before, when he was still young."[9] Indeed, the former First Lady ordered the preservation of a specific likeness, ageless and defiant against inevitable decay; she sought for her husband an immortality that challenged the finality of death and the certainty of deposal. Insisting that Malabed paint Marcos as he had once been rather than what he now was, Imelda Marcos attempted to revive the fictions that had buttressed their power to infuse them into the permanence of cultural memory. While she aimed to showcase the callousness of the Aquino administration's denial of the family's burial request, her proclamation of the body as spectacle insisted that the body, above all, be *seen*. In the face of the Aquino administration's quest to banish Marcos to the dregs of the historical past, the body as spectacle spurred a public memorial instead.

Mondo Marcos, an anthology edited by Frank Cimatu and Rolando Tolentino, is a collection of writings penned by so-called Marcos babies of the 1970s and 1980s who aim to bear witness to the legacies of the dictatorship. The collection includes two poems by writers Vince Gotera and R. Zamora Linmark that address the significance of Marcos's body to the memorialization of martial law. In Gotera's "Three Sonnetinas" and Linmark's "What Some Are Saying about the Body," Marcos's body catalyzes a *looking* that reckons with Marcos's power. Much of the regime's force depended on the ability to see and be seen, a mode of governance that rendered its power visible and its abuses invisible. The Marcoses' fixation with aestheticizing modernization and performing sentimentality, for instance, established visuality as a critical medium for interaction between the regime on display and the public as audience. Moreover, the regime's declaration of martial law sanctioned a system of surveillance (public curfew and censorship of the press) that constructed the frame of visibility in ways that rendered the public hypervisible.[10] Shifting their focus to the things that lie beneath this operation of display and surveillance—the things that transpire in between these renditions of public and private space, that breathe and whisper—Gotera's and Linmark's poems envision another optic for articulating the regime's violence. In these texts, seeing is discerning but unfocused, while looking is direct and piercing. Not passive but active, what Marita Sturken and Lisa Cartwright have described as "a social practice ... a means of navigating space organized around the sense of sight," looking underlines a public fascination with the body as spectacle to organize an unflinching interrogation and adjudication of the regime.[11] Whereas seeing functions as a modality of public control that treats the seen as subjects of the regime's state fictions and control, looking challenges the subjectivities pronounced by these fictions by rearticulating the terms of agency and will. Looking is also different from witnessing, which depends on a witness's capacity to replicate the extent of her sight. Whereas the witness is often inserted within juridical processes of redress, impelled to tell and confess, urged to reveal how it really happened, looking does not concern itself with the reassembly of the truth but, rather, describes truth as a vehicle that the regime weaponizes to propel its violence.[12] Looking reassembles configurations to reimagine these relations to power and possibility.

Born and raised in San Francisco but also a resident of the Philippines for a time, Vince Gotera is a poet and critic who has written about the Filipino experience in the United States as well as his life as a US soldier during the Vietnam War. In his own study of Vietnam War poetry written by veterans of the war, Gotera notes that "to 'tell it' is one of the dominant impulses informing Vietnam-war literature: the documentary urge, the drive to make the horrors, the senselessness of war, and the incredibility of Vietnam concrete to Americans back home."[13] He continues to explain that there is an "unquestioned assumption" within the literature that "poetry is *the* proper response to war."[14] While his poem "Three Sonnetinas" addresses the fall of the Marcoses and not the US war in Vietnam, Gotera's conceptualization of war poetry elucidates the poetic form as a critical vehicle with which to "tell" of the atrocities of violence. In "Three Sonnetinas," the omniscient masses watch a Marcosian comedy of errors unfold and see the Marcos family devolve into a state of inconsequence.[15] The first stanza finds Marcos shadowboxing in the front of a mirror as he instructs his wife to wear the "blue *terno*" to her arraignment hearing. In the second stanza, Imelda Marcos orchestrates a grand birthday celebration for her husband's corpse. She sings "happy birthday" to her "fair Andy," whose fairness is only the result of his frozenness within a "space-age polymer coffin." In the third stanza, Bongbong Marcos, the couple's politician son, visits Cardinal Jaime Sin for confession only to request an exorcism to banish the ghost of his "Daddy Marcos." In the first stanza, Marcos stares at himself, and jurists interrogate Imelda. In the second stanza, the First Lady gazes at her dead husband, and in the final stanza, Bongbong trembles at the sight of his father's ghost.

The poem redirects the regime's system of surveillance from the Filipino people to the Marcos family so that the Marcoses themselves become the objects of scrutiny. By the end of the poem, Marcos's ghost complains that he "doesn't deserve to be gawked at by sense- / less yokels. Hell would be better." The irony is in the looking: the attention that Marcos once craved from the masses is now the medium of his entrapment. Even as Marcos's ghost condemns the "senseless yokels," the Marcoses themselves are the targets of derision. In each stanza, the first-person singular voice details the banality of a Marcos life removed from the high echelons of power; and the rhyme constrains the immensity and ubiquity of the regime's control. Each stanza reveals a discrepancy between the way a Marcos views himself or herself and what he or she has inevitably become. The Marcoses performed authority through their rehearsal of what Talitha Espiritu has termed a "national family melodrama" to which the Filipino public subscribed for social instruction. Whereas the Marcoses intended this performance to be seen and admired, the sonnetinas stage and delight in a crumbling romance. The performance of grandness, for instance, through the terno and the posthumous birthday celebration renders the Marcoses' display absurd in relation to the solemnness of trial and death.

In the first stanza, the former president says to himself,

> The goddamn USA is hoping
> For billions, but Imelda's got more brains in her right
> Shoe than any federal judge—let the wife
> Show them.[16]

A series of US hearings and trials followed the Marcoses' exile in Honolulu. In 1987, the US House of Representatives Subcommittee on Asian and Pacific Affairs investigated the "Marcos tapes," recordings that captured the former president's plans to organize a coup and seize executive power from Aquino. By the end of the hearing, State Department legal adviser Abraham Soafer asserted that "it is unfair to suggest that if something happens in the Philippines, we will be responsible for it. It just is not so."[17] In 1988, a US grand jury indicted the Marcoses on charges of racketeering. The trial, which began in March 1990 in New York City, one year after Ferdinand Marcos's death in Honolulu, ended with Imelda Marcos's acquittal. Immediately after the trial, the former First Lady declared, "'I thank the almighty God for the vindication . . . and I am in great awe for the jury system that symbolizes the soul of the American people.'"[18] In the face of these outcomes, the poem juxtaposes the results of the trials with the dictator's declaration of the First Lady's deception. This looking peers into the intimate space of Marcos's room to expose the incongruity between the Marcoses' political maneuvering and US state determinations of justice. Although the judicial process cannot indict the Marcos family, looking indicts both the Marcos family and US law.

Dividing his time between Manila and Honolulu, R. Zamora Linmark is a poet, novelist, and playwright whose work explores the tensions between race, gender, and sexuality and the Filipino American experience. In "What Some Are Saying about the Body," the "some" summons a multiplicity of narrators, all of whom look, examine, interrogate, gawk at, and laugh at the body.[19] The speakers converge and diverge over their support for or denouncement of the regime and the truth of its efficacy. In their arbitration, much like the slum talk that guided Insiang's devolvement, they offer hearsay and tsismis to construct a history of the regime; yet the text never betrays one or the other as the most veritable form of knowledge. Instead, the poem suggests that this interplay between oppositions—testaments of Marcos's inspiring leadership and accusations of his blatant corruption, of his strength and vibrancy and his weakness and ineffectiveness—is precisely the legacy of his rule. The contradictions reveal the paradox of Marcosian logic: that the balance of power must be suspended to preserve the sanctity of liberal governance. Such a revelation undercuts the regime's gaze to uncover the unseen. Insofar as truth, often presented in the form of state-constructed official accounts, is rendered incapable of explicating the intricacy of this power, the poem replaces truth as the premier mode of acceptable knowledge. Instead, popular forms such as gossip operate as what Lisa Lowe has described as "the instrument of the people," serving as "the terrain for the critique of degrees of deception and for the organization of actions against the apparatuses of rule."[20]

The first two lines of the poem begin, "Some say the body in a glass display / in Batac, Ilocos Norte does not belong to you." What follows is a series of rumors: that the body is a "wax in a freezer," for example, or that "you never left Hawaii, / that you are buried in Aloha soil." For the poem's speakers, the body is the site on which people can lodge their grievances and testify against the regime. As they share stories and information with each other, they piece together an alternative history of the Marcos era, one that, as Lowe suggests, is nondevelopmental and belongs to no one and to everyone. Its aim is to enable other subjectivities in its expression and retelling. Justice here takes shape not as the enactment of a new constitution or as the restoration of democratic political institutions. Instead, nonstatist forms of knowledge illuminate that which other reconciliatory forms obscure, delimit, or delegitimize: the intimate and multifarious experiences of a people and the ways they engage the multimodal afterlives of a regime.[21]

The poem's speakers identify the regime's system of surveillance as an integral facet of its governance. They characterize Marcos as the "David Copperfield of Urban Planning," "Chief Editor of the *Encyclopedia of Missing Persons*," and "a magician . . . a grand illusionist." These roles distinguish the regime's reliance on visuality—whether in the construction of grand, brutalist structures or in the removal of persons from literal view—for establishing political and social control. On the contrary, the speakers' looking scrutinizes the body to uncover the mechanics that brace these illusions. While in power, the Marcoses fixated on newness and beauty as the predecessors to modernization. Decay, of course, signaled stagnancy and regression, and the regime's condemnation and eradication of degeneracy legitimized the expulsion of those said to enable its contagion.[22] In the poem, decay is the point of entrance for wrestling with the dictator and serves as the medium by which the masses interrupt the Marcoses' stories of themselves. The poem reads,

> It is brunettes, some say, brunettes in stilettos
> that pumped your muscles and lengthened your penis
> even till the last gasp;
> death found you
> under Honolulu sheets with a four-inch farewell.

The poem's speakers dissect and dismember the body, reducing the enormity of the autocrat into an assemblage of decaying parts. Against Marcos's enactment of masculinized force—embodied, for instance, in both the benevolence of his paternalism and in the aggressiveness of his military might—the designation of Marcos's manhood as a "four-inch farewell" diminishes his authority and makes insignificant his force in relation to the largeness of the masses' growing interrogation.

When interviewers for *Playboy* magazine, incidentally, asked Marcos in 1987 how he wished to be remembered by history, he responded that he wanted to be recalled as a "full man . . . a whole man."[23] The former First

Lady's attempt to maintain the intactness of her husband's body—her instruction to the embalmer to paint him in his youth—sought to control public memory over his legacy. Yet the masses' efforts to dismember Marcos's memory, to reduce the body to its singular parts, interrupts the public memorialization that Imelda Marcos sought to construct. Jocelyn Martinez has written that "*re/member*ing . . . can be understood, on the one hand, as a re*member*ing, a re-articulation of different 'members' or parts of a plot and as suturing, through narration, of disparate elements."[24] The poem's rendition of failed parts as well as its destruction of Marcos's solidity renders inoperative the power on which he relied to substantiate his mythology.

Even as looking requires a distinct closeness between the body and its visitor, a commitment to the right here and right now of the present place and time, it simultaneously conjures other people and locations that might not otherwise be discernable in this exchange. Looking at the body, a speaker addresses the dictator directly:

> Some say you built the city from the swamp up,
> that in one day, plants rose into skyscrapers,
> dust tracks became overpass, and,
> for the first time, people walked across the sky
> like street angels in rubber slippers.

Referencing the regime's infrastructural development program, which aimed to transform Manila into the City of Man, the speaker divulges that such projects effectively moved Filipinos out into and within the world. The "street angels in rubber slippers" who "[walk] across the sky" lay bare a Filipino social formation, a configuration, that emerged from the movement and migration activated by the regime's modernization program. The poem calls forward an unwieldy Filipino diaspora so that even as it urges a nation to remember, it might also reconceptualize that nation in the wake of the dictator's death.[25] Bound together neither by homeland nor by other singular conceptions of national belonging, this expression of diaspora exposes the meandering web of transnational dispersals that have characterized Filipino life under the collaborative governmentality of the racial cold war. Oscar Campomanes has described the literature of Filipinos in the United States as the expression of a "generalized condition of exile." Referring to it as an "ensemble of its many relations, degrees, and forms," Campomanes argues that this writing gestures toward an "incommensurable sense of nonbeing."[26] "Nonbeing" points to an exclusion or displacement from the nation, a subjectivity constituted by its marginalization from ideal forms of national citizenship. The poetic, with its stops and starts, pauses, and silences, captures this nonbeing.[27] Gotera's and Linmark's poems refuse the impetus of narrative ownership, allowing other voices to proliferate the space of the poem rather than overdetermine its speaker. Poetry here directs attention to nonbeing as another form of belonging, an imagined community that coheres in the collective experience of migration, displacement, and exile.

Where the former First Lady insisted on the intimacy, sorrow, and wonder that comes with seeing the body, looking appropriates this investment in a public memorialization by installing a mass audience as the mediators of the dictator's legacy. Drawing on gossip and other alternative forms of knowledge rather than on state processes of truth and reconciliation, looking makes possible another articulation of the regime's reign. The masses pierce the regime's system of visuality, subverting its gaze to render itself the judges of Marcos. They keep the dictator half-alive, interrupting the finality of peace and death to resuscitate him so that he is forced to answer their inquiries. In these poems, the people are no longer the object of surveillance: they are the arbiters of meaning, rearticulating the legacy of the regime beyond its totalizing narratives. While looking refuses the conclusiveness of forgetting, it also enjoins an unceasing deliberation with the past as a different kind of remembering. Remembering not simply to *not* forget, looking is a reckoning that describes survival not as perseverance or resilience but as transformation.

Reckoning makes clearer the mechanics of US coloniality and its function in establishing the paradigms for conceptualizing authoritarianism as the exception to US republicanism. Ronald Reagan's protection of Marcos in Honolulu, for instance, legitimized Hawai'i as a frontier for sanitizing the dregs of despotism and US imperialism gone awry. That is, Marcos's exile in Hawai'i and the maintenance of the islands as the landing spot for the dictator reinforced Hawai'i as a location for invisibilizing the conflict, turmoil, and paradox of the Philippine-US alliance. As an arm of the racial cold war, Marcos's exile further obscured the struggles of Kānaka Maoli and the extent to which they might be elucidated. Dean Saranillio has interrogated the role of Hawai'i within US Cold War geopolitics, especially as it functioned as a site for imagining US multiculturalism and US-led global integration in contradistinction to communism.[28] In the days following Marcos's death in 1989, the *Honolulu Advertiser* reported that the Filipino community expressed mixed feelings about his passing and his legacy. One writer explained, "[The Marcoses] could scarcely have chosen a more hospitable home than Hawaii.

Here, Filipinos who trace their roots to Ilocos and speak the Ilocano dialect predominate among the regionalistic sub-groups. That's an accommodation that could not be found anywhere in the world outside of Ilocos itself."[29] The writer rehearses Hawaiʻi's "alterity" as both a "hospitable" location for Filipino Ilocanos and a site on which Filipinos might struggle with and work through the complex ambivalence surrounding the dictatorship. The reconstitution of Hawaiʻi as the perfect place for the Marcoses' exile situates the Marcoses' within US state discourses about Hawaiʻi's multicultural exceptionalism and obfuscates US complicity in martial law. Such statements further obscure the continuity of Filipino and Asian settler colonialism in Hawaiʻi.

If, according to Raymond Williams, the preemergent is that which is "active and pressing but not yet fully articulated," Gotera and Linmark describe the formation of an emergent subjectivity born of the historical experience of martial law.[30] In Linmark's poem, a speaker explains, "Some say you were a magician indeed: / a grand illusionist who made hundreds of thousands / forget their identities." The lines describe a system of violence that attempted to eradicate critics of the regime as so-called enemies of the state. The distinct employment of "identity" here, however, recalls the power by which "multiple bodies, forces, energies, matters, desires, thoughts, and so on are gradually, progressively, actually and materially constituted as subjects."[31] Where Marcos deployed a magic to contain the multiplicity of experience into a singular subjectivity, the poem's aim is not to reclaim these forgotten identities. Instead, it offers another evocation of subjectivity as relationality. In the poem, Filipinoness designates survivors of the regime, those who endured the regime's torture and violence and others who were shaped by its policies: domestic workers, entertainers, seamen, nurses, teachers; those who left but also those who stayed. They are also those who did not survive in the same way, the dead and the disappeared whose presence is felt in the Filipino's invocation. The poem resituates Filipinoness not as any predetermined constitution—not as subject to the state nor defined through a global valuation system—but as a set of configurations, organized in a struggle with power, in relation to one another, on the way to something and somewhere else.

In response to the failure of US and Philippine governmental redress, looking offers a means of reckoning with the aftermath of the Marcos regime beyond the framework of adjudication. And reckoning requires the meticulousness of enumeration. It catalogues rather than documents. It repossesses rather than recovers. It demands not retribution but agitation. Reckoning wrestles with a past not as *the* past but as the terms of recognition that render the present utterable. To reckon is to understand that power often materializes as the frame that holds our memories intact and that resistance against this power may require the seizure of the very language by which the past can be made known so that something else might take its place. To reckon is to acknowledge that what was lost might never be recovered but that the violation and the absence that such violence produces instigates a profound change *in us* that commands new imaginations for conceiving of different ways of being in and of the world.

A BURIAL

In 2016, on the heels of his election to the presidency, Philippine president Rodrigo Duterte ordered the burial of Ferdinand Marcos, and Imelda Marcos finally fulfilled her life's mission to bury her husband in a hero's ceremony in the national cemetery of the Philippines. Responding to criticism around his mandate, Duterte explained that it was time for the nation to heal.[32] Who did Duterte implore when he invoked the nation here? What, in his estimation, needed healing—right now—and what did healing constitute?

Since his election to the presidency, Duterte's administration has garnered comparisons to Marcos's regime for their similar disregard for a political division of power as well as their display of exceptional violence as a vehicle for their rule. Marcos's body offers both a point of entry for considering Marcos's legacy in the present and a modality for illustrating the shifting landscape of Philippine-US collaboration, a racial cold war that has yet to end. The Marcos family (Imelda Marcos and Imee Marcos have both held or continue to hold political office in the country, and Ferdinand "Bongbong" Marcos Jr. is, at the time of this writing, in the first few months of a deeply contentious presidency offered its financial and political support to Duterte during his campaign, which many attribute to Duterte's decision to bury the dictator. The Marcoses' resolve for a national burial marked the emergence of a new kind of Marcosian politics embodied by the Marcoses' new rise to power. In this way, it functions as a further attempt to revise the narrative about Marcos's presidency in a way that legitimizes the Marcoses' reemergence and renewed access to the executive office. In response to Duterte's decision to bury Marcos, massive protests took shape to urge the country to "never again, never forget" Marcos's crimes. This politics of looking practiced a consistent articulation of martial law as the site of historical trauma. In a mock funeral of Marcos's effigy at the Inayawan landfill in

Cebu, protestors argued that officials sanitized Marcos's legacy.[33] The effigy, "constructed from chicken wire, stuffed with assorted trash, and dressed in a used barong, dark pants, black shoes, and fake medal," allowed Cebuano artists Raymund Fernandez and Linya Ocampo Fernandez and protestors to create and perform alternative funeral rites and burial. Describing Marcos as "dili bayani," or "not a hero," they portrayed the administration's historical revisionism as literal rubbish, a composite of haphazard and decaying parts. The procession itself articulated the magnitude of the people's labor on which that legacy depends. By constructing the body itself and then returning that body to the trash heap, they forced Marcos to reckon with the materiality of Filipino social conditions that his regime established and which continues into the present day. This reckoning, more than simply remembering, gestures toward the nuance of Marcosian power as well as its multiple manifestations well beyond the end of the regime.

Duterte's mandate to lay Marcos to rest in the national cemetery departed from past administrations' refusal to bury the late dictator. Duterte established a critical distance from the liberal regimes of post–EDSA Revolution presidential administrations. Indeed, the protestors' instruction to never forget used the past to contextualize the present to indict Duterte's presidency as a legacy of authoritarianism in the Philippines, that is, a call to look at Marcos through Duterte. Both presidents have declared martial law as a means of establishing order over the chaos of political dissent. Both have sanctioned the use of torture and killings as a means of punishing such dissidents. There are distinct departures, of course, between Marcos and Duterte that are worth exploring. Marcos's partnership with the United States functioned through the regime's own capacity to utilize US liberal reforms in the service of national modernization. Duterte's distinct admonition of the United States (famously admonishing it for its colonial wars and calling President Barack Obama a son of a bitch) as well as his threats to discard the Visiting Forces Agreement between the United States and the Philippines has signaled an attempt to collaborate with the Chinese government. It might be worth noting the ways that authoritarianism functions as responses to liberalism, the first to its capacity to structure a new world order and the latter to its failures. For both Marcos and Duterte, it is the distinct plight of the Filipino in the present that provokes a state of emergency. For both leaders, authoritarian rule marked a radical departure from the ineffectiveness of past administrations. The claim that a radical shift in governance is necessary to save the Filipino people also necessitates the abjection of those deemed a threat to the Filipino people—communists, leftists, drug users. The determination to protect the Filipino constructs a subjectivity that validates the rule of law required to maintain it. In other words, the resolve of authoritarianism to protect the Filipino from all that seeks to undermine it articulates a configuration that advances the power and violence of authoritarianism itself.

The insidiousness of Duterte's mandate to bury Marcos is not only in his rejection of the masses' insistence to reckon but also in the assumption of a continuity between the nation he invoked and the one he addressed. He presumed the coherence of a subjectivity tied to a version of nation whose invocation is used over and over again to sanction the desires and ambitions of the people who run it. It is these invocations of nation that the masses undermine in their protests and in their lifemaking practices. Their looking and reckoning articulates other subjectivities that refuse these discourses in their name. In Linmark's poem, recall that the "some" never fully congeals as a distinct identity traced to a particular temporal or spatial location. It is allowed—even encouraged—to be deliberate in its ambiguity, moving across the times and places it has been forced to inhabit and experience. It gains power in this movement rather than in its loyalty to time and place; in so doing, it makes possible other worlds, where the former First Lady holds onto her blue terno as the dregs of her failing relevance, where witches cast spells on the autocrat's limp penis, where first families are haunted by the ghosts of their pasts, and where dictators are left to decay and the people get to watch. By the end of the poem, when the dictator's "fingers move . . . beckoning the world to come," it is not Marcos who returns to life but the *some* who emerge in his wake.

The poem gestures toward another kind of people power, where both people and power are not predetermined, where power describes the force it takes to bring people's energies to life. When Duterte ordered that the nation must heal, he made the terrible mistake of assuming the limits of national belonging. Because the force of Filipino subjectivity has never been in its conclusion but always in its becoming.

* * *

I began this book with a proposition to treat Filipino America as a project of memorialization and to defamiliarize Filipino from America as a way to interrogate the alliances and collaborations that suture them. I end it here with the dictator's body as a mechanism by which Filipino America might again be unmade, to unravel the configurations and the possibilities that lie within and beyond it.

NOTES

INTRODUCTION. UNMAKING CONFIGURATIONS

1. See the "Bantayog ng mga Bayani" informational website at https://bantayog.org/about/. Lisandro E. Claudio has written about the tensions that constitute the memorial ("Memories of the Anti-Marcos Movement").
2. Chew, *Remembering Silme Domingo and Gene Viernes*, 53.
3. Bantayog, "About."
4. Bantayog, "About."
5. "Never again" has become a rallying cry against the historical revisionism that has sought to redefine the legacy of the dictatorship as the Marcos family regains political power in the Philippines. In her study of millennial activism against martial law in the Philippines, Joy Sales notes that "'Never again, never again, never again to martial law!' and 'Stop, stop, stop the killings. End martial law!'— encapsulated how Filipinos around the world refuse the repeating of history, while acknowledging how Duterte's administration is not merely a copycat of Marcos" ("#NeverAgainToMartialLaw").
6. Bantayog, "About."
7. I draw from Walter Benjamin, who noted that "the past carries with it a temporal index by which it is referred to [as] redemption" ("Theses on the Philosophy of History," 254).
8. Wendy Brown writes, "Institutionalized, freedom arrayed against a particular image of unfreedom sustains that image, which dominates political life with its specter long after it has been vanquished and preempts appreciation of new dangers to freedom posed by institutions designed to hold the past in check. Yet the very institutions that are erected to vanquish the historical threat also recuperate it as a form of political anxiety; so, for example, functions the 'state

of nature' or the 'arbitrary sovereign' in the liberal political imagination" (*States of Injury*, 8).

9. Benjamin, "Theses on the Philosophy of History," 262.
10. See Churchill, *Triumph over Marcos*; and Chew, *Remembering Silme Domingo and Gene Viernes*.
11. Domingo, "Building a Movement."
12. Antonio Tiongson has described the term "Filipino American" as a "troubled and uneven coupling" that must be positioned "within a much broader historical context, in imperial and global terms that take into account the imbrication of U.S. national formation and its imperial history" (Tiongson, Gutierrez, and Gutierrez, *Positively No Filipinos Allowed*, 4–5). Perhaps similarly, Jessica Hagedorn's novel *Dogeaters* is, beyond a rumination on martial law, an interrogation of the uneasiness of Filipino American subjectivity. Her characterization of Freddie, Dolores, and Rio Gonzaga, in particular, is telling. Freddie "believes in dual citizenships, dual passports, as many allegiances to as many countries as possible at any given time . . . a 'guest' in his own country" (7). Dolores "carries American papers because of her father, feels more viscerally connected to the Philippines than he ever could. She used to argue with him. . . . 'You are definitely a Filipino! A mestizo, yes—but definitely a Filipino'" (8).
13. To date, FANHS holds a Pinoy Archive in Seattle, boasts more than thirty chapters around the United States, and holds yearly national conferences dedicated to the cultural and historical representation of Filipino America.
14. Cordova, *Filipinos*, xiii.
15. In *Racial Formation in the United States*, Michael Omi and Howard Winant note, "We should think of race as an element of social structure rather than as an irregularity within it; we should see race as a dimension of human representation rather than an illusion. Such a perspective informs what we mean by racial formation" (112).
16. US multiculturalism refers to a specific post-1965 discourse of racial pluralism that heralded the end of racial strife in exchange for the rhetoric of individualism that gained traction throughout the 1970s and 1980s. Also see Iyko Day's *Alien Capital*.
17. In the introduction to the formative anthology *Positively No Filipinos Allowed*, Tiongson writes that the anthology aims "to signify the ways Filipinos endure the burdens and legacies of empire past and present, which cannot be understood simply in terms of exclusion but more in terms of the coerced incorporation of Filipinos into the nation, underwritten by the violence of conquest, empire building, white supremacy, and global capital" (Tiongson, Gutierrez, and Gutierrez, *Positively No Filipinos Allowed*, 1).
18. The October celebration of Filipino American History Month is another example. Robyn Rodriguez explains that "October was designated 'Filipino American History Month' by its originator, the Filipino American National Historical Society (FANHS), not only because it is the birth month of Filipino American labor leader,

Larry Itliong (Itliong was born on October 25th), but because October 18, 1587[,] marks the first known landing of Filipinos on the shores of (what is now) the continental United States at Morro Bay, California.... This narrative along with the fact that groups like FANHS worked to ensure the marking of the site with a commemorative plaque and struggled for the recognition of Filipino American History Month more broadly are but a few examples of the kinds of investments Filipino Americans have in staking a claim to Americanness and belonging in America" (*Filipino American Transnational Activism*, 1).

19 N. V. M. Gonzalez and Oscar Campomanes ("Filipino American Literature") and Robyn Rodriguez ("Toward a Critical Filipino Studies Approach to Philippine Migration") have each addressed the ways that the "three waves" approach to the historicization of Filipino immigration to the United States presents problems for conceptualizing the dynamism of Filipino American history.

20 Cordova, *Filipinos*, 228.

21 Some have noted that the organizational tensions between FANHS and KDP during the 1970s and 1980s illuminates disagreements about the shape and scope of Filipino American political work. For more about the intersecting histories between FANHS and the KDP, see Augusto Espiritu, "Journeys of Discovery and Difference"; Dorothy Fujita-Rony, "Illuminating Militarized Rupture"; Schulze-Oechtering and Jopanda, "Transpacific Freedom Dreams"; and L. Joyce Zapanta Mariano, *Giving Back*. See also Ligaya Domingo's critique of FANHS as unable to contend with the transnational politics of anti–martial law activism ("Building a Movement," 66–69). Recent studies of martial law have shed new light on the details of the Marcos dictatorship and have complicated the history of anti–martial law activism.

22 When using the term "racial capitalism," I draw specifically from Cedric Robinson's work. Robinson wrote: "The development, organization, and expansion of capitalist society pursued essentially racial directions, so too did social ideology. As a material force, then, it could be expected that racialism would inevitably permeate the social structures emergent from capitalism. I have used the term 'racial capitalism' to refer to this development and to the subsequent structure as a historical agency" (*Black Marxism*, 2).

23 In her formative work on subjectless critique, Kandice Chuh has written that questions about identity are always questions about memory and forgetting, an amnesiac struggle in which forgetting strives toward a racial sameness. Chuh explains that subjectless critique addresses the cohesion or "achievement" of Asian American subjectivity as a project of US nationalism. In its attention to the "irremedial complexity of 'Filipino America,'" Chuh's analysis contends with subjectivity as it wrestles with the necessity of political representation and the limitations of representation to address the myriad forms of power and violence that constitute such formations (*Imagine Otherwise*). Laura Kang has written about the enfiguration of "Asian American women" as both a "historiographical dilemma" and shorthand "for the ways that 'Asian,' 'American,' and 'Asian

American' come to bear on the gendered ontology of 'women'" (*Compositional Subjects*).
24 Chuh, *Imagine Otherwise*, 44, 33–35.
25 Chuh, *Imagine Otherwise*, 32.
26 Lisa Yoneyama theorizes that "what matters is not how much we know about the past but rather through what structural access, and under what personal, social, and historical conditions, we come to an awareness of it" ("For Transformative Knowledge and the Postnationalist Public Spheres," 331).
27 For more on the citizen-subject as national agent, see Lowe, *Immigrant Acts*.
28 Neferti Tadiar offers a useful discussion of the ways that the categorization of the "people" excises "the exploitative classes from the term [and] arrives at the category of 'the masses,' which in its positive form is articulated as the political unity forged against imperialism and feudalism." Moreover, in her theorization of "life-times" as living labor, Tadiar warns of the dangers of subscribing to forms of political emancipation that replicate the logics of capital and disregard or foreclose other forms of lifemaking ("Life-Times of Becoming Human," 7).
29 Chuh, *Imagine Otherwise*, 56.
30 Arendt, *Origins of Totalitarianism*, 316.
31 Stuart Hall wrote of Raymond Williams: "He sees both the dangers of reconstructing a spuriously unified cultural identity and a falsely continuous national history when the real history is one of ruptures and discontinuities—'industrial conflict within rapid economic development and agrarian conflict within impoverishment, depopulation, and marginalization'—and even the resistance to cultural colonization was itself a deeply differentiated response, governed as much by what it was responding to as what it was in itself" ("Culture, Community, Nation," 359).
32 Here I take up Wendy Brown's provocations in *States of Injury* about the left's abandonment of freedom as a statist political project. One of the things that Brown accomplishes is a deep consideration of the ways that discourses of empowerment are intricately intertwined with state power (23–24).
33 Fanon, *Wretched of the Earth*, 148.
34 Raymond Williams, *Marxism and Literature*, 121–27.
35 Neferti Tadiar describes the Philippine historical experience as "both the imaginary, affective, sociosubjective activity that impels and shapes prevailing notions of production in a sociohistorical formation and the hermeneutic perspective that recognizes alternative agencies in the making of history, which such activity affords" (*Things Fall Away*, 15).
36 This is Angela Davis's directive to organize identity around politics and not politics around identity ("Interview with Lisa Lowe," 318).
37 See Antonio Gramsci's notion of "social formation" (via Ferreira da Silva's *Toward a Global Idea of Race*, xxv). While Paul Gilroy's theorization of a "politics of transfiguration" is imperative for conceptualizing the "hidden internal fissures in the concept of modernity" (*Black Atlantic*, 38), I point to configurations, too, as a formation invested with the aspirations of state governmentalities.

38 Poblete, *Islanders in the Empire*.
39 Baldoz, *Third Asiatic Invasion*.
40 In her discussion of the Commonwealth period and the complexity of the postcolonial marker to describe the period, Amanda Solomon argues that the "moment is ironic in that ... this time of seemingly official separation is actually when the Philippines and U.S. are tied even closer to each other through economic, martial and cultural policies." Further, Solomon notes that "there is no progress from colonial to post-colonial; rather, the islands seem to permanently inhabit a space and time of deferred decolonization, never arriving at any 'post-colonial' telos" ("Managing the [Post]colonial," 10).
41 In his analysis of Juan C. Laya's *His Native Soil*, Paul Nadal writes that Laya's realism presents a "depiction of a colony in transition tasked to incorporate its racially disenfranchised populations in the United States, and this in view of its future-oriented imagining of Philippine modernity" ("Literary Remittance"). See also Estella Habal's discussion of anti-Filipino riots, in which she contends that "racial violence in Watsonville embodied a clear social statement by the local white community—the unassimilability of the Filipino" ("Radical Violence in the Fields").
42 See, *Decolonized Eye*.
43 Garcia, "One Hundred Years of the Ateneo de Manila."
44 Augusto Espiritu, "'To Carry Water on Both Shoulders,'" 179.
45 Augusto Espiritu's study of Carlos Romulo and the Bandung Conference is an illuminating historical look into Romulo's ambivalent expressions of anticolonialism and sovereignty. Espiritu writes that Romulo "created a space for a discourse of both friendship (however unequal) *and* criticism, and of a shared anti-communist, free-market ideology *and* a principled disagreement on the questions of nationalism, racism, and colonialism. This is a synthesis critical to understanding the post–Bandung Conference history of various modes of transcending the East-West conflict, such as the idea of a Third World, as well as that of NAM [Non-aligned Movement], for indeed Romulo and others had helped to formulate a kind of third way that transcended the binaries of American imperial capitalism and Soviet communist support for revolution" ("'To Carry Water on Both Shoulders,'" 186–87).
46 Klein, *Cold War Orientalism*.
47 See Tadiar, *Fantasy Production*; and Ong, *Neoliberalism as Exception*.
48 Choy, "From Exchange Visitor to Permanent Resident," 160–61.
49 Choy, "From Exchange Visitor to Permanent Resident," 165–67.
50 Renato Constantino and Letizia Constantino, "The Miseducation of the Filipino."
51 Tadiar has rightly noted that Constantino's conceptualization of the crisis of Philippine culture treats "true culture" as a static form that could be otherwise realized if it were not for its oppression by US colonialism. She writes, "To the anti-imperialist nationalists, Philippine culture was suffocating under the weight of Western powers, duped by colonial mentality, weakened through brain drain,

alienated and divided from itself, all to the economic and political detriment of the people. In Renato Constantino's version of this narrative, a version widely held in the wake of national political independence 'granted' by the United States in 1946, true Philippine culture was itself oppressed, prevented from coming into authentic, unalienated, and empowered being" (*Things Fall Away*, 27).

52   Joaquin, *Culture and History*.
53   Diaz, "'We Were War Surplus, Too.'"
54   Cruz, *Transpacific Femininities*, 18.
55   Rafael, *White Love and Other Events in Filipino History*, 32.
56   Blanco, "Race as Praxis in the Philippines at the Turn of the Twentieth Century," 361.
57   There is, according to Tadiar, an "effective historical role that the very trope of modernity has played in creating the conditions it designates," and Ferdinand Marcos's knowingness of such trope "stir[red] the desires for modern development and . . . undergird[ed] the transnational model of modernization, which the technocratic architects of the regime attempted to follow" (*Things Fall Away*, 153).
58   Michel Foucault's notion of governmentality as an "art of government" is instructive here: "The art of government must therefore fix its rules and rationalize its way of doing things by taking as its objective the bringing into being of what the state should be. What government has to do must be identified with what the state should be. Governmental *ratio* is what will enable a given state to arrive at its maximum being in a considered, reasoned, and calculated way. What is it to govern? To govern according to the principle of *raison d'état* is to arrange things so that the state becomes sturdy and permanent, so that it becomes wealthy, and so that it becomes strong in the face of everything that may destroy it" (*Birth of Biopolitics*, 4).
59   See Ferdinand Marcos's *New Filipinism* as well as Naoki Sakai and Hyon Joon Yoo's discussion of injured masculinity (*Trans-Pacific Imagination*).
60   Ferdinand Marcos, *Notes on the New Society of the Philippines*.
61   Casumbal-Salazar, "Indeterminacy of the Philippine Indigenous Subject," 79.
62   "Declaration of the United Nations."
63   Reddy, "Globality and the Ends of the Nation-Form."
64   Chen, *Asia as Method*, 8.
65   Benjamin, "Critique of Violence," 295.
66   Arendt explains, "Political consequences such as postwar pacifism, for example, derived from the general fear of war, not from the experiences in war. Instead of producing a pacifism devoid of reality, the insight into the structure of modern wars, guided and mobilized by fear, might have led to the realization that the only standard for a necessary war is the fight against conditions under which people no longer wish to live—and our experiences with the tormenting hell of the totalitarian camps have enlightened us only too well about the possibility of such conditions. Thus the fear of concentration camps and the resulting insight into the nature of total domination might serve to invalidate all obsolete political differentiations from right to left and to introduce beside and above them the

politically most important yardstick for judging events in our time, namely: whether they serve totalitarian domination or not" (*Origins of Totalitarianism*, 442).

67 Agamben, *State of Exception*, 4.
68 Robinson, *Black Movements in America*, 124.
69 Dudziak, *Cold War Civil Rights*.
70 Melamed, "Spirit of Neoliberalism."
71 Ching, *Becoming "Japanese,"* 53.
72 The three-waves approach to the study of Filipino immigration to the United States has shaped the epistemological and discursive boundaries of Filipino America as a social formation.
73 Labor Code of the Philippines, Art. 12, g.
74 In 1977, Marcos bestowed on Cesar Chavez the Presidential Appreciation Award for his work to "improve the lot of Filipino migrant workers in California" (*Washington Post*, "Cesar Chavez Hails Philippines' Rule"). See Fujita-Rony, "Coalitions, Race, and Labor"; and San Juan, "Philip Vera Cruz."
75 Denise Ferreira da Silva contends that "the racial subaltern is always already inscribed as a historical subject who finally comes into representation as a *transparent 'I'* when articulating an emancipatory project" (*Toward a Global Idea of Race*, xxiv).
76 Lowe, "International within the National," 32.
77 Campomanes, "Figures of the Unassimilable," 46.
78 Dylan Rodriguez, *Suspended Apocalypse*, 33.
79 Dylan Rodriguez, *Suspended Apocalypse*, 26.
80 In her discussion of the absence of "Asia's necrohistories" from US and Canadian studies of the Cold War, Lisa Yoneyama contends that "the areas that appeared as postcolonies in the aftermath of Japan's defeat have been perceived for the most part as unproductive sites for anthropologically theorizing 'violence in war and peace'" (*Cold War Ruins*, 23).
81 Yến Lê Espiritu, *Body Counts*.
82 David Price has investigated the alignment of postwar anthropology with the expansion of US empire. He argues that "many who took part in transforming the postwar world did so while continuing to use the previous war as an ideological reference point. Most anthropologists working on occupations or aid programs conceived of their role as that of a stabilizer or liberator, not an active agent of a new American empire" and that "anthropology has long been ambivalent about how to cope with the political processes in which it is enveloped" (*Cold War Anthropology*, 51).
83 Manalansan and Espiritu, *Filipino Studies*, 9.
84 Robinson, *Black Movements in America*, 134.
85 Lisa Yoneyama theorizes that the lowercase "cold war" designation points to "an alternative to the Cold War geography, which emerged out of transwar, interimperial, and transnational entanglements" and enlivens "a conjunctive cultural critique of the transpacific in order to elucidate the still-present Cold War frame of knowledge" (*Cold War Ruins*, x).

86 See also Denise Cruz, *Transpacific Femininities*; Chen, *Asia as Method*; and Lin, "Resignifying 'Asia' in the Transnational Turn of Asian/American Studies."

87 Kim, *Ends of Empire*, 3.

88 See Stuart Hall's theory of popular culture ("Notes on Deconstructing the Popular") as well as Lisa Lowe and David Lloyd's discussion of culture in *The Politics of Culture in the Shadow of Capital*.

89 Challenging limited readings of Filipino writing, Oscar Campomanes insists on a reconceptualization of "Filipino (American)" cultural production that gravitates toward the Filipino imagination: "Are we actually confronted with unrecognizably different or alternative kinds of imagination and nationality in Filipino literatures and predicaments? . . . It is precisely their perceivable intermixtures of alternations *between* Filipino (American) texts and conditions that demand more critical attention than they have received. If Filipinos seemed to have failed in the 'epic' effort to forge a nation, and their intellectuals have only 'lyrically' bewailed this miserable 'failure,' is it possible that this prevalent judgment can only be the result of the critic's own failure of 'discriminating' imagination, and a function of residually (neo)colonial reading regimes?" (Gonzalez and Campomanes, "Filipino American Literature," 84).

90 Raymond Williams, "Culture Is Ordinary," 96.

91 Lowe, "International within the National," 38–39.

92 Chakrabarty, *Provincializing Europe*, 88–89.

93 Hall, "Cultural Identity and Diaspora," 225.

94 Here I am drawn to Sylvia Wynter's conceptualization of the Coloniality of Being/Power/Truth/Freedom, especially "the logical inference that one cannot 'unsettle' the 'coloniality of power' without a redescription of the human outside the terms of our present descriptive statement of the human, Man, and its overrepresentation" ("Unsettling the Coloniality of Being/Power/Truth/Freedom," 268). Denise Ferreira da Silva's theorization of being not as interiority but as constituted by modern fields of representation is also instructive. Ferreira da Silva writes that the transparency thesis is "the ontoepistemological account that institutes 'being and meaning' as effects of interiority and temporality. What this reading provides is the delineation of an other ontoepistemological context, globality, in which being and meaning emerge as an effect of exteriority and spatiality, a mode of representing human difference as an effect of scientific signification. By showing how the *transparent 'I,'* which the representation of the subject historicity presupposes and (re)produces, emerges always already in a contention with others that both institute and threaten its ontological prerogative, my reading displaces the transparency thesis to refashion the modern subject as *Homo modernus*, the global-historical being produced with tools yielded by both fields of modern representation, namely, history and science" (emphasis in original, *Toward a Global Idea of Race*, 4). I am also informed by Dipesh Chakrabarty's distinction between "being" and "becoming" as ways to conceptualize History 2 not as the "dialectical Other of the necessary logic of History 1" and its historical drive to

articulate the ends of capital; rather, "History 2 is better thought of as a category charged with the function of constantly interrupting the totalizing thrusts of History 1" (*Provincializing Europe*, 66).

95 Benjamin, *Arcades Project*, 5.
96 "Lifeworlds" refers to the phenomenological concept of experience of the world, as outlined by Edmund Husserl and theorized by Jürgen Habermas. My usage of it here, however, draws from postcolonial and feminist scholars. Neferti Tadiar's concept of life-times, moreover, is "a concept for reckoning with the diverse array of acts, capacities, associations, aspirations in practice, and sensibilities that people engage in and draw upon in the effort to make and remake social life in situations of life-threatening hardship, deprivation, and precariousness" ("Life-Times of Becoming Human," 1).
97 Denise Ferreira da Silva has written, "From an analytical position that engages modern representation as a political-symbolic context composed by strategies of engulfment, I show how the spelling of the proper name of man, the writing of the transparent I, is also an effect of raciality. For I choose engulfment" (*Toward a Global Idea of Race*, 33).

CHAPTER ONE. THE FICTIONS OF NATIONAL CULTURE

1 Curtis, "First Lady Adds to Glitter; Musicians' Strike Is Settled."
2 In addition to the grand plan of the Lincoln Center for the Performing Arts, the brainchild of Robert Moses and John D. Rockefeller, the opera house was a part of the broader project of cultural rejuvenation, as some explain, a showcase of American cultural excellence during a period of Soviet propaganda and threat. As a case in point, the overdetermined celebration of American arts and culture depended precisely on the dislocation of mostly poor, working-class, immigrant, and minority communities in the Upper West Side, as Moses described, the elimination of the city's slums. It is important to recall that that Johnson's war on poverty served, in many ways, as a function of liberal governance that could not often account for this kind of "slum clearance." See Foulkes, "Other West Side Story."
3 Naima Prevots (*Dance for Export*) has detailed the ways that the US State Department sponsored the travel of African American dancers abroad to evidence to international audiences the weight that the country assigned to African American cultural production even as Black life was characterized by aggressive assaults of exclusion by that very state. Christina Klein (*Cold War Orientalism*) has theorized the ways that the sentimentality of US cultural production about Asia instilled within US audiences ideas about global economic cooperation and military containment. Likewise, scholars of the Philippines have interrogated the role of the Cultural Center of the Philippines to Marcos's justification of authoritarianism. Gerard Lico's (*Edifice Complex*) analysis of Marcosian architecture, for instance,

points to the Marcoses' cultural ideation of modernity to the advancement of their programs for development. Pearlie Baluyut's (*Institutions and Icons of Patronage*) study of the Marcoses' patronage, moreover, describes the role that arts and culture played in the formation of a "national culture" that cohered in its transnational potential.

4 Man, *Soldiering through Empire*, 121–23.
5 Gamalinda, *Empire of Memory*, 16.
6 Gamalinda, *Empire of Memory*, 162.
7 Gamalinda, *Empire of Memory*, 77.
8 The "arts and humanities" refers to the artistic and literary forms of cultural production that communicated intrinsic truths about national life through creative self-expression, in many ways, the construction of a national imaginary. In its 1964 report, the Commission on the Humanities declared that "one cannot speak of history or culture apart from the humanities. They not only record our lives; our lives are the very substance they are made of. Their subject is every man. We propose, therefore, a program for all our people, a program to meet a need no less serious than that for national defense. We speak in truth, for what is being defended—our beliefs, our ideals, our highest achievements" (*Report of the Commission on the Humanities*, 1).
9 Binkiewicz, *Federalizing the Muse*, 94–97.
10 Peters and Woolley, "Lyndon B. Johnson: Remarks at the Signing of the Arts and Humanities Bill."
11 *Report of the Commission on the Humanities*, 4.
12 Peters and Woolley, "Lyndon B. Johnson: Commencement Address at Howard University." In his discussion of postwar Black diasporic art in Britain, Stuart Hall theorizes the problem and possibility of Blackness that helpfully challenges the overdetermination that Johnson presents here: "With this putting of the black body into question we come face to face, not with some essential 'truth' about blackness, but with what elsewhere I called 'the end of the essential black subject'—triggering a kaleidoscopic proliferation of meanings around blackness, and bringing to light the hidden connections between the racialized, the gendered, and the sexualized body—a space of condensation which for so long had been the privileged operational zone of racial discourse" ("Black Diaspora Artists in Britain," 20).
13 Melamed, *Represent and Destroy*.
14 Brock, "Nation and the Cold War," 12–13.
15 Melamed, "Spirit of Neoliberalism," 6.
16 Peters and Woolley, "Lyndon B. Johnson: Address on Vietnam before the National Legislative Conference, San Antonio, Texas."
17 This definition of justice is driven by what Reynaldo Ileto has noted as the "singl[ing] out of wars for their ability to organize memory and experience in socially comprehensible terms" ("Philippine Wars and the Politics of Memory," 216).

18 Lady Bird Johnson, *White House Diary*, 432.
19 Lady Bird Johnson, *White House Diary*, 435. Christine Bacareza Balance notes that Imelda Marcos herself dedicated and sang these songs ("Dahil Sa Iyo," 125–26).
20 Lady Bird Johnson, *White House Diary*, 435.
21 Balance, "Dahil Sa Iyo," 130.
22 Camacho, *Cultures of Commemoration*.
23 Jin-kyung Lee, "Surrogate Military, Subimperialism, and Masculinity."
24 US Office of the Historian, "Memorandum from the President's Special Assistant (Rostow) to President Johnson"; "Memorandum for the Record."
25 Balance, "Dahil Sa Iyo."
26 See Gonzalves, *Day the Dancers Stayed*. The Bayanihan dance troupe that performed for national leaders simultaneously imaged the internationalism of the Cold War and a distinct kind of national culture that advanced the regime's policies. Barbara Gaerlan ("In the Court of the Sultan," 272) has explored the troupe's political utility over time. Discussing its role during the Marcos regime, Gaerlan notes, "Who could doubt that Moros were actively integrated into the Philippine state if one of their dances was the 'signature piece' of the national dance troupe?" Bayanihan's performance of Moro dance during a period when the regime actively suppressed a war against Moro separatists against the state attempted to include Moros within Marcos's narrative of Philippine sovereignty.
27 Sturken, *Tangled Memories*.
28 US Office of the Historian, "Memorandum from the President's Special Assistant (Valenti) to President Johnson."
29 Johnson, "Remarks at Dulles International Airport upon Returning from the Asian-Pacific Trip"; and US Office of the Historian, "Memorandum from the Officer in Charge of Philippine Affairs (Kattenburg) to the Assistant Secretary of State for Far Eastern Affairs (Bundy)."
30 Johnson, "Remarks at Dulles International Airport upon Returning from the Asian-Pacific Trip."
31 Jin-kyung Lee has noted that antiauthoritarian opposition in South Korea during the Park Chung Hee regime "lay in [the] reassessment of South Korea's relations with the United States, rather than with Japan" and that "mounting anti-American sentiment was further reinforced by the dissidents' recognition of the military regime's comprador alliance with U.S. capital" (*Service Economies*, 133).
32 Balance, "Dahil Sa Iyo," 130.
33 Pedrosa, *Imelda Marcos*, 11.
34 Peters and Woolley, "Lyndon B. Johnson: Toasts of the President and President Marcos of the Philippines."
35 *Life*, "Visit," 133.
36 Ferdinand Marcos, "Fourth State of the Nation Address."
37 Flores, "'Total Community Response,'" 14.

38 Ferdinand Marcos, "Sixth State of the Nation Address."
39 Ferdinand Marcos, "Sixth State of the Nation Address." In his discussion of the US transformation of Japan as Asia's economic center, Shunya Yoshimi explains that "there was a shift from an Americanism modelled directly on America, to an Americanism more deeply embedded in a particularistic national consciousness and more focused on the images of consumer lifestyles" (Yoshimi and Buist, "'America' as Desire and Violence," 443).
40 Benito Lim notes that "Philippine foreign policy was precipitated to a large degree by international developments. By the 1960s, a serious rift occurred between China and the Soviet Union; Nixon announced the withdrawal of American forces in Asia, the relaxation of cold war tensions, and America's détente with the Soviet Union. The looming worldwide monetary crisis, coupled with worsening domestic economic difficulties as a consequence of deteriorating trade with the US and other industrialized nations, led President Marcos to announce a new policy which was to normalize commercial relations with the socialist states" ("Political Economy of Philippines-China Relations," 9).
41 Lim, "Political Economy of Philippines-China Relations."
42 Government of the Republic of the Philippines, "Proclamation No. 1081."
43 Ferdinand Marcos, "Fourth State of the Nation Address."
44 Rommel Curaming writes, "The grand narrative of Philippine historical development that runs through Tadhana coincided almost perfectly with Marcos' [sic] interest to present martial law and the New Society it sought to create as a natural or a logical conclusion of the evolutionary process in the development of the Filipino nation. The choice of title Tadhana, which means 'destiny,' is strongly indicative of this aspiration. It was supposedly a destiny for the Filipino nation to see the rise of the New Society (Bagong Lipunan) characterized by peace, prosperity and national pride" ("Official History Reconsidered"). In the introduction to the text, Marcos explains that volume 1 serves as a prehistory but cannot yet be published due to the ongoing research required for its completion.
45 Curaming, "Official History Reconsidered," 246. In an extensive study of Marcos's "intellectual fraud," Miguel Paolo P. Reyes argues that it is imperative to acknowledge that "there is evidence that Marcos did not write 'his' books" and that "the myth of Marcos the scholar has to die" ("Producing Ferdinand E. Marcos," 210). I note the importance of Reyes's caution here. At the same time, what remains most important to me, beyond the verifiable origins of Marcos's books, is the intellectual and political logic that guided the regime's power and violence.
46 Ferdinand Marcos, *Marcos Reader*, 5.
47 Ferdinand Marcos, *Marcos Reader*, 9.
48 Ferdinand Marcos, *Marcos Reader*, 4.
49 See Bliss Cua Lim, *Translating Time*; and Chakrabarty, *Provincializing Europe*.
50 Ferdinand Marcos, *Marcos Reader*, 8.

51 Ferdinand Marcos, *Marcos Reader*, 149.
52 Sturken, *Tangled Memories*.
53 Camacho, *Cultures of Commemoration*, 93.
54 Flores, "'Total Community Response,'" 13.
55 Ferdinand Marcos, *Marcos Reader*, 147, 152.
56 Flores, "'Total Community Response,'" 14.
57 Lico, *Edifice Complex*.
58 Baluyut, *Institutions and Icons of Patronage*.
59 See Baluyut, *Institutions and Icons of Patronage*, 16–19; and Flores, "'Total Community Response.'"
60 U.S. Information Agency, "Statement of Albert Harkness, Jr., Director, Information Center Service, Re Philippine-American Cultural Foundation," 780.
61 McKenna, *American Imperial Pastoral*, 3.
62 Hines, "Imperial Façade," 45.
63 Quoted in Hines, "Imperial Façade," 48.
64 Fujitani, White, and Yoneyama, *Perilous Memories*, 16.
65 US Office of the Historian, "Memorandum from the President's Special Assistant (Rostow) to President Johnson."
66 Schein, "War Damage Compensation through Rehabilitation," 533.
67 Schein, "War Damage Compensation through Rehabilitation," 532.
68 Raymond Williams, "Culture Is Ordinary," 96.
69 Schein, "War Damage Compensation through Rehabilitation," 522.
70 Schein, "War Damage Compensation through Rehabilitation," 540.
71 I often turn to Ninotchka Rosca's 1988 novel *State of War* to think about Filipino subjectivity through the framework of unending war.
72 Lico, *Edifice Complex*.
73 Mananquil, "'There's a Little Imelda in All of Us.'"
74 Imelda Marcos, "Sanctuary of the Filipino Soul," in *The Compassionate Society*, 19–20.
75 For more on the the Katipunan society and the emergence of Filipino nationalism, see Rafael, *Promise of the Foreign*.
76 Rafael's reading of Apolionario Mabini's theorization of sovereignty is useful for reconsidering the Philippine Revolution away from this historicism: "Other accounts of the Revolution left behind by Filipino fighters suggest that it was always something more than the practical unraveling of the received notions of sovereignty as we have seen in our reading of Mabini. They also reveal how the Revolution occasionally opened up the possibility of another kind of sovereignty, one that did not entail the exercise of power and the delusions of empowerment. Rather, it was a kind of sovereignty that stemmed from a vernacular experience of freedom, or what in Tagalog is called kalayaan: that is, freedom from the necessity of labor and the violence of law" ("Afterlife of Empire," 105–6).
77 Benedicto, "Queer Afterlife of the Postcolonial City," 583.
78 Tadiar, *Things Fall Away*, 261.

79 For the regime, "Filipino culture" was a configuration that, as Chandan Reddy theorizes about representational archival terms, "enunciated from within forms of knowledge that enabled the substantive violation of nonwhite peoples and their social imaginaries as coincident with the extension of 'autonomous' and 'universal' knowledge to all 'members' of the globe ("Globality and the Ends of the Nation-Form," 475).
80 Singh, "Author Q&A: Eric Gamalinda."
81 Cimatu and Tolentino, *Mondo Marcos*, 191.
82 The novel references the controversy of the Tasaday, which experts heralded as an anthropological marvel before finding that the Marcos administration may have fabricated its existence. It also references the Bataan Refugee Processing Center, which I discuss in chapter 4.
83 In her discussion of Filipino novels in English, Caroline Hau notes that this conflict is characteristic of novels that grapple with postindependence history. She explains that such novels illustrate the "many specters haunting Philippine society," which "do not simply take the form of the exploitative foreigner or outsider, but appear as the other within, the 'other' who is also Filipino, something of and within the nation that has been marginalized or suppressed in the name of the nation" ("Filipino Novel in English," 327).
84 Gamalinda, *Empire of Memory*, 29.
85 I think of Gamalinda's anti-history alongside Jason Magabo Perez's urgent inquiry: "Where & when & how is it that we have come to do what we do with little or no regard for what has been done to us?" (*This Is for the Mostless*, 22).
86 Fujitani, White, and Yoneyama, *Perilous Memories*, 19.
87 Gamalinda, *Empire of Memory*, 43.
88 Schirmer and Shalom, *Philippine Reader*, 200.
89 Benjamin, "Theses on the Philosophy of History," 255.
90 Gamalinda, *Empire of Memory*, 80–81.
91 The archipelagic disrupts national time. See Isaac, "Offshore Identities."
92 Lowe, *Intimacies of Four Continents*.
93 Gamalinda, *Empire of Memory*, 106.
94 Gamalinda, *Empire of Memory*, 107.
95 Tucker, *Insatiable Appetite*, 191.
96 Tadiar, *Things Fall Away*, 311.
97 Gamalinda, *Empire of Memory*, 122.
98 Benjamin, "Theses on the Philosophy of History."
99 Gamalinda, *Empire of Memory*, 120.
100 Gamalinda, *Empire of Memory*, 20–21.
101 Hall, "Cultural Identity and Diaspora," 226.
102 Imelda Marcos, *Compassionate Society*, 19.
103 Imelda Marcos, *Compassionate Society*, 20.
104 Gamalinda, *Empire of Memory*, 57.
105 Lady Bird Johnson, *White House Diary*, 433.

106 Roberts and Stephens, *Archipelagic American Studies*.
107 Burns, *Puro Arte*.
108 Reading Homi Bhabha, Celine Parreñas Shimizu writes that "if there is mimicry at work, it is not just a one-way mimicry of the colonized mimicking the colonizer. It is not just a one-way assimilation of the minor into the major. But the major subsumes the lessons from the other in order to transform oneself, to be more conscious, and to see beyond oneself the conditions of others" ("Can the Subaltern Sing, and in a Power Ballad?," 58–59).
109 Balance, *Tropical Renditions*, 152.
110 Writing against America as constant political and cultural referent, Shunya Yoshimi argues for a nuanced transpacific analysis that encourages one to "consider cultural relations between Japan and the Philippines up to the 1950s from the perspective of personnel interchange within the military base network in the region, which had an effect on the development of music and sexuality during that period. There is also a need to examine how, in Korea and Taiwan, 'America' was incorporated into peoples' consciousness just as the previously dominant presence of 'Japan' was being negated" (Yoshimi and Buist, "'America' as Desire and Violence," 434).
111 See Ileto, *Pasyon and Revolution*; and Kramer, *Blood of Government*, 77.
112 Gamalinda, *Empire of Memory*, 137.
113 Gamalinda, *Empire of Memory*, 238.
114 I credit Susan Buck-Morss here. In her delineation of Vodou and Freemasonry, she discusses the latter's attendance to the lessons of ancient civilization in contradistinction to the former's adherence to decay and death. Pointing to Haitian Vodou practices, she writes, "The skull and crossbones—a variant of the pervasive emblem of the deaths-head—signifies not merely the transiency of life, but the transiency of meaning, the impermanence of truth itself. The gods are radically distant. They have deserted the living. They must be recalled, physically reembodied, literally 'possessing' the body of a believer at every Vodou ceremony, just as the elaborately conceived vèvès, the Vodou cosmograms figured on the ground in poured powder and erased by the dancers' feet, must be created every time anew" (*Hegel, Haiti, and Universal History*, 127–28). I do not mean to conflate Vodou with the Pasyon, only to point to Buck-Morss's articulation of universal history and its practices as afforded to the living. In her estimation, the temporality that underscores Vodou relies not on this kind of historicity but, rather, on the understanding of impermanence within the discourses of European universalism.
115 Gamalinda, *Empire of Memory*, 259.
116 Edkins, *Trauma and the Memory of Politics*.
117 Casper, "Review: *The Empire of Memory*," 285.
118 Gamalinda, *Empire of Memory*, 265.
119 In "The Storyteller: Reflections on the Works of Nikolai Leskov," Walter Benjamin wrote, "What announces itself in these passages is the perpetuating remembrance of

the novelist as contrast with the short-lived reminiscences of the storyteller. The first is dedicated to one hero, one odyssey, one battle; the second, to many diffuse occurrences. It is, in other words, remembrance which, as the Muse-derived element of the novel, is added to reminiscence, the corresponding element of the story, the unity of their origin in memory having disappeared with the decline of the epic" (43).

120 Sonza, "'Is There a Contrary in the Empire of Memory?,'" 89.

CHAPTER TWO. BALIKBAYAN MOVEMENTS

An earlier version of this chapter was published as "Balikbayan Configurations and a U.S.-Philippine Politics of Modernization," *Journal of Asian American Studies* 21, no. 1 (February 2018): 1–29.

1 *Philippine Quarterly*, "Old and New Manila."
2 Government of the Republic of the Philippines, "Letter of Instruction No. 105."
3 Ibarra, "FM Launches 'Homecoming Season.'" Linda Richter (*Politics of Tourism in Asia*) also provides a detailed elaboration of the ways that the balikbayan program sought to silence overseas Filipinos' concerns about martial law.
4 *Filipino Tribune*, "Martial Law Lecture."
5 Ibarra, "FM Launches 'Homecoming Season.'" A 1976 *New York Times* profile of Filipinos living in the city pointed to a Mr. Sarda, who explained, "'I've been carrying my application for citizenship around for six months and I haven't signed it yet. I'm pretty sure I will eventually, but somehow I haven't been able to take that final step" (Sterne, "Manila Strip on Ninth Ave. Is Bit of Home for Filipinos"). In 1975, Philippine secretary of labor Blas F. Ople visited Filipino officials in New York, Washington, and California to promote a Philippine campaign to funnel US dollar remittances from Filipino overseas workers to the Philippines, expecting the Philippines to receive about $100 million from the remittances (US Department of State, "Labor Secretary Ople's Comments to Press upon Return").
6 Yến Lê Espiritu notes that "the returnees were offered a combination of reduced airfares, extended visas, tax breaks, and priority immigration and customs service upon arrival at the international airport in Manila" (*Home Bound*, 81).
7 Yến Lê Espiritu, *Home Bound*, 81.
8 Viola, "Toward a Filipino/a Critical (FilCrit) Pedagogy," 86.
9 Ibarra, "FM Launches 'Homecoming Season.'"
10 Ibarra, "FM Launches 'Homecoming Season.'"
11 In contextualizing the timeliness of Marcos's declaration of martial law, Linda Richter has helpfully suggested that Marcos "had to assure that martial law would neither jeopardize the flow of foreign capital investment into the country nor encourage cuts in foreign aid or new trade barriers to Philippine exports" ("Political Uses of Tourism," 242).
12 World Bank, "Current Economic Position and Prospects of the Philippines," 9.

13 Ricardo Manapat's impressive investigation of crony capitalism indicts several key businessmen within the Marcos regime for producing national economic crises—namely, the sugar monopoly that resulted in billion-dollar losses for producers (see Manapat, *Some Are Smarter Than Others*; and Branigin, "'Crony Capitalism' Blamed for Economic Crisis"). For Marcos's discussion of the 1973 oil crisis, see Government of the Republic of the Philippines, "Fourteenth State of the Nation Address, July 23, 1979."
14 *Balikbayan Magazine*, "Letters from Home," December 1981.
15 Geoffrey Rhoel Cruz provides a helpful history of "Calle de Escolta" through a discussion of contemporary historical conservation efforts ("The Cultural Heritage–Oriented Approach to Economic Development in the Philippines").
16 Quintos, "Escolta Revisited," 15.
17 Quintos, "Escolta Revisited," 15.
18 Benjamin, *Arcades Project*, 62–63.
19 Elmo Gonzaga has studied the Escolta of the 1930s, locating Filipino consumers as "transitional" figures between different decades of US colonial rule that grappled with "the capacity of modern commodities to deliver the miraculous benefits of modernity to everyday life" ("Consuming Capitalist Modernity," 82).
20 Quintos, "Escolta Revisited," 15.
21 Quintos, "Escolta Revisited, 17.
22 Vernadette Vicuña Gonzalez, *Securing Paradise*, 58.
23 Delia Aguilar offers a different articulation of the past and the present. In her rumination on Escolta and the politics of exile, she references Thomas Wolfe to write, "You can never go back home again" ("Memory Work," 480).
24 Quintos, "Escolta Revisited," 17.
25 Johnson, "Remarks at the Signing of the Immigration Bill."
26 Eithne Luibhéid, for instance, has written that "it is possible to reconstruct how Asian-origin peoples substantially exceeded the predictions of the numbers who would enter the United States under the provisions of the 1965 INA. Yet the subsequent surge was clearly an unintended consequence of the 1965 act and did not occur because lawmakers set out to right a wrong done to Asians" ("1965 Immigration and Nationality Act," 507).
27 See Dudziak, *Cold War Civil Rights*.
28 Writing for the *New York Times*, Michael Sterne explained that Filipino immigrants in New York "are quite unlike the earlier migrant generation of Filipino house servants, ship stewards and farm laborers who settled on the West Coast." In response to a question asking why Filipinos remain unrecognized, Mr. Nicanor explained, "We work hard. We study hard. We're like Americans" ("Manila Strip on Ninth Ave. Is Bit of Home for Filipinos"). See Baik, *Reencounters*.
29 Catherine Ceniza Choy's study of Filipino health care professionals (*Empire of Care*) offers an insightful historical trajectory of Filipino migration to the United States throughout the twentieth century. Additionally, Lucy Mae San Pablo Burns's interrogation of Filipino performance in taxi dance halls in *Puro*

Arte and Dawn Mabalon's analysis of Filipino community-building in Stockton in *Little Manila Is in the Heart* provide the necessary framework for exploring the means by which Filipino immigrants to the United States navigated the uncertain yet restrictive economic and social realities of life before the passage of the Immigration and Nationality Act of 1965.

30   Lowe, *Immigrant Acts*, 1–36.
31   Lowe notes that the US management of the Asian alien and the Asian citizen has been an attempt to resolve the contradictions of capital and labor that have seen the development of late capitalism from the nineteenth century into the twentieth. Lowe writes, "The history of the legislation of the Asian as *alien* and the administration of the Asian American as *citizen* is at once the genealogy of this attempt at resolution and the genealogy of a distinct 'racial formation' for Asian Americans, defined not primarily in terms of biological racialism but in terms of institutionalized legal definitions of race and national origin" (*Immigrant Acts*, 10).
32   Lowe, *Immigrant Acts*, 23–24.
33   Trinidad, "Conpuso," 15.
34   Vernadette Vicuña Gonzalez, *Securing Paradise*, 51.
35   Nicholas De Genova has written about the production of "illegality" through the quantitative evaluation of migrants from Mexico and throughout the Western Hemisphere. He explains, "With the end of the national-origins quota system, predictably, the 1965 amendments have been typically celebrated as a liberal reform, and U.S. immigration policy suddenly appeared to be chiefly distinguished by a broad inclusiveness, but with respect to Mexico, the outcome was distinctly and unequivocally restrictive. These same 'liberal' revisions (taking effect in 1968) established for the first time in U.S. history an annual numerical quota to restrict 'legal' migration from the Western Hemisphere. Indeed, the new cap imposed for the Western Hemisphere came about as a compromise with those who sought to maintain the national-origins quota system" ("Legal Production of Mexican/Migrant 'Illegality,'" 169).
36   Hernandez, *Migra!*, 215.
37   Reyes, *Global Borderlands*, 75.
38   See Yoneyama, *Cold War Ruins*; and Jin-kyung Lee, *Service Economies*.
39   Niu, "Wives, Widows, and Workers," 97.
40   Rick Bonus's study of Filipino American racial formation references the so-called third wave of Filipino migration to the United States to assert that "the significant movement of Filipinos to the United States during this period has also been attributed to the close and sustained economic, political, and cultural relationship between the Philippines and the United States" and that "with modern means of transportation, it has been relatively easy to bring Filipinos to the United States through recruitment and business connections" (*Locating Filipino Americans*, 45). Additionally, in his description of the emergence of a goods and remittance system that materialized in the aftermath of this wave of migration, Jonathan Okamura explains, "Insofar as these transnational services and Philippine-made

goods are desired and consumed by Filipino Americans, the widespread advertising for them is indicative of a diasporic consciousness and identity among Filipinos to sustain a connection with their homeland and with one another, in addition to their ongoing efforts to establish themselves in American society" (*Imagining the Filipino Diaspora*, 45). These foundational studies are importantly attuned to a persistent connection to the homeland and the built infrastructures that sustained it. At the same time, each maintains wedded to an articulation of post-1965 Filipino immigrants in the United States as affected by but discursively outside the Philippine nation rather than as fundamentally integrated within both state and national systems. Extending such conversations about the means by which Filipino Americans ground their racial consciousness in articulations of displacement and irresolution, the exploration of the *politics* of return complicates an *apart*ness that tends to naturalize a diasporic divide that often does not address the multiple and variegated ways that a Filipino American attachment to the homeland has been and remains a constructed and fraught formation (see Tiongson, Gutierrez, and Gutierrez, *Positively No Filipinos Allowed*; and Shankar and Srikanth, *Part Yet Apart*).

41 Hagar Kotef has noted that citizenship denotes a process of regulating mobility: "movement and stability thus precondition each other." Kotef's theorization of the regulation of movement as undergirding political liberalism helpfully situates US citizenship as enabling Filipino movement and return to the Philippines (*Movement and the Ordering of Freedom*, 11).

42 In his exploration of the spectral presence of the overseas Filipino, Vicente Rafael has argued that "Filipinos abroad simultaneously signify the failure of the nation-state to contain its excess population and the success of global capitalism in absorbing and accommodating this failure." He adds that while "they originate from the Philippines they can, thanks to the workings of global capital, now return to the nation in a form that is at once abstract and exterior to it" ("'Your Grief Is Our Gossip,'" 268). Rafael's postulation necessarily contends that the overseas Filipino is both a product of the nation and emblematic of its failure and that the balikbayan returns to the Philippines in a form different from the one in which it left. Yet the discourse of excess, failure, and abstraction is limited in its capacity to articulate the ways that the balikbayan as a political formation has been instrumental to the functionality of both Philippine and US modernity. This turn to mobility—and the infrastructures that enabled it—challenges the stasis underlined by excess and national failure to highlight the ways that movement to and from, that is, the promise and continuity of movement, was integral to conceptualizations of productivity and modernization in the Cold War era. That this mobility was fashioned by Philippine and US law and urban development offers alternative ways to imagine the balikbayan not as abstraction but as the realization of relational state projects that are grounded by a sustained history of Filipino labor and migration to the United States.

43 Government of the Republic of the Philippines, "Letter of Instruction No. 163."

44 At the same time, Marcos's push to nationalize the airline did well to attach these advancements to Marcos's New Society. As the Marcoses positioned themselves as the bearers of political and social progress, PAL, as it long had before, continued to serve the interests of the reigning administration (Meynardo P. Mendoza, "Binding the Islands," 77–104).
45 US Department of State, "Civair: Philippine Homecoming Fair Subsidy."
46 US Department of State, "Civair: Philippine Homecoming Fair Subsidy."
47 Pan American Airways contested the legality of the fare, questioning the extent to which such incentives could be offered only to a particular ethnic subset of customers.
48 US Department of State, "Civair: Homecoming Fair Suspension."
49 Lohr, "Isle for Divers—and Nondivers."
50 A telegram from the US embassy on March 22, 1974, noted: "The department of tourism announced yesterday new airline fare for filipinos in the united states wishing to take advantage of balikbayan ii. Secretary of tourism jose d. Aspiras emphasized that the reduced round trip fares, ordered by president marcos under letter of instruction no. 163, were good only on philippine airlines planes. Pal serves only honolulu, hawaii and san francisco, california in the united states. The net round trip fare is $500 san francisc-manila-san francisco and $410 honolu-manila-honolulu, individual, economy class and for groups of 70 persons" (US Department of State, "Civair: Philippine Homecoming Fair Subsidy."
51 Residual formations of past migration legacies, PAL's routes privileged overseas Filipinos located in Honolulu and San Francisco in ways that forced into the foreground the US colonial program that brought Filipino laborers to agricultural centers in the US West throughout the earlier decades of the twentieth century. PAL's recruitment of overseas Filipinos in these places, through advertisements such as these, relied on a map of migration and return that reinvigorated well-worn transpacific routes.
52 Even before the commencement of the balikbayan program, tourist officials in 1971 readied themselves for an unprecedented influx of Filipino tourists arriving from Hawai'i. Called on by the Phil-American Cultural Club of Honolulu to address the double taxation that Filipino tourists incurred in their homeland, government officials made efforts to assure the tourists that the government would take adequate steps to ensure their pleasant stay. Officials continuously speculated about the amount of foreign dollars that Filipino tourists would spend in the country during their visits.
53 See Baldoz, *Third Asiatic Invasion*; and Poblete, *Islanders in the Empire*.
54 Saulog, "Philippine Airlines Ad." In her discussion of *Reader's Digest*'s "middle-brow mission," Christina Klein explains that the magazine "understood itself as a tool that would guide the average person through the confusions of the twentieth century by providing clarity and reassurance" and that it "appealed to readers at the level of feeling rather than intellect." Klein's reading helpfully illustrates

the importance of such periodicals to the circulation of US Cold War discourse (*Cold War Orientalism*, 68).

55 General Assembly Resolution 2658 (XXV) safeguards, "the role of modern science and technology in the development of nations and the need to strengthen economic and technico-scientific co-operation among States."

56 The *Sarasota Herald Tribune* reported on January 24, 1972, that arson was suspected as the cause of the fire. The party responsible for the fire was (and continues to be) under speculation ("Cause of Manila Airport Fire Remains Subject to Suspicion").

57 In considering the airport as entry facility, I am particularly drawn to Lucy Mae San Pablo Burns's discussion of "contact zones" in *Puro Arte* and Nayan Shah's discussion in *Stranger Intimacy* of the regimes of regulation that South Asian labor migrants encountered at ports of entry.

58 Yến Lê Espiritu, *Home Bound*, 81.

59 According to the Manila International Airport Authority (https://www.miaa.gov.ph), the Manila International Airport, now the Ninoy Aquino International Airport, developed from a former US Air Force base that underwent major renovations in the 1950s and '60s. While Marcos formed the airport authority and developed plans for the airport's reconstruction in 1972, the new airport was not completed until the 1980s.

60 Executive Order No. 381.

61 Cresswell, *On the Move*, 221–24.

62 *New York Times*, "Manila Airport Seeks Expansion."

63 Brian Edwards writes that "the international airport is a modern kind of placeless city. . . . The big, busy multinational airport derives its logic from the distribution of world trade, the spatial pattern of international cities, and the often irrational location of national boundaries. This has led some observers to contend that the airport is a new type of city" (*Modern Airport Terminal*, 27).

64 Lico, *Edifice Complex*.

65 Maguigad, "Airport as a Cultural and Functional Showcase," 14.

66 Describing the home of the Centeno family, a reporter for the *New York Times* wrote that it was "a tiny metal and board shanty erected two years ago on land across from the two-month-old ultramodern Manila International Airport" and "is one of thousands of shantytown homes that were ordered demolished last week by Imelda R. Marcos, the First Lady and Human Settlements Minister. Acting quickly, the airport authority has signed an agreement to begin the demolition and relocation of the residents whose shacks give arriving visitors to the Philippines their first look at Manila's growing urban poor" (Hollie, "Manila Squatters Are an Eyesore for Mrs. Marcos").

67 *Manila Times*, "Christmas Tour Flights Okayed."

68 Clifford, "Tainted Cultures," 39.

69 In her analysis of urban excess and Marcos-constructed Manila, Neferti Tadiar has written that "the authoritarian state has converted Metro Manila into a

state-corporate body, and therefore anything that cannot be incorporated in this transnationally shaped, practical organon of autocratic desire is decreed lawless or criminal" (*Things Fall Away*, 161).

70 Laquian, *Slums and Squatters in Six Philippine Cities*, 36.
71 Laquian, *Slums and Squatters in Six Philippine Cities*, 14.
72 PhilRights, "From 'Squatters' into 'Informal Settlers.'"
73 Rolando Tolentino's study *Contestable Nation-Space* is a particularly apt and incisive exploration of the ways that Marcos's modernization program radically departed from earlier administrations.
74 I draw here from Filipino statesman Claro Recto's 1951 address at the University of the Philippines, in which he famously lambasted the Philippine government for continuing to adhere to Washington's self-serving policies ("Our Mendicant Foreign Policy"). Marcos's passage of the Mendicancy Law of 1978 (Presidential Decree No. 1563) sought to manage squatter populations by outlawing beggars in city spaces. I highlight these two events in order to draw connections between Marcos's articulation of national progress and his identification of the most unproductive members of Philippine society. That is, part of his presidential agenda relied on resolving the latter to realize a Philippine nationalism characterized by reinvigoration and self-reliance.
75 Squatters, according to Neferti Tadiar, are the "by-products of maldevelopment and mismanagement . . . people who engage in activities recognized as nonproductive, unregulated and, hence, illegitimate according to the standards of the national economy." Tadiar's analysis, drawing from the work of Neil Smith, helpfully posits that capital produces "the effect *of* subjectivity" in the likeness of its own image and adheres to the desires of the state while struggling to contain capital's antagonisms (that is, the poor classes that are simultaneously suppressed and necessitated by capital). Her discussion of flyovers that span across the skies of Metro Manila identifies the extent to which these highways managed excess Philippine populations that could not access them and regulated Filipino middle-class desire to remain distinct from the chaotic elements of the city. For the latter, flyovers "serve as the site of transnational identification" and "[raise] them out of their urban immersion in the contradictory conditions of their economic upliftment" (*Fantasy Production*, 80–85)." Tadiar thus pointedly historicizes flyovers as emerging from the work of the Aquino administration to reinstate free-market capitalism and privatization in the aftermath of the Marcoses' overregulation of the Philippine economy. Extending this conversation, the Marcoses' infrastructural reforms, enacted before Aquino's presidency, remain an important avenue for investigating the ways that their nationalization paradigm also wrestled with free-market liberalism. Where Tadiar posits that subjectivity offers a modality with which to interrogate the intersections of state and collective desire, Marcosian modernization remains a critical axis point for examining the ways that subjectivities also contended with and emerged from the regulatory regime of martial law.

76 Butterfield, "Mrs. Marcos."
77 Imelda Marcos, *Compassionate Society*, 121–22.
78 Benedicto, "Queer Afterlife of the Postcolonial City," 580–97.
79 Robles, "Manila without Madness," 13.
80 *Balikbayan Magazine*, "Balikbayan Reports," 18.
81 Government of the Republic of the Philippines, "Official Week in Review: March 22–March 31, 1982." Eric Pido's study of balikbayans provides an important analysis of the ways that Marcos's policies set the stage for overseas Filipinos' ongoing investment in real estate and development in the Philippines (*Migrant Returns*).
82 Basch, Schiller, and Blanc, *Nations Unbound*, 258–59.
83 Lelyveld, "Stark Contrasts Persist in Philippines's 'New Society.'"
84 Pante, "Politics of Flood Control," 582.
85 Karaos, "Manila's Squatter Movement," 84.
86 Hollie, "Manila Squatters Are an Eyesore for Mrs. Marcos."
87 *New York Times*, "Slum Evictions in Manila Embarrass the World Bank."
88 Tadiar's reading of Jun Cruz Reyes's novel *Tutubi, Tutubi, 'Wag Kang Magpahuli Sa Mamang Salbahe* (1981) presents a particularly lucid analysis of scavenging in Metro Manila as it posits a practice of movement that challenges the regime's sanction of transnational mobility: "Shaped by the conditions of the dispossessed into whose lot he is thrown, [the character, Jo's] liquidity enables him to make this moving picture of protest out of the negative remains and forgotten, castaway times of the Marcoses' modernist urban spectacle. This defiant urban social film smears the solid, cleaned-up, timeless social edifice of the New Society with the presences of the erased, the abandoned, the eliminated, and especially the subversive, like the strokes of red paint that smear its repressive white walls" (*Things Fall Away*, 199).
89 *Los Angeles Times*, "Manila Burial Turns into Political Protest."
90 Vasuvedan, "Autonomous City," 9.
91 Shabecoff, "Grievances Boiling Out of Manila Slums."
92 *New York Times*, "Slum Evictions in Manila Embarrass the World Bank."

CHAPTER THREE. THE NEW FILIPINA MELODRAMA

An earlier version of this chapter was published as "Chaos and Order in Lino Brocka's *Insiang*," ALON: *Journal for Filipinx American and Diasporic Studies* 1, no. 3 (2021): 311–29.

1 Imelda Marcos, *Imelda Romualdez Marcos*, 17.
2 Imelda Marcos, *Imelda Romualdez Marcos*, 18.
3 Scholars of migration and globalization Robyn Rodriguez and Anna Guevarra historicize the contemporary Philippine national economy through the interrogation of US colonial occupation. I argue here that an investigation of the Cold War period, specifically, is fundamental to threading such coloniality to the present.

4   Rodriguez, *Migrants for Export*.
5   Rafael, "Patronage and Pornography," 285.
6   Imelda Marcos biographer Katherine Ellison explained that Ferdinand Marcos "insist[ed] he had won more medals for bravery than any Filipino or American in history. He commissioned a movie about his exploits called Maharlika, christened a government broadcasting network 'Maharlika,' dubbed the main north-south highway on the island of Luzon, 'Maharlika,' and named a hall in the presidential palace, again, 'Maharlika'" (*Imelda*, 40). James Hamilton-Patterson relays a story about Lyndon B. Johnson's tendency to swim naked in order to intimidate his guests. Yet Marcos "had an athletic, even beautiful body in those days, beside which the naked LBJ would have looked like an ogre" (*America's Boy*, 218).
7   Balance, "Dahil Sa Iyo."
8   Ellison, *Imelda*, 9.
9   Ferdinand Marcos, *New Filipinism*.
10 Tolentino, "Post-national Family," 126.
11 Roces, *Women, Power, and Kinship Politics*, 10.
12 Baik, *Reencounters*, 38. See also Christina Klein, who has studied the ways that white Americans' adoption of South Korean and Vietnamese children rehearsed Orientalist discourses about the aberrance of Asian sexualities and emboldened ideas about the United States as the exemplar of benevolent modernity (*Cold War Orientalism*, 147).
13 Lowe, "Globalization."
14 This connection between family and US empire precedes the Cold War but gains new importance in a post–World War II era of US imperial dominance and postcolonial nation-building. To illustrate, Amy Kaplan's work on national expansion, "imperial domesticity," and US empire in the nineteenth century is fundamental here: "My point here is not to survey foreign policy but to suggest how deeply the language of domesticity suffused the debates about national expansion. Rather than stabilizing the representation of the nation as home, this rhetoric heightened the fraught and contingent nature of the boundary between the domestic and the foreign, a boundary that breaks down around questions of the racial identity of the nation as home. If we begin to rethink women's sphere in this context, we have to ask how the discourse of domesticity negotiates the borders of an increasingly expanding empire and a divided nation" ("Manifest Domesticity," 585).
15 Rafael, "Patronage and Pornography," 284.
16 Ellison describes that "in his toast at the White House dinner, Lyndon Johnson said he had long awaited meeting Marcos, particularly after [Hubert] Humphrey and other emissaries to Manila had returned with identical three-part reports: 'The Philippines are on the march. President Marcos is a great man. He sure has a beautiful wife'" (*Imelda*, 80).
17 Roces, "Women in Philippine Politics and Society," 173.

18 Quijano de Manila, *Reportage on the Marcoses*, 133. Quijano de Manila is Nick Joaquin's pen name.
19 Tadiar, *Things Fall Away*, 146.
20 The construction of the Cultural Center of the Philippines and Manila International Airport, for instance, mandated the eradication of squatters (see chaps. 1 and 2).
21 Bareng, "Steeling the Butterfly."
22 Villadolid, "What's Doing in Manila." Genevieve Clutario's study of the Carnival Queen contests in Manila in the first decades of the twentieth century points to the ways that beauty pageants illuminated racial tensions between Westerners and Filipinos during key years of Philippine state formation ("Pageant Politics").
23 Mina Roces's point is important here. In her discussion of the radical politics of Filipina women's groups and organizations, she points out that MAKIBAKA arrived to the political scene at a demonstration outside the venue of a Miss Philippines contest. Roces writes that "beauty . . . in the Philippine context is associated with female power and not with objectification, subjugation, or victimization" (*Women, Power, and Kinship Politics*, 127). By contending with a Western feminist politics that conceptualizes the promotion of beauty as a form of subjugation, Roces's point illustrates the dialectic at hand in Filipina contentions with beauty.
24 Mijares, *Conjugal Dictatorship of Ferdinand and Imelda Marcos*.
25 Vernadette Vicuña Gonzalez has also described the "feel of modernity" as "founded on the continuing unmodernity of human labor" ("Military Bases, 'Royalty Trips,' and Imperial Modernities," 32).
26 Mimi Thi Nguyen, *Gift of Freedom*, 364.
27 Imelda Marcos, *Imelda Romualdez Marcos*, 24–25.
28 Imelda Marcos, *Compassionate Society*, 17.
29 Imelda Marcos, *Imelda Romualdez Marcos*, 24.
30 Parreñas, "Migrant Filipina Domestic Workers," 569.
31 See Ong, *Neoliberalism as Exception*; and Hong, *Ruptures of American Capital*.
32 Hardt, "Affective Labor," 96–99.
33 Hardt, "Affective Labor," 100.
34 Parreñas, "Migrant Filipina Domestic Workers," 563.
35 Ding, "Prostitutes, Parasites, and the House of State Feminism," 315.
36 Jin-kyung Lee, *Service Economies*, 130.
37 Enloe, *Maneuvers*, 72–76.
38 US Department of State, "World Conference International Women's Year (WCIWY)."
39 AP, "Mexico International Women's Conference."
40 United Nations, *Report of the World Conference of the International Women's Year Conference*.
41 United Nations, *Report of the World Conference of the International Women's Year Conference*, 2.

42 United Nations, *Report of the World Conference of the International Women's Year Conference*, "Introduction," Point 25, 13.
43 See Grewal, *Transnational America*; and Hua, *Trafficking Women's Human Rights*.
44 Randall Williams, *Divided World*, xx.
45 Randall Williams, *Divided World*, 40.
46 Kaplan, "Manifest Domesticity"; Anne McClintock, *Imperial Leather*.
47 Olcott, "Cold War Conflicts and Cheap Cabaret," 736.
48 Hua, *Trafficking Women's Human Rights*, xxii.
49 Cruz, "Notes on Trans-Pacific Archives," 11.
50 Lisa Yoneyama has analyzed the ways that the postwar reconstruction of Japan into a "junior partner" of the United States materialized, in part, through the "rescue" of Japanese women (*Cold War Ruins*).
51 Sakai and Yoo, *Trans-Pacific Imagination*, 10.
52 Cho, *Haunting the Korean Diaspora*, 21.
53 See Roces, *Women, Power, and Kinship Politics*; and Cruz, *Transpacific Femininities*.
54 Imelda Marcos, *Compassionate Society*, 83.
55 NCRFW, *Annual Report* (1975), 35.
56 NCRFW, *Annual Report* (1975), 35.
57 NCRFW, *Annual Report* (1975), 82.
58 Cruz, *Transpacific Femininities*, 198.
59 Government of the Republic of the Philippines, "Presidential Decree No. 633."
60 NCRFW, *Annual Report* (1975), 16–18.
61 Imelda Marcos, *Compassionate Society*, 91–92.
62 NCRFW, *Annual Report* (1977), 20.
63 Marcos's martial law decree (Proclamation No. 1081) identified Zambales specifically as the location of "subversion and insurgency in this country." Yet Presidential Decree No. 705 pinpointed Zambales as an important site for forestry development.
64 NCRFW, *Annual Report* (1978), 28–36.
65 Imelda Marcos, *Compassionate Society*, 51.
66 NCRFW, *Annual Report* (1978), 29–30.
67 Family Health Care, Inc., *A Review of the Philippines' Population Program*, 10.
68 Hickey and Wilkinson, *Agrarian Reform in the Philippines*, 20.
69 See Solomon, "Managing the (Post)colonial"; Ponce, *Beyond the Nation*; and Victor Román Mendoza, *Metroimperial Intimacies*.
70 Lopez and Nemenzo, "Formulation of Philippine Population Policy."
71 Khiun, *Liberalizing, Feminizing and Popularizing Health Communications in Asia*, 159; Rierson, "Country Report: Philippines."
72 Family Health Care, Inc., *A Review of the Philippines' Population Program*, 23. Many women who received intrauterine devices (IUDs) had to be treated for infections. One group of Catholic nuns operated a program in Manila to treat women who experienced difficulties with IUDs (23).
73 Kerkvliet, "Land Reform in the Philippines since the Marcos Coup," 289.

74 Describing discourses of poverty that cohered during the US Cold War, Alyosha Goldstein writes, "The postwar ascendancy of the behavioral sciences focused attention on the family as the crucible of culture and personality, and isolated psychological dynamics from social and economic conditions. During the Cold War, social scientists set about enumerating the psychological traits that they argued personified a distinctive national character. The American character—as a singular, homogenous disposition—was supposedly oriented toward achievement, acquisition, individualism, and deferred gratification in the service of long-term objectives. This psychological and cultural explanation for affluence and American exceptionalism positioned poor people in the United States as foreign to white middle-class familial heteronormativity and as lacking the national character" (*Poverty in Common*, 81).

75 Arminda Santiago, "Struggle of the Oppressed," 15.
76 Capino, *Martial Law Melodrama*, 50.
77 See David, *Manila by Night*.
78 Beller, *Acquiring Eyes*, 152.
79 Arminda Santiago, "Struggle of the Oppressed," 32.
80 Naficy and Brocka, "Americanization and Indigenization of Lino Brocka through Cinema," 147.
81 Imelda Marcos banned filming in Tondo in the early 1980s (Lim, *Translating Time*, 121).
82 In *Servants of Globalization*, Rhacel Salazar Parreñas defines reproductive labor as "the labor needed to sustain the productive labor force." She writes that this includes "household chores; the care of elders, adults, and youth; the socialization of children; and the maintenance of social ties in the family" (29).
83 Tolentino, "Vaginal Economy." While the term "vaginal economy" refers specifically to the feminization of labor, it also relies on a problematic determination of who constitutes "women."
84 Tadiar, *Things Fall Away*.
85 Tadiar, *Things Fall Away*, 55.
86 Manalansan, "Servicing the World," 222.
87 Tolentino, *Contestable Nation-Space*, 133.
88 Lowe, *Immigrant Acts*.
89 Arminda Santiago describes this as Brocka's Brechtian critique ("Struggle of the Oppressed," 114). Brocka explained that Koronel's striking beauty was important for illuminating the squalor of Manila's slums. The daughter of a Filipina mother and an American GI father once stationed at Clark Air Force Base, Koronel was raised in an impoverished area of Pasay City. As Brocka's muse, Koronel only rose to fame after Brocka featured her in several of his films.
90 Babiera, "FDCP Gets Ownership Rights of Lino Brocka's 'Insiang.'"
91 Honculada, "Case Study," 13.
92 Beltran, "Concept of Urban Renewal," 41–42.

93 World Bank, *Report and Recommendation of the President of the International Bank*, 10.
94 Tondo residents often "propelled many an aspiring lawyer into the city government and even Congress. In exchange for continued delivery of votes, the politician provided some measure of protection but failed to perform on the issue of land" (Honculada, "Case Study," 13).
95 Honculada, "Case Study," 17. One World Bank report noted that "commmmunity relations" had been "made more difficult because the [National Housing Authority] considers Zoto/Ugnayan to be anti-government and does not want to enhance their credibility in the community" (World Bank, *Philippines: Manila Urban Development Project*, 12).
96 Brocka, *Artist and His Times*.
97 Naficy and Brocka, "Americanization and Indigenization of Lino Brocka through Cinema," 153.
98 Gutierrez, "Realist Cinema of Lino Brocka," 175.
99 Gutierrez, "Realist Cinema of Lino Brocka," 175.
100 Tolentino, *Contestable Nation-Space*, 141–42.
101 Lilia Quindoza Santiago, "Rebirthing Babaye."
102 Honculada and Ofreneo, "The National Commission on the Role of Filipino Women," 134.
103 Roces, *Women, Power, and Kinship Politics*, 152.
104 Diaz, "Subject Case."
105 Butterfield, "Filipinos Say Marcos Was Given Millions for '76 Nuclear Contract."
106 *New York Times*, "Westinghouse Nuclear Center."
107 Lynn Lee, "Contemporary Women's Movement in the Philippines," 217.
108 Roces, *Women, Power, and Kinship Politics*, 153.
109 Aquino, "Filipino Women and Political Engagement," 38.

CHAPTER FOUR. THE FILIPINO HUMANITARIAN

1 Government of the Republic of the Philippines, "Speech of President Marcos during the Inauguration," my translation.
2 National Housing Authority, *Philippine Refugee Processing Center*.
3 Government of the Republic of the Philippines, "Speech of President Marcos during the Inauguration."
4 National Housing Authority, *Philippine Refugee Processing Center*, 15.
5 National Housing Authority, *Philippine Refugee Processing Center*, 9.
6 Government of the Republic of the Philippines, "Speech of President Marcos during the Inauguration."
7 Gonzalez, *Securing Paradise*.
8 Lowe, *Intimacies of Four Continents*.

9   Government of the Republic of the Philippines, "Speech of President Marcos during the Inauguration."
10 Ileto, "Philippine Wars and the Politics of Memory."
11 Tana and Takagi, "Japan's Foreign Relations with the Philippines," 312.
12 Sakai and Yoo, *Trans-Pacific Imagination*.
13 Philippines, Bureau of National and Foreign Information, *Development for the New Society*.
14 Philippines, Bureau of National and Foreign Information, *Development for the New Society*, 87.
15 As Aihwa Ong notes, "EPZs were given a free hand to exploit abundant low-wage workers, most of whom were female" (*Neoliberalism as Exception*, 103).
16 Mimi Thi Nguyen, *Gift of Freedom*, 35.
17 Montes, "Refugees."
18 See Tydings-McDuffie Act of 1934.
19 Kotlowski, "Breaching the Paper Walls." Allan Isaac has written about the Philippines' centrality to "America" even as the Philippines is obfuscated by US narratives. He writes that the Philippines "constitute[es] part of the American Tropics . . . where 'America' meets its aporia, its impasse—a contingent but not contiguous source of difficult passages in legal, cinematic, and literary narratives, giving texture to the American story" (*American Tropics*, 3).
20 The United Nations High Commissioner for Refugees' "Convention and Protocol Relating to the Status of Refugees" states: "As a result of events occurring before 1 January 1951 and owing to wellfounded fear of being persecuted for reasons of race, religion, nationality, membership of a particular social group or political opinion, is outside the country of his nationality and is unable or, owing to such fear, is unwilling to avail himself of the protection of that country; or who, not having a nationality and being outside the country of his former habitual residence as a result of such events, is unable or, owing to such fear, is unwilling to return to it." See also the Refugee Policy Group's "Of Special Humanitarian Concern: U.S. Refugee Admissions Since Passage of the Refugee Act" (1985).
21 Mimi Thi Nguyen, *Gift of Freedom*.
22 Mimi Thi Nguyen, *Gift of Freedom*.
23 Brown, "'The Most We Can Hope For . . . ,'" 459.
24 Baik, *Reencounters*, 54.
25 Yến Lê Espiritu, *Body Counts*, 35.
26 Kennedy, "Refugee Act of 1980."
27 Wendy Brown poses the following questions: "Whatever their avowed purpose, then, do human rights only reduce suffering? Do they (promise to) reduce it in a particular way that precludes or negates other possible ways? And if they reduce suffering, what kinds of subjects and political (or antipolitical) cultures do they bring into being as they do so, what kinds do they transform or erode, and what kinds do they aver?" ("'The Most We Can Hope For . . . ,'" 453).
28 Ferdinand Marcos, *New Filipinism*.

29 Foucault, "Nietzsche, Genealogy, History," 79.
30 Blanco, "Race as Praxis in the Philippines at the Turn of the Twentieth Century," 371.
31 Ferdinand Marcos, *Marcos Reader*.
32 Manuel, *Tao*, 9.
33 Ferdinand Marcos, *Marcos Reader*.
34 Ferdinand Marcos, *Marcos Reader*, 4.
35 Ferdinand Marcos, *Marcos Reader*, 7–8.
36 Schirmer and Shalom, *Philippine Reader*, 200.
37 Randall Williams's discussion of Fanon's theorization of anticolonial resistance is especially incisive. He writes, "As long as the power to confer or withhold the recognition of the Other's humanity remains a decision made elsewhere, there will be no substantial alteration of the material conditions that serve as the basis for the very possibility of a distinction between the human and the inhuman. What Fanon suggests here is that all appellative modes of recognition and/or redress are doomed to reproduce the power of the state and the cultural-economic structures indispensable to the smooth functioning of racist-colonial capitalism. As Fanon's closing allegory in *Black Skin, White Masks* figures the problem of nonviolence, it is in the absence of actional struggle to the death that the Negro is handed over to constitutional freedom under Law, and there he or she remains subject to the exploitative vagaries of the gift" (*Divided World*, 100). Williams's reading generates important insight into the ways that colonial knowledge production withstands the terms of freedom granted by the state.
38 Foucault's questions are useful here: "The guiding thread that seems the most useful for this inquiry is constituted by what one might call the 'techniques of the self,' which is to say, the procedures, which no doubt exist in every civilization, suggested or prescribed to individuals in order to determine their identity, maintain it, or transform it in terms of a certain number of ends, through relations of self-mastery or self-knowledge. In short, it is a matter of placing the imperative to 'know oneself'—which to us appears so characteristic of our civilization—back in the much broader interrogation that serves as its explicit or implicit context: What should one do with oneself? What work should be carried out on the self? How should one 'govern oneself' by performing actions in which one is oneself the objective of those actions, the domain in which they are brought to bear, the instrument they employ, and the subject that acts?" (*Ethics*, 87).
39 Ferdinand Marcos, "Ferdinand Marcos's Republican Principles."
40 Ferdinand Marcos, *Marcos Reader*, 213.
41 Ferdinand Marcos, *Marcos Reader*, 214.
42 United Nations, "United Nations General Assembly 32nd Session."
43 Imelda Marcos, *Compassionate Society*, 170.
44 Spivak, "Righting Wrongs," 531.
45 Mimi Thi Nguyen, *Gift of Freedom*, 38.
46 Mimi Thi Nguyen, *Gift of Freedom*, 38.
47 Brown, *States of Injury*, 8.

48 Brown, *States of Injury*, 24–25.
49 Ferdinand Marcos, *Marcos Reader*, 142.
50 Ferdinand Marcos, *Marcos Reader*, 178.
51 Ferdinand Marcos, *Marcos Reader*, 149.
52 Government of the Republic of the Philippines, "Speech of President Marcos during the Inauguration."
53 Imelda Marcos, *Compassionate Society*, 13.
54 Mankekar and Gupta, "Intimate Encounters."
55 US General Accounting Office, "Construction and Operation of the Philippine Refugee Processing Center in Bataan, the Philippines," 12–13.
56 Overseas Refugee Training Program, *Passage* (1985), 35.
57 Overseas Refugee Training Program, *Passage* (1988), 96; *Cultural Orientation Resource Manual* (1983), 5.
58 Jan Padios's study of call centers in the Philippines and the concept of "Filipino/American relatability" is especially useful for considering the ways that claims about Filipino affability rely on an understanding of the colonization of the Philippines that structures the conditions of Filipino and American relations in the present (what Padios calls "colonial recall") (*A Nation on the Line*, 82–84).
59 Tupas and Lorente, "'New' Politics of Language in the Philippines," 172.
60 US Philippine Commission, *Eighth Annual Report of the Philippine Commission to the Secretary of War, 1907*, 258.
61 Torres, *Americanization of Manila*, 154–55.
62 See Center for Applied Linguistics (CAL), http://www.cal.org/, accessed May 16, 2022.
63 Fox, "U.S. International English Language Policy," 14.
64 Alyosha Goldstein's study of US Cold War discourses of underdevelopment reveals the ways that agencies and officials constructed notions of domestic poverty (especially through termination policies aimed to restrict Native sovereignty) and applied these frameworks of underdevelopment to foreign nations. Goldstein's work underscores the importance of US Indian policy to Cold War foreign policy (*Poverty in Common*).
65 Nash, "Education Mission of the Bureau of Indian Affairs," 3. See also Eugene Briere's "English Language Testing Project for the Bureau of Indian Affairs."
66 Healy, "Progress Report on the President's Commission on Foreign Languages and International Studies," 3.
67 Center for Applied Linguistics, *Passage* (1988).
68 Center for Applied Linguistics, *Passage* (1988), 64.
69 Center for Applied Linguistics, *Passage* (1985), 21.
70 Center for Applied Linguistics, *Passage* (1988), 63.
71 Center for Applied Linguistics, *Passage* (1988), 65.
72 Center for Applied Linguistics, *Passage* (1988), 61.
73 Rafael, *Motherless Tongues*, 108.
74 Rafael, *Motherless Tongues*, 111.

75 Mankekar and Gupta, "Intimate Encounters," 28.
76 Rafael, *Motherless Tongues*, 7.
77 Rafael, *Motherless Tongues*, 6.

CONCLUSION. RECKONING WITH THE BODY

1 Morella, "Mortician to Marcos Reveals Trade Secrets."
2 Morella, "Mortician to Marcos Reveals Trade Secrets."
3 Office of Research and Publications (Ateneo de Manila University), *Memory, Truth-Telling, and the Pursuit of Justice*, 25.
4 Office of Research and Publications (Ateneo de Manila University), *Memory, Truth-Telling, and the Pursuit of Justice*, 74.
5 In a 2017 opinion piece for the *New York Times*, novelist Gina Apostol writes that "salvage" means to be "tortured and killed in unknown circumstances . . . a cross of two words: 'to savage' and to be 'salvaje,' which means wild in Spanish, but naughty or abusive in Tagalog. Add to that obscene joke the play on its meaning in English: to redeem, to extract from a wreck" ("Speaking in Fascism's Tongues"). In 2013, over a decade after this conference and during the presidential administration of Benigno "Noynoy" Aquino III (the son of slain senator Benigno Aquino, Jr.), the Philippine Congress passed Republic Act No. 10368. The act "provided for reparation and recognition of victims of human rights violations during the Marcos regime, documentation of said violations."
6 Franco, *Cruel Modernity*, 21.
7 The Aquino administration, with the support of Washington, deemed the return of the body a national security risk. Numerous coups, led by Marcos loyalists, plagued the Aquino presidency.
8 Ohira and Ryan, "Imelda Vows Again."
9 Morella, "Mortician to Marcos Reveals Trade Secrets."
10 In her discussion of Steve Mann's concept of "sousveillance" as "a way of naming an active inversion of the power relations that surveillance entails," Simone Browne theorizes dark sousveillance "to situate the tactics employed to render one's self out of sight, and strategies used in the flight to freedom from slavery as necessarily ones of undersight." According to Browne, dark sousveillance offers a critique of racialized surveillance in order to conceptualize other freedom practices (*Dark Matters*, 21).
11 Cartwright and Sturken, *Practices of Looking*, 9.
12 Yoneyama, *Cold War Ruins*.
13 Gotera, *Radical Visions*, 4.
14 Gotera, *Radical Visions*, 25.
15 Gotera, "Three Sonnetinas," 158–60.
16 Gotera, "Three Sonnetinas," 158.
17 *Marcos Tapes*, 80.

18 Wolff, "Marcos Verdict."
19 Linmark, "What Some Are Saying about the Body," 184–87.
20 Lowe, *Immigrant Acts*, 118.
21 Christine Bacareza Balance ("Just in Time for FAHM: Afterlives of Martial Law") has theorized the "afterlives" of the regime. Further, Martin Manalansan's theorization of the "everyday" practices of queer diasporic people is instructive for considering the poem as an archive of the language and humor of quotidian storytelling. Manalansan writes, "The everyday . . . troubles, if not resists, the conventional time-space binary by expressing the ways in which memory is spatialized and space is entangled with intimate habits, routines, personal histories, and deviant chronologies. . . . Everyday life is a site for critically viewing and 'reading' modernity. Unlike traditional historiography, which depends on grand narratives of 'famous men' and great events, the narrative of everyday life reveals the rich intricacies of the commonplace" ("Migrancy, Modernity, Mobility," 148).
22 Tadiar (*Things Fall Away*) has theorized scavenging as the capacity of the poor masses to transform decay into lifemaking practices that sustain the lives of the poor and provoke resistances against a state that seeks to obliterate them.
23 Kelley and Bronstein, "Interview: Imelda and Ferdinand Marcos."
24 Martin, "RIP, Rest in Pieces."
25 I draw here from Saidiya Hartman's work on tourism, memory, and the Black diaspora. While speaking in/of a different context and set of historical circumstances, namely, the place of Africa in the Black diasporic consciousness, Hartman's notion that "the ideological construction of the past is guided by the current political interests of the diaspora" has been helpful for articulating the constructedness of the idea of diaspora itself ("Time of Slavery," 765).
26 Campomanes, "Filipinos in the United States and Their Literature of Exile," 57, 50.
27 I am particularly struck by Louise Glück's observation here: "What I share with my friends is ambition; what I dispute is its definition. I do not think that more information always makes a richer poem. I am attracted to ellipsis, to the unsaid, to suggestion, to eloquent, deliberate silence. The unsaid, for me, exerts great power: often I wish an entire poem could be made in this vocabulary. It is analogous to the unseen; for example, the power of ruins, to works of art either damaged or incomplete" ("Disruption, Hesitation, Silence," 30).
28 Saranillio, "Why Asian Settler Colonialism Matters."
29 Glauberman, "It Was a Sad Day for Many Hawai'i Filipinos," September 29, 1989.
30 Raymond Williams, *Marxism and Literature*, 126.
31 Foucault, *"Society Must Be Defended,"* 28.
32 Ranada, "Duterte on Marcos Burial."
33 SunStar, "Editorial: 'Never Forget.'"

BIBLIOGRAPHY

PRIMARY SOURCES

AP. "Mexico International Women's Conference." *AP Archive*, June 22, 1975. Accessed December 15, 2021. http://www.aparchive.com/metadata/youtube/399ad28610 85b4deac6bd8788cac2400.
Balikbayan Magazine. "Balikbayan Reports: Land Ownership for Balikbayan Filipinos." *Balikbayan Magazine* 1, no. 2 (1981): 18.
Branigin, William. "'Crony Capitalism' Blamed for Economic Crisis." *Washington Post*, August 16, 1984.
Briere, Eugene. "English Language Testing Project for the Bureau of Indian Affairs." US Department of Health, Education, and Welfare, Office of Education. Washington, DC: Bureau of Indian Affairs, 1969.
Butterfield, Fox. "Filipinos Say Marcos Was Given Millions for '76 Nuclear Contract." *New York Times*, March 7, 1986.
Butterfield, Fox. "Mrs. Marcos: A Mix of Beauty and Power." *Milwaukee Journal*, March 5, 1976.
Center for Applied Linguistics. *Cultural Orientation Research Manual, Volume III*. Washington, DC: Center for Applied Linguistics, Bureau of Refugee Programs of the U.S. Department of State, 1983.
Commission on the Humanities. *Report of the Commission on the Humanities*. New York: American Council of Learned Societies, 1964.
Comptroller General of the United States. *Review of U.S. Assistance to the Philippine Government in Support of the Philippine Civic Action Group*. Washington, DC: Comptroller General of the United States, 1970.
Curtis, Charlotte. "First Lady Adds to Glitter; Musicians' Strike Is Settled." *New York Times*, September 17, 1966.

Family Health Care, Inc. *A Review of the Philippines' Population Program: The Family Health Care Report*. Washington, DC: Agency for International Development, 1977.

Filipino Tribune. "Martial Law Lecture." August 1–15, 1973.

Fox, Melvin. "U.S. International English Language Policy." In *Language in Public Life, Georgetown University Round Table on Languages and Linguistics*, edited by James E. Alatis and G. Richard Tucker, 8–22. Washington, DC: Georgetown University Press, 1979.

GABRIELA-Mindanao. *Babaye*. Davao City: GABRIELA-Mindanao and Women and Studies Resource Center, 1986.

Glauberman, Stu. "It Was a Sad Day for Many Hawai'i Filipinos." *Honolulu Advertiser*, September 29, 1989.

Gotera, Vince. *Radical Visions: Poetry by Vietnam Veterans*. Athens: University of Georgia Press, 1994.

Gotera, Vince. "Three Sonnetinas." In *Mondo Marcos: Writings on Martial Law and the Marcos Babies*, edited by Frank Cimatu, Rolando Tolentino, and Andy Zapata, 158–60. Pasig City: Anvil, 2010.

Government of the Republic of the Philippines. "Fourth State of the Nation Address, January 27, 1969." *Official Gazette*, January 27, 1969. https://www.officialgazette.gov.ph/1969/01/27/ferdinand-e-marcos-fourth-state-of-the-nation-address-january-27-1969/.

Government of the Republic of the Philippines. "Fourteenth State of the Nation Address, July 23, 1979." *Official Gazette*, July 23, 1979. https://www.officialgazette.gov.ph/1979/07/23/ferdinand-e-marcos-fourteenth-state-of-the-nation-address-july-23-1979/.

Government of the Republic of the Philippines. "Letter of Instruction No. 105, July 31, 1973." *Official Gazette*, July 31, 1973. http://www.officialgazette.gov.ph/1973/07/31/letter-of-instruction-no-105-s-1973/.

Government of the Republic of the Philippines. "Letter of Instruction No. 163, February 7, 1974." *Official Gazette*, February 7, 1974. http://www.officialgazette.gov.ph/1974/02/07/letter-of-instruction-no-163-s-1974/.

Government of the Republic of the Philippines. "Official Week in Review: March 22–March 31, 1982, March 29, 1982." *Official Gazette*, April 26, 1982. http://www.officialgazette.gov.ph/1982/04/26/official-week-in-review-march-22-march-31-1982/.

Government of the Republic of the Philippines. "Presidential Decree No. 633, s. 1975." *Official Gazette*, July 1, 1975. https://www.officialgazette.gov.ph/1975/01/07/presidential-decree-no-633-s-1975/.

Government of the Republic of the Philippines. "Proclamation No. 1081, s. 1972." *Official Gazette*, September 21, 1972. https://www.officialgazette.gov.ph/1972/09/21/proclamation-no-1081/.

Government of the Republic of the Philippines. "Republic Act No. 10368." *Official Gazette*, February 25, 2013. https://www.officialgazette.gov.ph/2013/02/25/republic-act-no-10368/.

Government of the Republic of the Philippines. "Sixth State of the Nation Address, January 25, 1971." *Official Gazette*, January 25, 1971. https://www.officialgazette.gov.ph/1971/01/25/ferdinand-e-marcos-sixth-state-of-the-nation-address-january-25-1971-2/.

Government of the Republic of the Philippines. "Speech of President Marcos during the Inauguration of the Philippine Refugee Processing Center, January 21, 1980." *Official Gazette*, January 21, 1980. https://www.officialgazette.gov.ph/1980/01/21/speech-of-president-macros-during-the-inauguration-of-the-philippine-refugee-processing-center/.

Healy, S. J. "A Progress Report on the President's Commission on Foreign Languages and International Studies." In *Language in Public Life, Georgetown University Round Table on Languages and Linguistics*, edited by James E. Alatis and G. Richard Tucker. Washington, DC: Georgetown University Press, 1979.

Hickey, Gerald, and John L. Wilkinson. *Agrarian Reform in the Philippines*. Washington, DC: RAND Corporation, 1977.

Hollie, Pamela G. "Manila Squatters Are an Eyesore for Mrs. Marcos." *New York Times*, June 30, 1982.

Human Rights Library. "Labor Code of the Philippines." University of Minnesota. http://hrlibrary.umn.edu/research/Philippines/PD%20442%20-%20Labor%20Code%20of%20the%20Philippines.pdf.

Ibañez, Ruby. "Teacher, It's Nice to Meet You, Too." *Passage: A Journal of Refugee Education* 1, no. 1 (1985): 35. https://files.eric.ed.gov/fulltext/ED254099.pdf.

Ibarra, Crisostomo D. Ibarra. "FM Launches 'Homecoming Season.'" *Filipino Tribune*, August 1–15, 1973.

Johnson, Lady Bird. *A White House Diary: Lady Bird Johnson*. Austin: University of Texas Press, 1970.

Kelley, Ken, and Phil Bronstein. "Playboy Interview: Imelda and Ferdinand Marcos." *Playboy*, August 1987, 36–45.

Laquian, Aprodicio A. *Slums and Squatters in Six Philippine Cities*. Final Report on a Research Grant from the Southeast Asia Development Advisory Group of the Asia Society, March 23, 1972.

Lelyveld, Joseph. "Stark Contrasts Persist in Philippines's 'New Society.'" *New York Times*, November 5, 1973.

Library of Congress. "God Bless America." Library of Congress. Accessed December 3, 2020. https://www.loc.gov/item/ihas.200000007/.

Life. "Visit: Mutual Admiration Alliance." *Life* 61, no. 14 (September 30, 1966): 133–34.

Linmark, R. Zamora. "What Some Are Saying about the Body." In *Mondo Marcos: Writings on Martial Law and the Marcos Babies*, edited by Frank Cimatu, Rolando Tolentino, and Andy Zapata, 184–87. Pasig City: Anvil, 2010.

Lohr, Steve. "An Isle for Divers—and Nondivers." *New York Times*, September 22, 1985.

Los Angeles Times. "Manila Burial Turns into Political Protest." August 7, 1985.

Manila Times. "Christmas Tour Flights Okayed." December 9, 1971.

Manning, Jack. "At the Opening Night of the New Metropolitan Opera House in Lincoln Center." *New York Times*, September 16, 1966. https://www.nytsyn.com/archives/photos/751823.html.

Marcos, Ferdinand E. "Ferdinand Marcos's Republican Principles." *Executive Intelligence Review* 12, no. 32 (1985): 36.

Marcos, Ferdinand E. *The Marcos Reader: Selected Essays and Speeches by Ferdinand E. Marcos, President of the Philippines*. Manila: Office of Media Affairs, 1982.

Marcos, Ferdinand E. *New Filipinism: The Turning Point (State of the Nation Message to the Congress of the Philippines, 27 January 1969)*. Manila: Office of the President of the Philippines, 1969.

Marcos, Ferdinand E. *Notes on the New Society of the Philippines*. Manila: Marcos Foundation, 1976.

Marcos, Ferdinand E. *Tadhana: The History of the Filipino People*. Manila: Ferdinand E. Marcos, 1977.

Marcos, Imelda. *The Compassionate Society and Other Selected Speeches*. Manila: National Media Production Center, 1977.

Marcos, Imelda. *Imelda Romualdez Marcos: The New Filipina*. Manila, 1969.

Marcos Tapes: Ferdinand Marcos' Plan to Invade the Philippines. Hearing before the Subcommittee on Asian and Pacific Affairs of the Committee on Foreign Affairs, House of Representatives, 100th Congress, 1st sess., July 9, 1987. Washington, DC: US Government Printing Office.

Montes, Sylvia P. "The Refugees: A Global Movement in Humanism." *Catholic Lawyer* 25, no. 2 (1980): 187–93.

Nash, Philleo Nash. "The Education Mission of the Bureau of Indian Affairs." *Journal of American Indian Education* 3, no. 2 (1964): 1–4.

National Executive Board. "Dictator's Nationalist Appeals Ring Hollow in U.S. Filipino Community." *Ang Katipunan* 7, no. 8 (April 25–30, 1980): 2.

National Housing Authority. *Philippine Refugee Processing Center: A Philippine Response to the Refugee Problem*. 198?. https://www.filipinaslibrary.org.ph/biblio/55559/.

NCRFW (National Commission on the Role of Filipino Women). *Annual Report*. Manila: Office of the President, 1975.

NCRFW (National Commission on the Role of Filipino Women). *Annual Report*. Manila: Office of the President, 1976.

NCRFW (National Commission on the Role of Filipino Women). *Annual Report*. Manila: Office of the President, 1977.

NCRFW (National Commission on the Role of Filipino Women). *Annual Report*. Manila: Office of the President, 1978.

NCRFW (National Commission on the Role of Filipino Women). *Annual Report*. Manila: Office of the President, 1980.

NCRFW (National Commission on the Role of Filipino Women). *Annual Report*. Manila: Office of the President, 1981.

New York Times. "Filipinos Throng to Foreign Jobs and Send Their Families Money." November 14, 1977.

New York Times. "Manila Airport Seeks Expansion." August 27, 1967.

New York Times. "Slum Evictions in Manila Embarrass the World Bank." October 7, 1976.

New York Times. "Westinghouse Nuclear Center." December 3, 1979.

Ohira, Rod, and Tim Ryan. "Imelda Vows Again: Body Will Go Home." *Honolulu Star-Bulletin*, September 29, 1989.

Overseas Refugee Training Program. *Passage: A Journal of Refugee Education* 1, no. 1 (1985). Washington, DC: Center for Applied Linguistics, Bureau of Refugee Programs of the U.S. Department of State, 1985.

Overseas Refugee Training Program. *Passage: A Journal of Refugee Education* 4, nos. 1–2 (1988). Washington, DC: Center for Applied Linguistics, Bureau of Refugee Programs of the U.S. Department of State, 1988.

Peters, Gerhard, and John T. Woolley. "Lyndon B. Johnson: Address on Vietnam before the National Legislative Conference, San Antonio, Texas." *American Presidency Project.* Accessed December 6, 2018. https://www.presidency.ucsb.edu/node/237536.

Peters, Gerhard, and John T. Woolley. "Lyndon B. Johnson: Commencement Address at Howard University: 'To Fulfill These Rights.'" Accessed December 6, 2018. *American Presidency Project.* https://www.presidency.ucsb.edu/node/241312.

Peters, Gerhard, and John T. Woolley. "Lyndon B. Johnson: Remarks at Dulles International Airport upon Returning from the Asian-Pacific Trip." *American Presidency Project.* Accessed December 6, 2018. https://www.presidency.ucsb.edu/documents/remarks-dulles-international-airport-upon-returning-from-the-asian-pacific-trip.

Peters, Gerhard, and John T. Woolley. "Lyndon B. Johnson: Remarks at the Signing of the Arts and Humanities Bill." *American Presidency Project.* Accessed December 6, 2018. https://www.presidency.ucsb.edu/node/241335.

Peters, Gerhard, and John T. Woolley. "Lyndon B. Johnson: Remarks at the Signing of the Immigration Bill, Liberty Island, New York." *American Presidency Project.* Accessed December 6, 2018. https://www.presidency.ucsb.edu/documents/remarks-the-signing-the-immigration-bill-liberty-island-new-york.

Peters, Gerhard, and John T. Woolley. "Lyndon B. Johnson: Toasts of the President and President Marcos of the Philippines." *American Presidency Project.* Accessed December 6, 2018. https://www.presidency.ucsb.edu/node/238621.

Philippine Quarterly. "Old and New Manila." *Philippine Quarterly* 8, no. 1 (1976): 62–66.

Philippines, Bureau of National and Foreign Information. *Development for the New Society: The Philippine Economy in the Mid-Seventies.* Foreword by Ferdinand E. Marcos. Manila: Department of Public Information, 1974.

Quintos, Floy. "Escolta Revisited." *Balikbayan Magazine* 1, no. 3 (1982): 12–17.

Refugee Policy Group. "Of Special Humanitarian Concern: U.S. Refugee Admissions since Passage of the Refugee Act." *Migration News* 35, no. 1 (1985): 3–36.

Rierson, Michael. *Country Report: Philippines.* Washington, DC: Interdisciplinary Communications Program, Smithsonian Institution, 1976.

Robles, Francisco. "Manila without Madness." *Focus Magazine*, November 25, 1972.

Sarasota Herald Tribune. "Cause of Manila Airport Fire Remains Subject to Suspicion." January 24, 1972.

Saulog, Jon Uy. "Philippine Airlines Ad." *Flickr*. Accessed December 6, 2018. https://www.flickr.com/photos/8223500@N05/13981875487.

Schein, Ernest. "War Damage Compensation through Rehabilitation: The Philippine War Damage Commission." *Law and Contemporary Problems* 16 (1951): 519–42.

Shabecoff, Philip. "Grievances Boiling Out of Manila Slums." *St. Petersburg Times*, March 16, 1970.

Sterne, Michael. "Manila Strip on Ninth Ave. Is Bit of Home for Filipinos." *New York Times*, December 30, 1976.

SunStar. "Editorial: 'Never Forget.'" November 21, 2016.

Trinidad, Recah. "Conpuso: A Filipino First in California." *Balikbayan Magazine* 1, no. 2 (1981): 14–17.

UNESCO. *International Women's Year*. UNESCO Courier 28 (March 1975). https://unesdoc.unesco.org/ark:/48223/pf0000074836.

United Nations. "Declaration of the United Nations." Accessed December 4, 2018. http://www.un.org/en/sections/history-united-nations-charter/1942-declaration-united-nations/index.html.

United Nations. "General Assembly Resolution 2658 (XXV)." December 7, 1970. https://documents-dds-ny.un.org/doc/RESOLUTION/GEN/NR0/349/23/IMG/NR034923.pdf?OpenElement.

United Nations. *Report of the World Conference of the International Women's Year Conference: Mexico City, 19 June–2 July 1975*. New York: United Nations, 1976.

United Nations. "United Nations General Assembly 32nd Session." Accessed December 7, 2018. http://www.un.org/ga/search/view_doc.asp?symbol=A/32/PV.15.

United Nations High Commissioner for Refugees. "Convention and Protocol Relating to the Status of Refugees." Accessed December 6, 2018. http://www.unhcr.org/en-us/protection/basic/3b66c2aa10/convention-protocol-relating-status-refugees.html.

US Department of State. "Civair: Homecoming Fair Suspension, April 17, 1975." Wikileaks. Review July 5, 2006. Accessed December 6, 2018. https://wikileaks.org/plusd/cables/1975MANILA04904_b.html.

US Department of State. "Civair: Philippine Homecoming Fair Subsidy, September 25, 1973." Wikileaks. Review June 30, 2005. Accessed December 6, 2018. https://wikileaks.org/plusd/cables/1973STATE191117_b.html.

US Department of State. "Labor Secretary Ople's Comments to Press upon Return, July 17, 1975." Wikileaks. Review July 6, 2006. Accessed December 6, 2018. https://wikileaks.org/plusd/cables/1975MANILA09777_b.html.

US Department of State. "World Conference International Women's Year (WCIWY), June 6, 1975." Wikileaks. Review July 6, 2006. Accessed December 6, 2018. https://www.wikileaks.org/plusd/cables/1975MANILA07797_b.html.

US General Accounting Office. "Construction and Operation of the Philippine Refugee Processing Center in Bataan, the Philippines." Washington, DC: United States General Accounting Office, 1981.

US Information Agency. "Statement of Albert Harkness Jr., Director, Information Center Service, Re Philippine-American Cultural Foundation US Congress. Hearings before the Subcommittee of the Committee on Appropriations, 86th Congress, 2nd sess., June 30, 1961." Washington, DC: US Government Printing Office.

US Office of the Historian. "Memorandum for the Record." *Foreign Relations of the United States, 1964–1968*. Vol. 26: *Indonesia; Malaysia-Singapore; Philippines*. Accessed December 6, 2018. https://history.state.gov/historicaldocuments/frus1964-68v26/d344.

US Office of the Historian. "Memorandum from the Officer in Charge of Philippine Affairs (Kattenburg) to the Assistant Secretary of State for Far Eastern Affairs (Bundy)." *Foreign Relations of the United States, 1964–1968*. Vol. 26: *Indonesia; Malaysia-Singapore; Philippines*. Accessed December 6, 2018. https://history.state.gov/historicaldocuments/frus1964-68v26/d336.

US Office of the Historian. "Memorandum from the President's Special Assistant (Rostow) to President Johnson, September 14, 1966." *Foreign Relations of the United States, 1964–1968*. Vol. 26: *Indonesia; Malaysia-Singapore; Philippines*. Accessed December 6, 2018. https://history.state.gov/historicaldocuments/frus1964-68v26/d342.

US Office of the Historian. "Memorandum from the President's Special Assistant (Valenti) to President Johnson, January 4, 1966." *Foreign Relations of the United States, 1964–1968*. Vol. 26: *Indonesia; Malaysia-Singapore; Philippines*. Accessed May 19, 2022. https://history.state.gov/historicaldocuments/frus1964-68v26/d322.

US Philippine Commission (1899–1900). *Eighth Annual Report of the Philippine Commission to the Secretary of War, 1907*. Washington, DC: US Government Printing Office, 1908.

Villadolid, Alice. "What's Doing in Manila." *New York Times*, April 14, 1974.

Virginia Polytechnic Institute. *Nutrition and Related Services Provided to the Republic of the Philippines*. Blacksburg, VA: AID/ASIA, 1979.

Wolff, Craig. "The Marcos Verdict: Marcos Is Cleared of All Charges in Racketeering and Fraud Case." *New York Times*, July 3, 1990. https://www.nytimes.com/1990/07/03/nyregion/marcos-verdict-marcos-cleared-all-charges-racketeering-fraud-case.html.

World Bank. "Current Economic Position and Prospects of the Philippines. Vol. 1: The Main Report." *Document of International Bank for Reconstruction and Development: International Development Association* (April 20, 1973). Accessed May 16, 2022. https://documents.worldbank.org/en/publication/documents-reports/documentdetail/244051468296153407/the-main-report.

World Bank. "Current Economic Position and Prospects of the Philippines. Vol. 2: Special Annexes." *Document of International Bank for Reconstruction and Development: International Development Association* (July 25, 1973). Accessed May 16, 2022. https://documents.worldbank.org/en/publication/documents-reports/documentdetail/771181468093853743/special-annexes.

World Bank. "Current Economic Position and Prospects of the Philippines. Vol. 3: Statistical Appendix." *Document of International Bank for Reconstruction and Development: International Development Association* (April 20, 1973). Accessed May 16, 2022. https://documents.worldbank.org/en/publication/documents-reports/documentdetail/424591468108545580/statistical-appendix.

World Bank. *Philippines: Manila Urban Development Project: Report on the Status of the Tondo Foreshore Development Project* (December 12, 1977). Accessed May 17, 2022. https://documents1.worldbank.org/curated/en/981461468296164467/pdf/855110BR0SecM10C0disclosed020270140.pdf.

World Bank. *Report and Recommendation of the President of the International Bank for Reconstruction and Development to the Executive Directors on Proposed Loans to the Republic of the Philippines for a Manila Urban Development Project* (May 17, 1976). Accessed May 18, 2022. https://documents1.worldbank.org/curated/en/730331468092654721/pdf/multiopage.pdf.

SECONDARY SOURCES

Agamben, Giorgio. *State of Exception*. Translated by Kevin Attell. Chicago: University of Chicago Press, 2005.

Aguilar, Delia D. "Memory Work." *Kritika Kultura* 26 (2016): 479–81.

Apostol, Gina. "Speaking in Fascism's Tongues." *New York Times*, May 19, 2017.

Aquino, Belinda. "Filipino Women and Political Engagement." *Review of Women's Studies* 4, no. 1 (1993–94): 32–53.

Arendt, Hannah. *The Origins of Totalitarianism*. San Diego: Harcourt Brace, 1976.

Babiera, Lester. "FDCP Gets Ownership Rights of Lino Brocka's 'Insiang.'" *Inquirer*, January 12, 2015. http://lifestyle.inquirer.net/181855/fdcp-gets-ownership-rights-of-lino-brockas-insiang/.

Baik, Crystal Mun-hye. *Reencounters: On the Korean War and Diasporic Memory Critique*. Philadelphia: Temple University Press, 2019.

Balance, Christine Bacareza. "Dahil Sa Iyo: The Performative Power of Imelda's Song." *Women and Performance: A Journal of Feminist Theory* 20, no. 2 (2010): 119–40.

Balance, Christine Bacareza. "Just in Time for FAHM: Afterlives of Martial Law." *Visual Communications*, October 10, 2017. Accessed May 16, 2022. https://vcmedia.org/latest-news/afterlives-of-martial-law.

Balance, Christine Bacareza. *Tropical Renditions: Making Musical Scenes in Filipino America*. Durham, NC: Duke University Press, 2016.

Balce, Nerissa. *Body Parts of Empire: Visual Abjection, Filipino Images, and the American Archive*. Ann Arbor: University of Michigan Press, 2016.

Balce, Nerissa. "Filipino Bodies, Lynching and the Language of Empire." In *Positively No Filipinos Allowed: Building Communities and Discourse*, edited by Antonio Tiongson Jr., Edgardo V. Gutierrez, and Ricardo V. Gutierrez, 43–60. Philadelphia: Temple University Press, 2006.

Baldoz, Rick. *The Third Asiatic Invasion: Empire and Migration in Filipino America, 1898–1946*. New York: New York University Press, 2011.

Baluyut, Pearlie Rose S. *Institutions and Icons of Patronage: Arts and Culture in the Philippines during the Marcos Years, 1965–1986*. Manila: University of Santo Tomas Publishing House, 2012.

Bantayog ng mga Bayani. "About: Preserving the Memory." Accessed December 15, 2021. https://bantayog.org.

Bareng, Eriza Ong. "Steeling the Butterfly: The Imperial Constructions of Imelda Marcos, 1966–1990." PhD diss., University of Hawai'i, Manoa, 2018.

Basch, Linda, Nina Glick Schiller, and Cristina Szanton Blanc, eds. *Nations Unbound: Transnational Projects, Postcolonial Predicaments, and Deterritorialized Nation-States*. New York: Routledge, 2003.

Beller, Jonathan. *Acquiring Eyes: Philippine Visuality, Nationalist Struggle, and the World-Media System*. Quezon City: Ateneo de Manila University Press, 2006.

Beltran, Jose V. "The Concept of Urban Renewal in Urban Manila: An Analysis." Master's thesis, University of Tasmania, 1982.

Benedicto, Bobby. "The Queer Afterlife of the Postcolonial City: (Trans)gender Performance and the War of Beautification." *Antipode* 47, no. 3 (2015): 580–97.

Benjamin, Walter. *The Arcades Project*. Cambridge, MA: Belknap Press of Harvard University Press, 2002.

Benjamin, Walter. "Critique of Violence." In *Reflections: Essays, Aphorisms, Autobiographical Writings*, translated by Edmund Jephcott, 277–300. New York: Schocken, 1978.

Benjamin, Walter. "The Storyteller: Reflections on the Works of Nikolai Leskov." In *Illuminations: Essays and Reflections*, edited by Hannah Arendt, translated by Harry Zohn, 26–55. Boston: Mariner, 2019.

Benjamin, Walter. "Theses on the Philosophy of History." In *Illuminations: Essays and Reflections*, edited by Hannah Arendt, translated by Harry Zohn, 253–64. New York: Schocken, 1968.

Bernad, Miguel A. "The First Year of the Philcag in Vietnam." *Philippine Studies* 16, no. 1 (1968): 131–54.

Binkiewicz, Donna M. *Federalizing the Muse: United States Arts Policy and the National Endowment for the Arts, 1965–1980*. Chapel Hill: University of North Carolina Press, 2004.

Blanco, John D. "Race as Praxis in the Philippines at the Turn of the Twentieth Century." *Southeast Asian Studies* 49, no. 3 (2011): 356–94.

Bonus, Rick. *Locating Filipino Americans*. Philadelphia: Temple University Press, 1991.

Brock, Lisa. "Nation and the Cold War: Reflections on the Circuitous Routes of African Diaspora Studies." *Radical History Review* 103 (2009): 7–15.

Brocka, Lino. *The Artist and His Times*. Edited by Mario Hernandez. Manila: Sentrong Pangkultura ng Pilipinas, 1993.

Brocka, Lino, dir. *Insiang*. Cinemanila, 1976.

Brown, Wendy. "'The Most We Can Hope For...': Human Rights and the Politics of Fatalism." *South Atlantic Quarterly* 103, nos. 2–3 (2004): 451–63.

Brown, Wendy. *States of Injury: Power and Freedom in Late Modernity*. Princeton, NJ: Princeton University Press, 1995.

Browne, Simone. *Dark Matters: On the Surveillance of Blackness*. Durham, NC: Duke University Press, 2015.

Buck-Morss, Susan. *Hegel, Haiti, and Universal History*. Pittsburgh: University of Pittsburgh Press, 2012.

Burns, Lucy Mae San Pablo. *Puro Arte: Filipinos on the Stages of Empire*. New York: New York University Press, 2012.

Butler, Judith. *Frames of War: When Is Life Grievable?* New York: Verso, 2009.

Camacho, Keith. *Cultures of Commemoration: The Politics of War, Memory, and History in the Mariana Islands*. Honolulu: University of Hawai'i Press, 2011.

Campomanes, Oscar. "Figures of the Unassimilable: American Empire, Filipino American Postcoloniality, and the U.S.-Philippine War of 1898–1910s." PhD diss., Brown University, 2011.

Campomanes, Oscar. "Filipinos in the United States and Their Literature of Exile." In *Reading the Literatures of Asian America*, edited by Shirley Lim and Amy Ling, 49–78. Philadelphia: Temple University Press, 1992.

Capino, Jose B. *Martial Law Melodrama: Lino Brocka's Cinema Politics*. Oakland: University of California Press, 2020.

Cartwright, Lisa, and Marita Sturken. *Practices of Looking: An Introduction to Visual Culture*. Oxford: Oxford University Press, 2009.

Casper, Leonard. "Review: *The Empire of Memory*." *Philippine Studies* 44, no. 2 (1996): 284–87.

Casumbal-Salazar, Melisa S. L. "The Indeterminacy of the Philippine Indigenous Subject: Indigeneity, Temporality, and Cultural Governance." *Amerasia* 41, no. 1 (2015): 74–94.

Celoza, Albert F. *Ferdinand Marcos and the Philippines: The Political Economy of Authoritarianism*. Westport, CT: Praeger, 1997.

Chakrabarty, Dipesh. *Provincializing Europe: Postcolonial Thought and Historical Difference*. Princeton, NJ: Princeton University Press, 2008.

Chen Kuan-Hsing. *Asia as Method: Toward Deimperialization*. Durham, NC: Duke University Press, 2010.

Chew, Ron. *Remembering Silme Domingo and Gene Viernes: The Legacy of Filipino American Labor Activism*. Seattle: Alaskero Foundation, University of Washington Press, 2012.

Ching, Leo. *Becoming "Japanese": Colonial Taiwan and the Politics of Identity Formation*. Berkeley: University of California Press, 2001.

Cho, Grace. *Haunting the Korean Diaspora: Shame, Secrecy, and the Forgotten War*. Minneapolis: University of Minnesota Press, 2008.

Choy, Catherine Ceniza. *Empire of Care: Nursing and Migration in Filipino History.* Durham, NC: Duke University Press, 2003.

Choy, Catherine Ceniza. "From Exchange Visitor to Permanent Resident: Reconsidering Filipino Nurse Migration as a Post-1965 Phenomenon." In *Re/collecting Early Asian American: Essays in Cultural History*, edited by Josephine D. Lee, Yuko Matsukawa, and Imogene L. Lim, 159–73. Philadelphia: Temple University Press, 2002.

Choy, Catherine Ceniza, and Judy Tsu-Chun Wu, eds. *Gendering the Trans-Pacific World.* Leiden: Brill, 2017.

Chuh, Kandice. *Imagine Otherwise: On Asian Americanist Critique.* Durham, NC: Duke University Press, 2003.

Churchill, Thomas. *Triumph over Marcos: A Story Based on the Lives of Gene Viernes and Silme Domingo, Filipino American Cannery Union Organizers, Their Assassination, and the Trial That Followed.* Greensboro, NC: Open Hand, 1995.

Cimatu, Frank, and Rolando B. Tolentino, eds. *Mondo Marcos: Writings on Martial Law and the Marcos Babies.* Pasig City: Anvil, 2010.

Claudio, Lisandro E. "Memories of the Anti-Marcos Movement: The Left and the Mnemonic Dynamics of the Post-authoritarian Philippines." *South East Asia Research* 18, no. 1 (2010): 33–66.

Clifford, James. "Tainted Cultures." In *Routes: Travel and Translation in the Late Twentieth Century*, 17–46. Cambridge, MA: Harvard University Press, 1997.

Clutario, Genevieve. "Pageant Politics: Tensions of Power, Empire, and Nationalism in Manila Carnival Queen Contests." In *Gendering the Trans-Pacific World*, edited by Catherine Ceniza Choy and Judy Tsu-Chun Wu, 257–83. Leiden: Brill, 2017.

Constantino, Renato, and Letizia Constantino. *The Miseducation of the Filipino.* Quezon City: Foundation for Nationalist Studies, 1987.

Cordova, Fred. *Filipinos: Forgotten Asian Americans: A Pictorial Essay/1763–circa 1963.* Dubuque, Iowa: Kendall/Hunt, 1983. https://archive.org/details/filipinosforgottoocord/mode/2up.

Cresswell, Tim. *On the Move: Mobility in the Western World.* London: Routledge, 2006.

Cruz, Denise. "Notes on Trans-Pacific Archives." In *Gendering the Trans-Pacific World*, edited by Catherine Ceniza Choy and Judy Tsu-Chun Wu, 10–19. Leiden: Brill, 2017.

Cruz, Denise. *Transpacific Femininities: The Making of the Modern Filipina.* Durham, NC: Duke University Press, 2012.

Cruz, Geoffrey Rhoel. "The Cultural Heritage–Oriented Approach to Economic Development in the Philippines: A Comparative Study of Vigan, Ilocos Sur and Escolta, Manila." Paper presented at the 10th DLSU Arts Congress, De La Salle University, Manila, Philippines, February 16, 2017.

Curaming, Rommel. "Official History Reconsidered: The Tadhana Project." In *The Palgrave Handbook of State-Sponsored History after 1945*, edited by Berber Bevernage and Nico Wouters, 237–53. London: Palgrave Macmillan, 2018.

David, Joel. *Manila by Night*. Vancouver: Arsenal Pulp, 2018.

Davis, Angela. "Interview with Lisa Lowe: Angela Davis: Reflections on Race, Class, and Gender in the USA." In *The Politics of Culture in the Shadow of Capital*, edited by Lisa Lowe and David Lloyd, 303–23. Durham, NC: Duke University Press, 1997.

Day, Iyko. *Alien Capital: Asian Racialization and the Logic of Settler Colonial Capitalism*. Durham, NC: Duke University Press, 2016.

De Genova, Nicholas. "The Legal Production of Mexican/Migrant 'Illegality.'" *Latino Studies* 2 (2004): 160–85.

De La Cruz, Dierdre. *Mother Figured: Marian Apparitions and the Making of a Filipino Universal*. Chicago: University of Chicago Press, 2015.

Diaz, Josen Masangkay. "The Subject Case: The Filipino Body and the Politics of Making Filipino America." PhD diss., University of California, San Diego, 2014.

Diaz, Josen Masangkay. "'We Were War Surplus, Too': Nick Joaquin and the Impossibilities of Filipino Historical Becoming." *Kritika Kultura* 24 (2015): 4–34.

Ding, Naifei. "Prostitutes, Parasites, and the House of State Feminism." *Inter-Asia Cultural Studies* 1, no. 2 (2000): 305–18.

Domingo, Ligaya. "Building a Movement: Filipino American Union and Community Organizing in Seattle in the 1970s." PhD diss., University of California, Berkeley, 2010.

Dudziak, Mary. *Cold War Civil Rights: Race and the Image of American Democracy*. Princeton, NJ: Princeton University Press, 2011.

Edkins, Jenny. *Trauma and the Memory of Politics*. Cambridge: Cambridge University Press, 2003.

Edwards, Brian. *The Modern Airport Terminal*. London: Taylor and Francis, 2005.

Ellison, Katherine. *Imelda: Steel Butterfly of the Philippines*. Lincoln, NE: iUniverse, 1988.

Enloe, Cynthia. *Maneuvers: The International Politics of Militarizing Women's Lives*. Berkeley: University of California Press, 2000.

Espiritu, Augusto. "Journeys of Discovery and Difference: Transnational Politics and the Union of Democratic Filipinos." In *The Transnational Politics of Asian Americans*, edited by Christian Collet and Pei-te Lien, 38–55. Philadelphia: Temple University Press, 2009.

Espiritu, Augusto. "'To Carry Water on Both Shoulders': Carlos P. Romulo, American Empire, and the Meanings of Bandung." *Radical History Review*, no. 95 (2006): 173–90.

Espiritu, Yến Lê. *Body Counts: The Vietnam War and Militarized Refugees*. Berkeley: University of California Press, 2014.

Espiritu, Yến Lê. *Home Bound: Filipino American Lives across Cultures, Communities, and Countries*. Berkeley: University of California Press, 2003.

Fanon, Frantz. *The Wretched of the Earth*. New York: Grove Weidenfeld, 1963.

Ferreira da Silva, Denise. *Toward a Global Idea of Race*. Minneapolis: University of Minnesota Press, 2007.

Flores, Patrick D. "'Total Community Response': Performing the Avant-Garde as a Democratic Gesture in Manila." *Southeast of Now* 1, no. 1 (2017): 13–38.

Foucault, Michel. *The Birth of Biopolitics: Lectures at the Collège de France, 1978–1979*. Translated by Graham Burchell. New York: Palgrave Macmillan, 2008.

Foucault, Michel. *Discipline and Punish: The Birth of the Prison*. Translated by Alan Sheridan. New York: Vintage, 1995.

Foucault, Michel. *Ethics: Subjectivity and Truth*. Edited by Paul Rabinow. New York: New Press, 1998.

Foucault, Michel. "Nietzsche, Genealogy, History." In *The Foucault Reader*, edited by Paul Rabinow, 76–100. New York: Pantheon, 1984.

Foucault, Michel. *"Society Must Be Defended": Lectures at the Collège de France, 1975–1976*. Translated by David Macey. New York: Picador, 1997.

Foulkes, Julia L. "The Other West Side Story: Urbanization and the Arts Meet at Lincoln Center." *Amerikastudien/American Studies* 52, no. 2 (2007): 227–47.

Franco, Jean. *Cruel Modernity*. Durham, NC: Duke University Press, 2013.

Fujitani, Takashi, Geoffrey M. White, and Lisa Yoneyama, eds. *Perilous Memories: The Asia-Pacific War(s)*. Durham, NC: Duke University Press, 2001.

Fujita-Rony, Dorothy. "Coalitions, Race, and Labor: Rereading Philip Vera Cruz." *Journal of Asian American Studies* 3, no. 2 (2000): 139–62.

Fujita-Rony, Dorothy. "Illuminating Militarized Rupture: Four Asian American Community-Based Archives." *Journal of Asian American Studies* 23, no. 1 (2020): 1–27.

Gaerlan, Barbara S. "In the Court of the Sultan: Orientalism, Nationalism, and Modernity in Philippine and Filipino American Dance." *Journal of Asian American Studies* 2, no. 3 (1999): 251–87.

Gamalinda, Eric. *The Empire of Memory*. Pasig City: Anvil, 1992.

Garcia, Carlos P. "One Hundred Years of the Ateneo de Manila." *Philippine Studies* 7, no. 3 (1959): 263–70.

Ghodsee, Kristin. "Revisiting the United Nations Decade for Women." *Women's Studies International Forum* 33, no. 1 (2010): 3–12.

Gilroy, Paul. *The Black Atlantic*. Cambridge, MA: Harvard University Press, 1995.

Glück, Louise. "Disruption, Hesitation, Silence." *American Poetry Review* 22, no. 5 (1993): 30–32.

Goldstein, Alyosha. *Poverty in Common: The Politics of Community Action during the American Century*. Durham, NC: Duke University Press, 2012.

Gonzaga, Elmo. "Consuming Capitalist Modernity in the Media Cultures of 1930s and 1960s Manila's Commercial Streets." *Journal of Asian Studies* 78, no. 1 (2019): 75–93.

Gonzalez, N. V. M., and Oscar Campomanes. "Filipino American Literature." In *An Interethnic Companion to Asian American Literature*, edited by King-Kok Cheung, 62–124. Cambridge: Cambridge University Press, 1997.

Gonzalez, Vernadette V. "Military Bases, 'Royalty Trips,' and Imperial Modernities: Gendered and Racialized Labor in the Postcolonial Philippines." *Frontiers: A Journal of Women's Studies* 28, no. 3 (2007): 28–59.

Gonzalez, Vernadette Vicuña. *Securing Paradise: Tourism and Militarism in Hawai'i and the Philippines*. Durham, NC: Duke University Press, 2013.

Gonzalves, Theo. *The Day the Dancers Stayed: Performing in the Filipino/American Diaspora*. Philadelphia: Temple University Press, 2009.

Grewal, Inderpal. *Transnational America: Feminisms, Diasporas, Neoliberalisms*. Durham, NC: Duke University Press, 2005.

Guevarra, Anna. *Marketing Dreams, Manufacturing Heroes: The Transnational Labor Brokering of Filipino Workers*. New Brunswick, NJ: Rutgers University Press, 2010.

Gutierrez, Jose, III. "The Realist Cinema of Lino Brocka." *Plaridel* 14, no. 2 (2017): 169–78.

Habal, Estella. "Radical Violence in the Fields: Anti-Filipino Riot in Watsonville." Accessed December 3, 2020. https://history.sfsu.edu/sites/default/files/EPF/1991_Estella%20Habal.pdf.

Hagedorn, Jessica. *Dogeaters*. New York: Penguin, 1990.

Hall, Stuart. "Black Diaspora Artists in Britain: Three 'Moments' in Post-war History." *History Workshop Journal* 61 (2006): 1–24.

Hall, Stuart. "Cultural Identity and Diaspora." In *Identity: Community, Culture, and Difference*, edited by Jonathan Rutherford, 222–37. London: Lawrence and Wishart, 1990.

Hall, Stuart. "Culture, Community, Nation." *Cultural Studies* 7, no. 3 (1993): 349–63.

Hall, Stuart. "Notes on Deconstructing the Popular." In *Cultural Theory and Popular Culture: A Reader*, edited by John Storey, 508–18. London: Pearson, 2007.

Hamilton-Patterson, James. *America's Boy: A Century of United States Colonialism in the Philippines*. New York: Henry Holt and Company, 1999.

Hardt, Michael. "Affective Labor." *boundary 2*, 26, no. 2 (1999): 89–100.

Hartman, Saidiya. "The Time of Slavery." *South Atlantic Quarterly* 101, no. 4 (2002): 757–77.

Hau, Caroline. "The Filipino Novel in English." In *Philippine English: Linguistic and Literary Perspectives*, edited by Ma Lourdes S. Bautista and Kingsley Bolton, 317–36. Hong Kong: Hong Kong University Press, 2008.

Hernandez, Kelly Lytle. *Migra! A History of the U.S. Border Patrol*. Berkeley: University of California Press, 2010.

Hines, Thomas S. "The Imperial Façade: Daniel H. Burnham and American Architectural Planning in the Philippines." *Pacific Historical Review* 41, no. 1 (1972): 33–53.

Honculada, Jurgette. "Case Study: ZOTO and the Twice-Told Story of Philippine Community Organizing." *Kasarinlan* 1, no. 2 (1985): 13–24.

Honculada, Jurgette, and Rosalinda Pineda Ofreneo. "The National Commission on the Role of Filipino Women, the Women's Movement and Gender Mainstreaming in the Philippines." In *Mainstreaming Gender, Democratizing the State? Institutional Mechanisms for the Advancement of Women*, edited by Shirin M. Rai, 131–145. Manchester: Manchester University Press, 2003.

Hong, Grace Kyungwon. *The Ruptures of American Capital: Women of Color Feminism and the Culture of Immigrant Labor*. Minneapolis: University of Minnesota Press, 2006.

Hong, Grace Kyungwon, and Roderick A. Ferguson, eds. *Strange Affinities: The Gender and Sexual Politics of Comparative Racialization*. Durham, NC: Duke University Press, 2011.

Hua, Julietta. *Trafficking Women's Human Rights*. Minneapolis: University of Minnesota Press, 2011.

Ileto, Reynaldo. *Pasyon and Revolution*. Quezon City: Ateneo de Manila University Press, 1997.

Ileto, Reynaldo. "Philippine Wars and the Politics of Memory." *positions: asia critique* 13, no. 1 (2005): 215–35.

Isaac, Allan Punzalan. *American Tropics: Articulating Filipino America*. Minneapolis: University of Minnesota Press, 2006.

Isaac, Allan Punzalan. "Offshore Identities: Ruptures in the 300-Second Average Handling Time." In *Archipelagic American Studies*, edited by Brian Russell Roberts and Michelle Ann Stephens, 411–26. Durham, NC: Duke University Press, 2017.

Joaquin, Nick. *Culture and History: Occasional Notes on the Process of Philippine Becoming*. Metro Manila: Solar Pub Corp., 1988.

Kang, Laura. *Compositional Subjects: Enfiguring Asian American Women*. Durham, NC: Duke University Press, 2002.

Kaplan, Amy. "Manifest Domesticity." *American Literature* 80, no. 3 (1998): 581–606.

Karaos, Anna Marie A. "Manila's Squatter Movement: A Struggle for Place and Identity." *Philippine Sociological Review* 41, no. 1 (1993): 71–91.

Kennedy, Edward. "Refugee Act of 1980." *International Migration Review* 15, nos. 1–2 (1981): 141–56.

Khiun, Liew Kai. *Liberalizing, Feminizing and Popularizing Health Communications in Asia*. London: Routledge, 2010.

Kim, Jodi. *Ends of Empire: Asian American Critique and the Cold War*. Minneapolis: University of Minnesota Press, 2010.

Klein, Christina. *Cold War Orientalism: Asia in the Middlebrow Imagination, 1945–1961*. Berkeley: University of California Press, 2003.

Kotef, Hagar. *Movement and the Ordering of Freedom: On Liberal Governances of Mobility*. Durham, NC: Duke University Press, 2015.

Kotlowski, Dean. "Breaching the Paper Walls: Paul V. McNutt and Jewish Refugees to the Philippines, 1938–39." *Diplomatic History* 33, no. 5 (2009): 865–96.

Kramer, Paul. *Blood of Government: Race, Empire, the United States, and the Philippines*. Chapel Hill: University of North Carolina Press, 2006.

Lee, Jin-kyung. *Service Economies: Militarism, Sex Work, and Migrant Labor in South Korea*. Minneapolis: University of Minnesota Press, 2010.

Lee, Jin-kyung. "Surrogate Military, Subimperialism, and Masculinity: South Korea in the Vietnam War, 1965–73." *positions: asia critique* 17, no. 3 (2009): 655–82.

Lee, Lynn. "The Contemporary Women's Movement in the Philippines." *Australian Feminist Studies* 3, nos. 7–8 (1988): 217–23.

Lico, Gerard. *Edifice Complex: Power, Myth, and Marcos State Architecture*. Quezon City: Ateneo de Manila University Press, 2003.

Lim, Benito. "The Political Economy of Philippines-China Relations." PASCN Discussion Paper No. 99-16. Philippine APEC Study Center Network. Makati City: Philippine Institute for Development Studies, September 1999.

Lim, Bliss Cua. *Translating Time: Cinema, the Fantastic, and Temporal Critique*. Durham, NC: Duke University Press, 2009.

Lin, Chien-ting. "Resignifying 'Asia' in the Transnational Turn of Asian/American Studies." *Review of International American Studies* 9, no. 2 (2016): 27–44.

Lopez, Maria Elena, and Ana Maria R. Nemenzo. "The Formulation of Philippine Population Policy." *Philippine Studies: Historical and Ethnographic Viewpoints* 24, no. 4 (1976): 417–38.

Lowe, Lisa. "Globalization." In *Keywords for American Cultural Studies*, 120–23. New York: New York University Press, 2007.

Lowe, Lisa. *Immigrant Acts: On Asian American Cultural Politics*. Durham, NC: Duke University Press, 1996.

Lowe, Lisa. "The International within the National: American Studies and Asian American Critique." *Cultural Critique* 40 (1998): 29–47.

Lowe, Lisa. *The Intimacies of Four Continents*. Durham, NC: Duke University Press, 2015.

Lowe, Lisa, and David Lloyd, eds. *The Politics of Culture in the Shadow of Capital*. Durham, NC: Duke University Press, 1997.

Luibhéid, Eithne. "The 1965 Immigration and Nationality Act: An 'End' to Exclusion?" *positions: east asia critique* 5, no. 2 (1997): 501–22.

Mabalon, Dawn. *Little Manila Is in the Heart: The Making of the Filipina/o American Community in Stockton, California*. Durham, NC: Duke University Press, 2013.

Maguigad, Virgilio. "The Airport as a Cultural and Functional Showcase: Case of the Ninoy Aquino International Airport." Paper presented at the Asian Media Cooperation and Cultural Exchange Conference, Quezon City, Philippines, October 2010.

Man, Simeon. *Soldiering through Empire: Race and the Making of the Decolonizing Pacific*. Oakland: University of California Press, 2018.

Manahan, Tats. "The Enduring Nightmare of the Manila Film Center." *Rogue*, November 2015. http://rogue.ph/enduring-nightmare-manila-film-center/.

Manalansan, Martin F., IV. "Migrancy, Modernity, Mobility: Quotidian Struggles and Queer Diasporic Intimacy." In *Queer Migrations: Sexuality, U.S. Citizenship, and Border Crossings*, edited by Eithne Lubhéid and Lionel Cantú Jr., 146–60. Minneapolis: University of Minnesota Press, 2005.

Manalansan, Martin, F., IV. "Servicing the World: Flexible Filipinos and the Unsecured Life." In *Political Emotions*, edited by Janet Staiger, Ann Cvetkovich, and Ann Reynolds, 215–28. London: Routledge, 2010.

Manalansan, Martin F., IV, and Augusto F. Espiritu, eds. *Filipino Studies: Palimpsests of Nation and Diaspora.* New York: New York University Press, 2016.

Mananquil, Millet M. "'There's a Little Imelda in All of Us.'" *Philstar*, September 6, 2009. https://www.philstar.com/lifestyle/sunday-life/2009/09/06/502262/theres-little-imelda-all-us.

Manapat, Ricardo. *Some Are Smarter Than Others: The History of Marcos' Crony Capitalism.* New York: Alatheia, 1991.

Mankekar, Purnima, and Akhil Gupta. "Intimate Encounters: Affective Labor in Call Centers." *positions: asia critique* 24, no. 1 (2016): 17–43.

Manuel, Maria Teresa, ed. *Tao: Humanism at Work in Filipino Society.* Manila: National Media Production Center, 1979.

Mariano, L. Joyce Zapanta. *Giving Back: Filipino America and the Politics of Diaspora Giving.* Philadelphia: Temple University Press, 2021.

Martin, Jocelyn. "R.I.P., Rest in Pieces: Mnemonic Transnationality, Travel, and Translation of the Marcos Burial in the Heroes' Cemetery." *International Journal of Politics, Culture, and Society* 32 (2019): 423–37.

McClintock, Anne. *Imperial Leather: Race, Gender, and Sexuality in the Colonial Contest.* New York: Routledge, 1995.

McKenna, Rebecca Tinio. *American Imperial Pastoral: The Architecture of US Colonialism in the Philippines.* Chicago: University of Chicago Press, 2017.

Melamed, Jodi. *Represent and Destroy: Rationalizing Violence in the New Racial Capitalism.* Minneapolis: University of Minnesota Press, 2011.

Melamed, Jodi. "The Spirit of Neoliberalism: From Racial Liberalism to Neoliberal Multiculturalism." *Social Text* 24, no. 4 (2006): 1–24.

Mendoza, Meynardo P. "Binding the Islands: Air Transport and State Capacity Building in the Philippines, 1946 to 1961." *Philippine Studies: Historical and Ethnographic Viewpoints* 61, no. 1 (2013): 77–104.

Mendoza, Victor Román. *Metroimperial Intimacies: Fantasy, Racial-Sexual Governance, and the Philippines in U.S. Imperialism, 1899–1913.* Durham, NC: Duke University Press, 2015.

Mijares, Primitivo. *The Conjugal Dictatorship of Ferdinand and Imelda Marcos.* San Francisco: Union Square, 1987.

Morella, Cecilia. "Mortician to Marcos Reveals Trade Secrets." *GMA Network*, November 24, 2016. http://www.gmanetwork.com/news/lifestyle/content/590061/mortician-to-marcos-reveals-trade-secrets/story/.

Muñoz, José Esteban. *Disidentifications: Queers of Color and the Performance of Politics.* Minneapolis: University of Minnesota Press, 1999.

Nadal, Paul. "A Literary Remittance: Juan C. Laya's *His Native Soil* and the Rise of Realism in the Filipino Novel in English." *American Literature* 89, no. 3 (2017): 591–626.

Naficy, Hamid, and Lino Brocka. "The Americanization and Indigenization of Lino Brocka through Cinema." *Framework: The Journal of Cinema and Media* 38/39 (1992): 133–55.

Nguyen, Mimi Thi. "The Biopower of Beauty: Humanitarian Imperialisms and Global Feminisms in an Age of Terror." *Signs* 36, no. 2 (2011): 359–83.

Nguyen, Mimi Thi. *The Gift of Freedom*. Durham, NC: Duke University Press, 2012.

Niu, Greta Ai-Yu. "Wives, Widows, and Workers: Corazon Aquino, Imelda Marcos, and the Filipina 'Other.'" *NWSA Journal* 11, no. 2 (1999): 88–102.

Office of Research and Publications (Ateneo de Manila University). *Memory, Truth-Telling, and the Pursuit of Justice: A Conference on the Legacies of the Marcos Dictatorship (Conference Report)*. Quezon City: Ortigas Peace Institute, 2001.

Okamura, Jonathan. *Imagining the Filipino Diaspora: Transnational Relations, Identities, and Communities*. London: Routledge, 1998.

Olcott, Jocelyn. "Cold War Conflicts and Cheap Cabaret: Sexual Politics at the 1975 United Nations International Women's Year Conference." *Gender and History* 22, no. 3 (2010): 733–54.

Omi, Michael, and Howard Winant. *Racial Formation in the United States: From the 1960s to the 1990s*. New York: Routledge, 1994.

Ong, Aihwa. *Neoliberalism as Exception: Mutations in Citizenship and Sovereignty*. Durham, NC: Duke University Press, 2006.

Orendain, Simone. "Philippine Nuns, Priests Say Role in Revolution Affected Their Faith." *Global Sisters Report*. Accessed December 1, 2018. http://www.globalsistersreport.org/news/spirituality/philippine-nuns-priests-say-role-revolution-affected-their-faith-37656.

Padios, Jan M. *A Nation on the Line: Call Centers as Postcolonial Predicaments in the Philippines*. Durham, NC: Duke University Press, 2018.

Pante, Michael. "Politics of Flood Control and the Making of Metro Manila." *Philippine Studies: Historical and Ethnographic Viewpoints* 64, nos. 3–4 (2016): 555–92.

Parreñas, Rhacel Salazar. "Migrant Filipina Domestic Workers." *Gender and Society* 14, no. 4 (2000): 560–80.

Parreñas, Rhacel Salazar. *Servants of Globalization: Migration and Domestic Work*. Redwood City: Stanford University Press, 2015.

Pedrosa, Carmen Navarro. *Imelda Marcos: The Rise and Fall of One of the World's Most Powerful Women*. New York: St. Martin's Press, 1987.

Perez, Jason Magabo. *This Is for the Mostless*. Cincinnati: WordTech Editions, 2017.

Pido, Eric. *Migrant Returns: Manila, Development, and Transnational Connectivity*. Durham, NC: Duke University Press, 2017.

PhilRights. "From 'Squatters' into 'Informal Settlers.'" PhilRights. Accessed December 6, 2018. http://philrights.org/from-squatters-into-informal-settlers/.

Poblete, JoAnna. *Islanders in the Empire: Filipino and Puerto Rican Laborers in Hawai'i*. Urbana: University of Illinois Press, 2014.

Ponce, Martin Joseph. *Beyond the Nation: Diasporic Filipino Literature and Queer Reading*. New York: New York University Press, 2012.

Prevots, Naima. *Dance for Export: Cultural Diplomacy and the Cold War*. Middletown, CT: Wesleyan University Press, 1999.

Price, David H. *Cold War Anthropology: The CIA, the Pentagon, and the Growth of Dual Use Anthropology*. Durham, NC: Duke University Press, 2016.

Quijano de Manila. *Reportage on the Marcoses, 1964–1970*. Manila: National Book Store, 1979.

Rafael, Vicente. "The Afterlife of Empire: Sovereignty and Revolution in the Philippines." *Cuaderno Internacional de Estudios Humanísticos y Literatura* 19 (2013): 99–109.

Rafael, Vicente. *Motherless Tongues: The Insurgency of Language amid Wars of Translation*. Durham, NC: Duke University Press, 2016.

Rafael, Vicente. "Patronage and Pornography." *Comparative Studies in Society and History* 32, no. 2 (1990): 282–304.

Rafael, Vicente. *The Promise of the Foreign: Nationalism and the Technics of Translation in the Spanish Philippines*. Durham, NC: Duke University Press, 2005.

Rafael, Vicente. *White Love and Other Events in Filipino History*. Durham, NC: Duke University Press, 2000.

Rafael, Vicente. "'Your Grief Is Our Gossip': Overseas Filipinos and Other Spectral Presences." *Public Culture* 9 (1997): 267–91.

Ranada, Pia. "Duterte on Marcos Burial: Let History Judge, I Followed Law." *Rappler*, November 18, 2016. https://www.rappler.com/nation/152854-duterte-marcos-burial-history-judge.

Recto, Claro. "Our Mendicant Foreign Policy." In *Vintage Recto: Memorable Speeches and Writings of Claro M. Recto*, edited by Renato Constantino, 63–83. Quezon City: Foundation for Nationalist Studies, 1986.

Reddy, Chandan. "Globality and the Ends of the Nation-Form." *American Literary History* 22, no. 2 (2010): 459–68.

Reyes, Miguel Paolo P. "Producing Ferdinand E. Marcos, the Scholarly Author." *Philippine Studies: Historical and Ethnographic Viewpoints* 66, no. 2 (2018): 173–218.

Reyes, Victoria. *Global Borderlands: Fantasy, Violence, and Empire in Subic Bay, Philippines*. Redwood City, CA: Stanford University Press, 2019.

Richter, Linda. "The Political Uses of Tourism." *Journal of Developing Areas* 14, no. 2 (1980): 237–57.

Richter, Linda. *The Politics of Tourism in Asia*. Honolulu: University of Hawai'i Press, 1989.

Roberts, Brian Russell, and Michelle Ann Stephens, eds. *Archipelagic American Studies*. Durham, NC: Duke University Press, 2017.

Robinson, Cedric. *Black Marxism: The Making of the Black Radical Tradition*. Chapel Hill: University of North Carolina Press, 2000.

Robinson, Cedric. *Black Movements in America*. New York: Routledge, 1997.

Roces, Mina. "Women in Philippine Politics and Society." In *Mixed Blessing: The Impact of American Colonial Experience on Politics and Society in the Philippines*, edited by Hazel M. McFerson, 159–90. Westport, CT: Greenwood, 2002.

Roces, Mina. *Women, Power, and Kinship Politics: Female Power in Post-war Philippines*. Westport, CT: Praeger, 1998.

Rodrigo, Raul. "How Journalists Covered the 1986 EDSA Revolt." In *The Power and the Glory: The Story of the Manila Chronicle, 1945–1988*, 308–12. Manila: Lopez Memorial Museum and Library, 2008. Accessed December 5, 2018. http://lopezseum.blogspot.com/2013/02/how-journalists-covered-1986-edsa.html.

Rodriguez, Dylan. *Suspended Apocalypse: White Supremacy, Genocide, and the Filipino Condition*. Minneapolis: University of Minnesota Press, 2010.

Rodriguez, Robyn, ed. *Filipino American Transnational Activism: Diasporic Politics among the Second Generation*. Leiden: Brill, 2019.

Rodriguez, Robyn. *Migrants for Export: How the Philippine State Brokers Labor to the World*. Minneapolis: University of Minnesota Press, 2010.

Rodriguez, Robyn. "Toward a Critical Filipino Studies Approach to Philippine Migration." In *Filipino Studies: Palimpsests of Nation and Diaspora*, edited by Martin F. Manalansan IV and Augusto F. Espiritu, 33–55. New York: New York University Press, 2016.

Rosca, Ninotchka. *State of War*. New York: Norton, 1988.

Sakai, Naoki, and Hyon Joo Yoo, eds. *The Trans-Pacific Imagination: Rethinking Boundary, Culture and Society*. Hackensack, NJ: World Scientific Publishing, 2012.

Sales, Joy. "#NeverAgainToMartialLaw: Transnational Filipino American Activism in the Shadow of Marcos and Age of Duterte." *Amerasia Journal* 45, no. 3 (2019): 299–315.

San Juan, E., Jr. "Philip Vera Cruz: In Search of Defamiliarizing Narrative." *St. John's University Humanities Review* 3, no. 1 (2005): 1–10.

Santiago, Arminda V. "The Struggle of the Oppressed: Lino Brocka and the New Cinema of the Philippines." PhD diss., University of North Texas, 1993.

Santiago, Lilia Quindoza. "Rebirthing Babaye: The Women's Movement in the Philippines." In *The Challenge of Local Feminisms: Women's Movements in Global Perspective*, edited by Amrita Basu, 110–28. Boulder, CO: Westview, 1995.

Saranillio, Dean. "Why Asian Settler Colonialism Matters: A Thought Piece on Critiques, Debates, and Indigenous Difference." *Settler Colonial Studies* 3, nos. 3–4 (2013): 280–94.

Schirmer, Daniel B., and Stephen Rosskam Shalom. *The Philippine Reader: A History of Colonialism, Neocolonialism, Dictatorship, and Resistance*. Boston: South End, 1987.

Schulze-Oechtering, Michael, and Wayne Jopanda. "Transpacific Freedom Dreams: The Radical Legacy of Silme Domingo and Gene Viernes." In *Filipino American Transnational Activism: Diasporic Politics among the Second Generation*, edited by Robyn Rodriguez, 227–47. Leiden: Brill, 2019.

See, Sarita. *The Decolonized Eye: Filipino American Art and Performance*. Minneapolis: University of Minnesota Press, 2009.

Shah, Nayan. *Stranger Intimacy: Contesting Race, Sexuality, and the Law in the North American West.* Berkeley: University of California Press, 2012.

Shankar, Lavina, and Rajini Srikanth. *A Part Yet Apart: South Asians in Asian America.* Philadelphia: Temple University Press, 1998.

Shimizu, Celine Parreñas. "Can the Subaltern Sing, and in a Power Ballad? Arnel Pineda and Ramona Diaz's *Don't Stop Believin': Everyman's Journey.*" *Concentric: Literary and Cultural Studies* 39, no. 1 (2013): 53–75.

Singh, Ajay. "Author Q&A: Eric Gamalinda." *South China Morning Post,* November 15, 2014.

Solomon, Amanda. "Managing the (Post)colonial: Race, Gender, and Sexuality in Literary Texts of the Philippine Commonwealth." PhD diss, University of California, San Diego, 2011.

Sonza, Jorshinelle T. "'Is There a Contrary in the Empire of Memory?': Eric Gamalinda's Transgression of the Narrative Act." *Journal of Commonwealth Literature* 32, no. 2 (1997): 85–97.

Spivak, Gayatri Chakravorty. "Righting Wrongs." *South Atlantic Quarterly* 103, nos. 2–3 (2004): 523–81.

Sturken, Marita. *Tangled Memories: The Vietnam War, the AIDS Epidemic, and the Politics of Remembering.* Berkeley: University of California Press, 1997.

Tadiar, Neferti. *Fantasy Production: Sexual Economies and Other Philippine Consequences for the New World Order.* Hong Kong: Hong Kong University Press, 2004.

Tadiar, Neferti. "Filipinas Living in a Time of War." In *Pinay Power: Peminist Critical Theory: Theorizing the Filipina/American Experience,* edited by Melinda de Jesus, 373–84. New York: Routledge, 2005.

Tadiar, Neferti. "Life-Times of Becoming Human." *Occasion: Interdisciplinary Studies in the Humanities* 3 (2012): 1–17.

Tadiar, Neferti. *Things Fall Away: Philippine Historical Experience and the Makings of Globalization.* Durham, NC: Duke University Press, 2009.

Tana, Maria Thaemar, and Yusuke Takagi. "Japan's Foreign Relations with the Philippines: A Case of Evolving Japan in Asia." In *Japan's Foreign Relations in Asia,* edited by James D. J. Brown and Jeff Kingston, 312–28. New York: Routledge, 2018.

Tiongson, Antonio, Jr., Edgardo V. Gutierrez, and Ricardo V. Gutierrez, eds. *Positively No Filipinos Allowed: Building Communities and Discourse.* Philadelphia: Temple University Press, 2006.

Tolentino, Rolando. *Contestable Nation-Space: Cinema, Cultural Politics, and Transnationalism in the Marcos-Brocka Philippines.* Quezon City: University of Philippines Press, 2014.

Tolentino, Rolando. "Post-national Family/Post-familial Nation: Family, Small Town, and Nation Talk in Marcos and Brocka." *Budhi: A Journal of Ideas and Culture* 3, no. 1 (2013): 119–38.

Tolentino, Rolando. "Vaginal Economy: Cinema and Sexuality in the Post-Marcos, Post-Brocka Philippines." *positions: asia critique* 19, no. 2 (2011): 229–56.

Torres, Cristina Evangelina. *The Americanization of Manila, 1898–1921*. Quezon City: University of the Philippines Press, 2010.

Tucker, Richard P. *Insatiable Appetite: The United States and the Ecological Degradation of the Tropical World*. Lanham, MD: Rowman and Littlefield, 2007.

Tupas, Ruanni, and Beatriz P. Lorente. "A 'New' Politics of Language in the Philippines: Bilingual Education and the New Challenge of the Mother Tongue." In *Language, Education and Nation-Building: Assimilation and Shift in Southeast Asia*, edited by Peter Sercombe and Ruanni Tupas, 165–80. London: Palgrave, 2014.

Vasuvedan, Alexander. "The Autonomous City: Towards a Critical Geography of Occupation." *Progress in Human Geography* 39, no. 3 (2014): 316–37.

Viola, Michael. "Toward a Filipino/a Critical (FilCrit) Pedagogy: A Study of United States Educational Exposure Programs to the Philippines." PhD diss., University of California, Los Angeles, 2012.

Wideman, Bernard. "Cesar Chavez Hails Philippines' Rule." *Washington Post*, July 19, 1977.

Williams, Randall. *The Divided World*. Minneapolis: University of Minnesota Press, 2010.

Williams, Raymond. "Culture Is Ordinary." In *Resources of Hope: Culture, Democracy, and Socialism*, edited by Robin Gable, 3–18. London: Verso, 1989.

Williams, Raymond. *Marxism and Literature*. Oxford: Oxford University Press, 2009.

Wynter, Sylvia. "Unsettling the Coloniality of Being/Power/Truth/Freedom: Towards the Human, after Man, Its Overrepresentation—an Argument." *New Centennial Review* 3, no. 3 (2003): 257–337.

Yoneyama, Lisa. *Cold War Ruins: Transpacific Critique of American Justice and Japanese War Crimes*. Durham, NC: Duke University Press, 2016.

Yoneyama, Lisa. "For Transformative Knowledge and the Postnationalist Public Spheres: The Smithsonian *Enola Gay* Controversy." In *Perilous Memories: The Asia-Pacific War(s)*, edited by Takashi Fujitani, Geoffrey M. White, and Lisa Yoneyama, 323–77. Durham, NC: Duke University Press, 2001.

Yoshimi, Shunya, and David Buist. "'America' as Desire and Violence: Americanization in Postwar Japan and Asia during the Cold War." *Inter-Asia Cultural Studies* 4, no. 3 (2003): 433–50.

INDEX

Page numbers in italics refer to figures.

abjection, 5, 15, 39, 45, 53, 59, 75, 87, 106, 133, 151
African Americans, 31, 87, 161n3. *See also* Black Americans
Agamben, Giorgio, 17
Aguilar, Delia, 169n23
Aldaba-Lim, Estafania, 98
Algiers Charter (1967), 37
Ali, Muhammad, 61
alien figure (immigration), 5, 10, 65, 170n31
Angeles City, 11, 35
anti-Blackness, 18, 31
anticolonialism, 14, 37, 45, 182n37
anticommunism, 11, 18–19, 28, 33, 101
anti-history, 24, 29, 47, 55–57, 166n85
anti-imperialism, 30, 157n51
anti–martial law movement, 1–4, 7, 110, 153n5, 155n21
anti–nuclear power activism, 110–12
Apostol, Gina, 184n5
Aquino, Benigno "Ninoy," Jr., 140, 184n5
Aquino, Benigno "Noynoy," III, 184n5
Aquino, Corazon, 140–42, 144, 174n75, 184n7
area studies, 22
Arendt, Hannah, 8, 158n66

arts and humanities, 27–32, 162n8
Arts and Humanities Act (1965), 29
Asian exclusion immigration laws, 10, 19, 64
Aspiras, Jose D., 172n50
assimilation, 88, 134–35, 157n41, 167n108; benevolent, 129
asylum, 113. *See also* refugees
Ateneo de Manila University, 128, 140
Australia, 33
Austria: Vienna, 42
authoritarianism, 9, 46, 57, 148, 161n3, 173n69; and balikbayan, 68–70; definition, 14; gendered, 110; and humanitarianism, 114, 119, 124–25, 137; in *Insiang*, 25, 102–3; and liberalism, 4, 6, 8, 17–19, 21, 26, 35, 38, 151–52; as postcolonial state of exception, 17–18; and racial cold war, 22, 97; resistance to, 80, 82, 102, 163n31; in *Tadhana*, 38, 41, 49

Baguio, 76–77, 126
Baik, Crystal Mun-hye, 88
Balance, Christine Bacareza, 54, 185n21; on Imelda Marcos, 33, 35–36, 87, 163n19
Baldoz, Rick, 10
Balikatan sa Kaunlaran program, 100

balikbayan, 24–25, 58, 168n3, 171n42, 172n52, 175n81; and air travel, 68–75, 172n50; in *Empire of Memory*, 56; and Escolata, 61–64; and Operation Homecoming, 59–60; and squatters, 75–84; and US immigration law, 64–68
Balikbayan Magazine, 25, 60–61, 66, 79
Baluyut, Pearlie, 161n3
Bandaranaike, Sirimavo, 98
Bandung Conference (1955), 11, 37, 157n45
Bantayog ng mga Bayani, 1–3, 7
Barber, Samuel, 27
Barrio Fiesta, 33–34
Bataan, 100, 110–11, 113, 114–17, 126–27, 166n82
Bataan Death March, 115
Bataan Nuclear Power Plant, 110
Batac, 138–39, 141, 145
Bayanihan, 33–34, 163n26
Beatles, 47, 56
Beller, Jonathan, 102
Bell Trade Act (1946), 11
benevolence, 120, 146, 176n12; benevolent assimilation, 129; benevolent empire, 10
Bengzon, Alfredo R. A., 140–41
Benjamin, Walter, 17, 26, 61, 153n7, 167n119
Bhabha, Homi, 167n108
biopolitics, 100, 132
biopower, 90, 92
Black Americans, 31. *See also* African Americans
Black liberation movement, 3, 18
Blanco, John D., 13–14, 121
Bonus, Rick, 170n40
British imperialism, 44, 61–62
Brock, Lisa, 31
Brocka, Lino, 179n89; *Insiang*, 25, 86, 102–9, 145; *Maynila sa mga Kuko ng Liwanag*, 102
Brown, Wendy, 119, 124–25, 153n8, 156n32, 181n27
Browne, Simone, 184n10
Buck-Morss, Susan, 167n114
Burnham, Daniel B., 41–42
Burns, Lucy Mae San Pablo, 54, 169n29, 173n57

cacique politics, 2
California, 59, 139, 159n74, 168n5; Exeter, 10; Los Angeles, 66; Morro Bay, 154n18; San Francisco, 60, 70, 111, 143, 172n50; Stockton, 169n29; Watsonville, 10, 157n41
Camacho, Keith, 33, 40
Cambodia, 21, 136
Campomanes, Oscar, 20–21, 147, 155n19, 160n89
Cannes Film Festival, 45, 102
Capino, José B., 102
capitalism, 8, 16, 97, 170n31, 171n42, 174n75; crony, 66, 70, 169n13; gendered, 104, 112; and humanitarianism, 126, 132; and integrationism, 14, 21, 120; and Marcos regime, 40, 45, 53, 70, 125, 169n13; racial, 6, 65, 155n22, 182n37; and rehabilitation, 12; and US empire, 10, 32, 70, 157n45. *See also* neoliberalism; remittances; structural adjustment policies
Capitol Golf Course and Country Club, 81
Carnival Queen contests, 177n22
Cartwright, Lisa, 143
Casper, Leonard, 55
Casumbal-Salazar, Melisa S. L., 16
Catholicism, 54, 101, 113, 117, 178n72
Cavite, 101
Cebu, 43, 81, 151
Center for Applied Linguistics (CAL), 130; *Passage: A Journal of Refugee Education*, 131–37
Central Intelligence Agency (CIA), 11
Chakrabarty, Dipesh, 160n94
Chen Kuan-Hsing, 17
China, 61, 151, 164n40; Chinese refugees, 117–19; and Marcos regime, 32, 37, 119
Choy, Catherine Ceniza, 12, 169n29
chrononormativity, 88
Chuh, Kandice, 155n23
Cimatu, Frank, 142
citizenship, 8, 18, 26, 54, 73, 109, 148; and balikbayan, 75, 80; dual, 154n12; Filipino, 117, 168n5; and immigration, 18–20, 65, 67; and squatters, 80–81; US, 5, 19, 65, 88, 128, 171n41. *See also* naturalization

City of Man, 77–78, 89, 147
civil rights, 6, 18, 24, 30, 124–25
Civil Rights Act (1964), 30
Clark Air Base, 11, 179n89
Claudio, Lisandro E., 153n1
Clifford, James, 76
Clutario, Genevieve, 177n22
Coconut Palace, 41
colonial epistemologies, 5, 9
commemoration, 40, 42, 115, 154n18
Commission on the Humanities, 30, 162n8
commonwealth period, 10, 65, 118, 157n40
communism, 12, 117, 119, 148, 151, 157n45; Marcos fight against, 14–15, 37, 82; South Korean fight against, 33; US fight against, 12, 17–19, 28, 32, 69, 101. *See also* anticommunism
Communist Party (Philippines), 82
Conference on the Legacies of the Marcos Dictatorship (1999), 140–41
Congress of the International Movement of Catholic Jurists, 117
conjugal dictatorship, 90
Constantino, Renato, 13, 157n51
Cordillera Mountains, 63
Cordova, Dorothy, 4–5
Cordova, Fred, 4–7
counterinsurgency, 14, 18, 34, 74, 101, 115, 117
creolization, 13
Croce, Benedetto, 39
Cruz, Denise, 13, 88, 97–99
Cruz, Geoffrey Rhoel, 169n15
Cubao, 63
Cultural Center of the Philippines (CCP), 41–46, 52, 61, 74, 89, 161n3, 177n20
cultural orientation, 113, 128–29, 131–32, 134, 137
cultural studies, 23–24
culture, 74, 80, 103, 109, 157n51, 160n88, 161n2, 162n8, 166n79, 179n74; definition, 23; Filipino American, 4, 22; and human rights, 181n27; and methodology of book, 23–26; national, 13–14, 23–24, 27–57, 60, 141, 161n3, 163n26; and unmaking, 9
Curaming, Rommel, 38, 164n44

"Dahil Sa Iyo," 35–36
Davao, 100
Davis, Angela, 156n36
decolonization, 11, 17–18, 32, 97, 130–31; deferred, 157n40; and Marcos regime, 14–15, 37, 45, 53, 83, 99, 125; and neoliberalism, 12, 25
De Genova, Nicholas, 170n35
democracy, 8, 40, 110, 119; and English-language teaching, 133, 135; and martial law, 59; post-Marcos, 2–3, 140, 146; US, 18, 30, 64, 67, 98
development, 48, 130, 156n31, 164n40, 173n55, 173n59, 175n81; agricultural, 10; and balikbayan, 24, 58–63, 68–84; and capitalism, 32; and CCP, 44–45; forestry, 178n63; gendered, 85–86, 89–102, 106–11; and humanitarianism, 114–17; and Marcos regime, 15, 24–25, 34, 37, 39–40, 122, 125, 147, 158n57, 161n3, 164n44; postcolonial, 33; and racial cold war, 22–23, 53; and squatters, 77–83, 174n74; and transpacific collaborations, 8; under-, 183n64; urban, 3, 14, 25, 83, 106, 171n42
diaspora, 3, 7, 9, 88, 147, 170n40, 185n25; and balikbayan identity, 63, 66, 68, 70, 83; and culture, 24, 31, 162n12; queer, 185n21; unidirectional, 5; and US immigration law, 19, 64–65. *See also* balikbayan
Ding, Naifei, 93
Dipolog, 42–43
discrimination, 3, 19–20, 99, 112
displacement, 3, 25, 75–76, 83, 107, 114, 127, 147–48, 170n40
dispossession, 16, 18, 25, 81, 83, 120, 129, 136
domestic workers, 91–93, 149
Domingo, Ligaya, 155n21
Domingo, Silme, 1–7, 10
Dularawan, 45
Duterte, Rodrigo, 139, 150–52, 153n5

Edkins, Jenny, 55
Edwards, Brian, 173n63
Egypt, 98
Ejército Zapatista de Liberación Nacional, 95

Ellis Island, 64
Ellison, Katherine, 176n6, 176n16
English as a second language (ESL) instruction, 126–37
English language, 166n83, 184n5; instruction, 25, 126–37
Epifanio de los Santos Avenue (EDSA), 140, 151
Espiritu, Augusto, 11, 22, 157n45
Espiritu, Talitha, 144
Espiritu, Yến Lê, 120, 168n6
Estrada, Joseph, 140
eugenics, 54. *See also* population control
exceptionalism, 2, 15, 22, 75, 110, 150; multicultural, 149; neoliberalism as exception, 12; state of exception, 17, 21, 114; US, 18–20, 32, 88, 118, 179n74
Exchange Visitor Program, 12
exclusion, 4–5, 31, 66–67, 80–81, 118, 147, 154n17, 161n3; Asian exclusion immigration laws, 10, 19, 64
Executive Order No. 381, 74, 76, 79
export processing zones (EPZs), 48, 92, 111, 116–17, 181n15

family planning, 100–101. *See also* population control
Fanon, Frantz, 9, 125, 182n37
fashionable Filipino figure, 61–63, 70
femininity, 33, 85–91, 99–100, 109
feminism, 85, 91–93, 96–99, 104, 109–10, 161n96, 177n23
feminization of labor, 25, 93, 104, 107, 179n83
Fernandez, Armando, 66
Fernandez, Linya Ocampo, 151
Fernandez, Raymund, 151
Ferreira da Silva, Denise, 159n75, 160n94, 161n97
Filipino American History Month, 154n18
Filipino American National Historical Society (FANHS), 4–7, 154n13, 154n18, 155n21
Filipino as Human, 120–26
Filipino First, 11
Filipino question, 9–14
Flores, Patrick, 37, 40
Focus Magazine, 78

Folk Arts Theater, 89
foreign policy, 8, 28, 33, 101, 164n40, 176n14, 183n64
Foucault, Michel, 92, 158n58, 182n38
Franco, Jean, 141
Frazier, Joe, 61
Freedom Village, 81
Freemasonry, 167n114
Free World Military Alliance, 28

GABRIELA, 110
Gaerlan, Barbara, 163n26
Gamalinda, Eric, 166n85; *Empire of Memory*, 24, 29, 38, 46–57
Garcia, Carlos, 11
gender, 4, 7–8, 74, 145, 155n23, 162n12; and balikbayan, 25; gendered labor, 12–13, 25, 33–34, 65, 88, 92, 135; and humanitarianism, 25, 114, 116, 128, 135; and memory, 50, 76; and the New Filipina, 85–112; racialized, 22, 65, 67, 114. *See also* femininity; feminism; masculinity; patriarchy
gendered violence, 25, 86, 98, 110–12, 116. *See also* sexual violence
Georgetown University Round Table on Languages and Linguistics (1979), 130–31
Germany, 117
Gilroy, Paul, 156n37
globalization, 17, 23, 92, 104, 105–6, 175n3
Glück, Louise, 185n27
Goldstein, Alyosha, 179n74, 183n64
Gonzaga, Elmo, 169n19
Gonzalez, N. V. M., 155n19
Gonzalez, Vernadette Vicuña, 63, 66, 90, 115, 177n25
"Good Manners and Right Conduct" bulletin, 129
Gotera, Vince: "Three Sonnetinas," 26, 142–44, 148–49
governmentality, 22, 102, 119, 127, 147, 156n37, 158n58
Gramsci, Antonio, 156n37
Great Britain, 162n12; British imperialism, 44, 61–62
Great Society, 18, 29–32

Greenhills, 63
Guam, 40, 118
Guevarra, Anna, 175n3
Gupta, Akhil, 135
Gutierrez, Jose, III, 109

Habal, Estella, 157n41
Habermas, Jürgen, 161
Habsburgs, 42
Hagedorn, Jessica: *Dogeaters*, 154n12
Haitian Vodou, 167n114
Hall, Stuart, 51, 156n31, 160n88, 162n12
Hardt, Michael, 92
Hart-Cellar Act (Immigration and Nationality Act, 1965), 19. See also post-1965 immigration
Hartman, Saidiya, 185n25
Hau, Caroline, 166n83
Hawai'i, 10, 118, 149; Honolulu, 70, 139, 141, 144–46, 148, 172nn50–52
Healy, Timothy, 131
Hegel, Georg Wilhelm Friedrich, 39
Hernandez, Kelly Lytle, 67
heroization, 7–8
heteronormativity, 66, 88, 109, 179n74
historiography, 9, 24, 38, 121–22, 155n23, 185n21
Hitler, Adolf, 117–18
Holt, Harold, 33
Holyoake, Keith, 33
Honculada, Jurgette, 110
Honolulu Advertiser, 148
Howard University, 30
Hua, Julietta, 97
Hukbalahap, 11
humanism, 25, 114, 123–28, 132, 135
humanitarianism, 25, 113–37
human rights, 16, 18, 94–96, 118, 123–25, 181n27, 184n5
Husserl, Edmund, 161n96

Ibañez, Ruby: "Teacher, It's Nice to Meet You, Too," 25, 114, 133–37
Ifugao, 100
Ileto, Reynaldo, 54, 116, 162n17

Ilocos Norte, 87, 138, 145, 149
Iloilo City, 76–77
imperial domesticity, 176n14
Inayawan landfill, 150–51
India, 62
Indigeneity, 16, 38
Indigenous Peoples, 3, 16, 18, 49, 56, 122, 130, 183n64
indios, 13
Indonesia, 113
Insular Cases (1901), 10
integrationism, 11, 14, 69
interimperialism, 10
International Catholic Migration Commission (ICMC), 113, 127–28
internationalism, 135, 163n26; liberal, 11
International Longshoremen's and Warehousemen's Union (Local 37), 1
International Monetary Fund, 16; IMF–World Bank Conference (1976), 61
International Women's Year Conference (IWY, 1975), 98–99; Report, 94–95
Intramuros, 42, 89
Isaac, Allan, 181n19
Isnegs, 47–48
isolationism, 11
Israel, 105
Itliong, Larry, 154n18

Japan, 11–12, 37; Japanese imperialism, 10, 33, 44, 49, 97; Okinawa, 93; Philippine-Japanese relations, 54, 115–16, 120
Japanese Imperial Army, 97
Jewish refugees, 117–18
Joaquin, Nick (Quijano de Manila), 13, 89, 177n18
Johnson, Lady Bird, 27, 33, 52
Johnson, Lyndon B., 18, 161n2, 162n12, 176n6, 176n16; and immigration law, 19, 64; and national culture, 24, 27–43
Joint US Military Assistance Group, 11

KALYAAN, 110
Kānaka Maoli, 148
Kang, Laura, 155n23

Kaplan, Amy, 176n14
Katipunan, 45
Katipunan ng Bagong Pilipina (KaBaPa), 110
Katipunan ng mga Demokratikong Pilipino (KDP), 3, 155n21
Kim, Jodi, 23
Kissinger, Henry, 125
Klein, Christina, 161n3, 172n54, 176n12
Komenich, Kim, *iii*
Korean War, 12, 88
Koronel, Hilda, 107, 179n89
Kotef, Hagar, 171n41

Labasbas, Aurora, 82–83
Labor Code of the Philippines (1974), 19–20
labor export system, 19, 84, 86, 91–92
Languido, Alberto, 81
Laos, 21
La Paz Naval Base, 47
Laurel-Langley Agreement (1955), 11
Laya, Juan C., 157n41
Lee, Jin-kyung, 93, 97, 163n31
Lennon, John, 56
Letter of Instruction No. 19, 76, 79
Leyte, 87
liberalism, 40, 44, 120, 145, 153n8, 161n2, 174n75; and authoritarianism, 4, 6, 8, 17–19, 21, 26, 35, 38, 151–52; and Cold War, 65, 88; gendered, 92, 95–98, 107; and humanitarianism, 119–20, 124–25, 129, 132–33, 136–37; and immigration law, 67, 119, 170n35; and internationalism, 11, 17; liberal internationalism, 11; and mobility, 70, 82, 171n41; and neocolonialism, 36; racial, 7, 31–32; and republicanism, 2
Lico, Gerard, 41, 161n3
Lim, Benito, 164n40
Lima Declarations (1972, 1975), 37
Lincoln Center for the Performing Arts, 27, 30, 41, 161n2
Linmark, R. Zamora: "What Some Are Saying about the Body," 26, 142–43, 145–49, 152
Lloyd, David, 160n88
Locsin, Leandro, 41, 74–75
Louisiana Manilamen, 5

Lowe, Lisa, 20, 24, 145–46, 160n88, 170n31
Luibhéid, Eithne, 169n26
Luna, Antonio, 39
Luzon, 176n6

Mabalon, Dawn, 169n29
Mabini, Apolionario, 39, 165n76
Macapagal, Diosdado, 34
Magsaysay, Ramon, 11
Maguigad, Virgilio, 74–75
Maharlika, 176n6
Makati, 63
Malabed, Frank, 138, 142
Malacañang Palace, *34*, 47
"Malakas at Maganda," 87–88, 94, 109
Malayang Kilusan ng Bagong Kababahian (MAKIBAKA), 109, 177n23
Malolos, 85
Manalansan, Martin, IV, 22, 105, 185n21
Manapat, Ricardo, 169n13
Mangahas, Fe, 110
Manila, 86, 102, 116–18, 145, 147, 176n16, 177n22, 178n72, 179n89; and air travel, 70–77, 168n6, 172n50, 173n66, 174n75; anti–nuclear power activism in, 110–12; and balikbayan, 25, 58, 61–63, 81, 83; Binondo, 61; and methodology of book, 138–39; Metro Manila, 41, 75–83, 89, 103, 173n69, 174n75, 175n88; and national culture, 27–28, 41–47, 52, 78; and New Filipina, 89, 100; Quezon City, 1, 52, *139*; and squatters, 75–83, 107, 174n74; Tondo, 107–8, 179n81, 180n94. *See also* City of Man
Manila Bay, 44, 77
Manila Film Center, 41, 45
Manila International Airport, 71, 73, 173n59, 173n66, 177n20
Manila International Airport Authority, 173n59
Manila International Festival, 45
Manila Summit (1966), 32, 52
Manila Urban Development Project, 107
Mankekar, Purnima, 135
Mann, Steven, 184n10
Maori People, 33

Marcos, Ferdinand, 144–45, 153n5, 158n57, 159n74, 164n40, 166n82, 175n88, 176n6; 1966 US state visit, 27–36, 42, 176n16; assassinations by, 1, 3–4, 6; as author, 38, 48, 164n45; and balikbayan, 25, 58–61, 63, 68–74, 76, 83; body of, 138–39, 141–43, 146–47, 150–51, 184n7; burial of, 141–42, 150–52; crony capitalism under, 70, 87, 92, 140, 169n13; development under, 34, 172n44, 172n50, 173n59, 173n69, 174n75; and Filipino American identity, 4, 8; and humanitarianism, 25, 113–28, 135; labor policy under, 6, 19; legacy of, 140–41, 148–49, 184n5; and martial law, 1, 3, 15–17, 38, 58, 114, 155n21, 164n44, 168n11, 178n63; modernization under, 14–15, 37, 58, 63, 70, 73, 79–84, 86, 174n75; and national culture, 24, 27–49, 52–57, 161n3, 163n26; and New Filipina, 25, 86–93, 99, 101–2, 108–11, 121; and Philippines national identity, 14–16; and sex work, 68; and squatters, 76–83, 174n74; State of the Nation address (1969), 15; State of the Nation address (1970), 73; *Tadhana*, 38–41, 49, 164n44. *See also* "Malakas at Maganda"

Marcos, Ferdinand "Bong," Jr., 150

Marcos, Imee, 150

Marcos, Imelda, 139, 142–46, 172n44, 179n81; 1966 US state visit, 27–28, 34–36, 42, 176n16; and balikbayan, 77–79; biographer of, 176n6; and development, 74, 78, 173n66, 175n88; and Ferdinand Marcos's body, 141–45, 147–48, 150, 152; in Hawai'i, 139, 144, 148–49; and humanitarianism, 120–27; and national culture, 27–28, 34–36, 41, 44–47, 49, 52–53, 55–56, 61, 161n3, 163n19; and New Filipina, 85–91, 94, 98–100, 102, 105, 107–10, 121; and squatters, 78, 80–83, 174n75; and *Tadhana*, 38. *See also* "Malakas at Maganda"

Marcos babies, 46, 57, 142

Marcos tapes, 144

Mariana Islands, 12

Marshall Islands, 12

martial law, 6, 80, 108, 141–42, 150–51, 154n12, 164n44, 168n11, 174n75, 178n63; and authoritarianism, 17; and balikbayan, 58–60, 78, 168n3; and Cold War culture, 23–26; in *Empire of Memory*, 55–56; and gender, 86, 109–10; justifications for, 15–16, 38, 47, 114; and Marcos babies, 46; and migration, 19, 59–60; resistance to, 1–4, 7, 110, 153n5, 155n21; US complicity in, 149. *See also* anti–martial law movement; Proclamation No. 1081

Martinez, Jocelyn, 147

Mascardo, Salvador, 75, 80

masculinity, 7, 13, 67, 86, 97, 135, 146; and balikbayan, 63, 68; and culture, 33; injured, 116, 158n59; militarized, 67

McKenna, Tinio, Rebecca, 42

Melamed, Jodi, 18, 31

melodrama, 85–112, 144

memorialization, 2–4, 25, 44, 115, 142, 147–48, 152

Mendicancy Law (1978), 174n74

mestizos, 13, 154n12

methodology of book, 23–26

Metropolitan Opera House, 27–28

Mexico, 67, 95, 170n35; Mexico City, 94

Mijares, Primitivo, 90

Military Bases Agreement (1947), 11, 37

Ministry of Social Services and Development, 117

Miss Philippines pageant, 177n23

Miss Universe pageant, 61, 89

modernization, 8, 14, 37, 142, 146–47, 151, 158n57, 171n42, 174n73, 174n75; and balikbayan, 58, 63, 66, 70, 73, 79–84; gendered, 86–87; and humanitarianism, 115, 117, 130; and national culture, 40, 43; and New Filipina, 86, 89, 91–92, 97, 99–101, 107, 110; and New Society, 15; and racial cold war, 22–23. *See also* development

Montes, Sylvia P., 117–19

Morong, 113–15, 126–27

Moros, 163n26

Moses, Robert, 161n2

motherhood, 85, 87, 90–91, 95, 100–101

Moynihan, Daniel Patrick: *The Negro Family* (Moynihan Report), 87

multiculturalism, 5–6, 30–32, 52, 65, 148–49, 154n16
Muslims, 16, 49

Nadal, Paul, 157n41
Naficy, Hamid, 103
National Advisory Council on the Teaching of English as a Second Language, 130
National Commission on the Role of Filipino Women (NCRFW), 85, 99–101, 109–10
National Council on the Arts, 29
national culture, 13–14, 24, 60, 141, 161n3, 163n26; and anti-history, 24, 55–57; and *Empire of Memory*, 46–57; and postwar rehabilitation, 41–46; and state power, 23; and US–Philippines relations, 27–40, 52–53
National Democratic Front, 108
national family, 87, 105, 109
National Historical Institute, 39
National Housing Authority, 180n95
national minorities, 48, 100, 122
naturalization, 65, 117. *See also* citizenship
Nayong Filipino Museum, 89
Nazi Party (Germany), 119
neocolonialism, 11, 18, 20, 36, 83, 111, 123, 125
neoliberalism, 12, 14, 25, 65, 91–92, 110. *See also* export processing zones (EPZs); structural adjustment policies
"never again," 1, 150, 153n5
New Cinema Movement, 102
New Filipina, 25, 85–112, 121
New Filipinism, 15, 36, 121
New People's Army, 47, 56
New Society, 15, 18, 36, 164n44, 172n44, 175n88; and balikbayan, 75–76, 81–83; and humanitarianism, 124; and national culture, 35–40, 47, 52–57; and New Filipina, 91–92, 94, 99–100, 106–7
New York City, 28, 144, 168n5; Upper West Side, 27
New Yorker, 71, 71–72
New York Times, 27, 89, 168n5, 169n28, 173n66, 184n5
New Zealand, 33
Nguyen, Mimi Thi, 90, 117, 124

Nicanor, Mr., 169n28
1986 presidential election, 140
1986 revolution, 2, 56, 140–42
Ninoy Aquino International Airport. *See* Manila International Airport
Nixon, Richard, 164n40
Non-Aligned Movement (NAM), 11, 125, 157n45

Obama, Barack, 151
Okamura, Jonathan, 170n40
Olcott, Jocelyn, 96
Olongapo, 11
Omi, Michael, 154n15
Ong, Aihwa, 12, 181n15
Operation Homecoming, 59–60, 64, 68–69
Ople, Blas F., 168n5
Orientalism, 22, 176n12

Pacific Islands, 97
Padios, Jan, 183n58
palabas, 87
PALakbayan, 70
Pan American Airways, 172n47
Pangasinan, 126
Paper Dolls, 105
Park Chung Hee, 17, 32–33, 163n31
Parreñas, Rhacel Salazar, 91–92, 179n82
Pasyon, 54
patriarchy, 33, 88, 97–99, 139
Peace Corps, 130, 133
Pennsylvania, 111
People Power Revolution/EDSA Revolution, 56, 140, 151
Perez, Jason Magabo, 166n85
Phil-American Cultural Club of Honolulu, 172n52
Philippine Airlines (PAL), 25, 68–72, 69, 172n50
Philippine American Cultural Foundation, 41
Philippine-American Friendship Day, 29
Philippine Army, 28
Philippine Civic Action Group (PHILCAG), 28, 34, 115
Philippine Civil Aeronautics Board, 69

Philippine Congress, 180n94, 184n5
Philippine Convention Center, 41
Philippine Department of Commerce and Industry (DCI), 73
Philippine Department of Tourism, 69
Philippine Foreign Trade Zone Authority, 116
Philippine Independence, 10–14, 37, 42, 66, 71, 157n51, 166n83
Philippine Independence Day, 139
Philippine Ministry of Foreign Affairs, 122
Philippine Normal School, 128
Philippine Quarterly, 58
Philippine Refugee Processing Center (PRPC), 25, 113–19, 126–28, 130, 133–37
Philippines' Population Commission, 101
Philippine War Damage Commission, 42–43
Philippine Women's University (PWU), 85
Pido, Eric, 175n81
PILIPINA, 110
Pinoy Archive, 154n13
Pioneer Square (Seattle), 1
Playboy, 146
population control, 100–101, 178n72
post-1965 immigration, 19, 21, 64–68, 83, 154n16, 170n40. *See also* Hart-Cellar Act (Immigration and Nationality Act, 1965)
postcolonial configuration, definition, 8
Presidential Assistant on National Minorities (PANAMIN), 48, 122
Presidential Decree No. 633, 99
Presidential Decree No. 705, 178n63
President's Commission on Foreign Languages and International Studies, 131
Prevots, Naima, 161n3
Price, David, 159n82
Proclamation No. 1081, 178n63. *See also* martial law
progressivism, 6, 18, 22, 24, 30, 64, 112
propaganda, 27, 30, 64, 128, 161n2
Puerto Rico, 118

Quiazon, Troadio, Jr., 60
Quijano de Manila. *See* Joaquin, Nick (Quijano de Manila)
Quintos, Floy, 61–63, 70, 80, 82

race as praxis, 13, 121
racial capitalism, 6, 65, 155n22, 182n37
racial cold war, 53, 57, 59, 147–48, 150; and balikbayan, 59, 68, 83; definition, 22–23; in *Empire of Memory*, 29, 57; and humanitarianism, 114, 137; and New Filipina, 94, 97, 100, 107, 112; and squatters, 80
racial liberalism, 7, 31–32
racial pluralism, 12, 32, 64, 66, 83, 154n16
racism, 3, 12, 28, 39–40, 96, 118, 155n22, 157n45, 182n37; anti-Black, 18, 31. *See also* eugenics
Rafael, Vicente, 133–35, 137, 165n76, 171n42
Ramos, Fidel, 141
Rand Corporation, 101
Reader's Digest, 172n54; *Reader's Digest Asia*, 71
Reagan, Ronald, 148
Recto, Claro, 174n74
Reddy, Chandan, 166n79
Refugee Act (1980), 119
refugees, 47, 115–16, 181n20; Chinese, 117–19; Jewish, 117–18; rehabilitation of, 25, 113–14, 117–37; Vietnamese, 117. *See also* asylum; Philippine Refugee Processing Center (PRPC)
rehabilitation, 12, 35, 40, 41–46, 74, 77, 79; of refugees, 25, 113–14, 117–37
re/membering, 147
remittances, 12, 19, 24, 60, 168n5, 170n40. *See also* balikbayan
reproductive labor, 25, 90–92, 104, 107, 179n82. *See also* domestic workers; motherhood; vaginal economy
Republic Act No. 10368 (2013), 184n5
republicanism, 2, 8, 22, 98, 119, 148
Research and Documentation Committee, 1
Reyes, Jun Cruz, 175n88
Reyes, Miguel Paolo P., 164n45
Reyes, Victoria, 67
Richter, Linda, 168n11
Rizal, Jose, 38–39, 85, 121
Robinson, Cedric, 18, 155n22
Robles, Francisco, 78–80
Roces, Mina, 87–88, 110, 177n23
Rockefeller, John D., 27, 44, 161n2

Rodriguez, Dylan, 21
Rodriguez, Robyn, 154n18, 155n19, 175n3
Romulo, Carlos, 11, 157n45
Rotary Club of Manila, 77–78, 80
Russia, 93, 117, 119

Sadat, Jehan, 98
Sales, Joy, 153n5
Samoa, 12
Sanchez, Segundino, 82
Santiago, Arminda, 179n89
Saranillio, Dean, 148
Sarasota Herald Tribune, 173n56
Sarda, Mr., 168n5
Schein, Ernest, 42–43
self-determination, 7, 23, 32, 41, 65, 81, 109, 122; and liberalism, 18; national, 38, 40; women's, 94–96
separatism, 45, 163n26
Seven Years' War: Battle of Manila, 44
sexual labor, 93–94, 104
sexual violence, 97, 103–5
sex work, 67–68, 93–94, 97, 112
Shah, Nayan, 173n57
Shimizu, Celine Parreñas, 167n108
Smith, Neil, 174n75
Soafer, Abraham, 144
socialism, 37, 119, 164n40
Solomon, Amanda, 157n40
Sombath, 133–37
sousveillance, 184n10
South China Sea, 52–53
Southeast Asian Development Advisory Group, 101
South Korea, 12, 32–33, 35, 93, 97, 176n12
Soviet Union, 22, 30, 37, 96, 157n45, 161n2, 164n40
Spain, 9, 47
Spanish-American War: Battle of Manila Bay, 44
Spanish colonialism, 9, 13, 42, 44–45, 47, 49, 61, 77, 88
Special Education Fund, 42
special relationship (US–Philippines), 115
Spivak, Gayatri Chakravorty, 123

squatters, 59, 75–83, 106–7, 174nn74–75, 177n20
state of exception, 17, 21, 114
Sterne, Michael, 169n28
structural adjustment policies, 12, 66, 105, 117. *See also* neoliberalism
Sturken, Marita, 143
Subic Bay Naval Base, 11, 35, 94
surveillance, 18, 142–48, 184n10

Tadiar, Neferti, 44, 51, 81, 105, 156n28, 156n35, 157n51, 158n57, 161n96, 173n69, 174n75, 175n88
Tagalog language, 133, 165n76, 184n5
tago nang tago (TNTs), 66
Taiwan, 12, 17, 93, 167n110
Tamad, Juan, 15, 121, 126
Tasaday, 166n82
Task Force Morong, 113
Tatalon, 52
Thailand, 33, 113
Third World, 3, 11, 15, 18–19, 37, 96, 125, 157n45
third world cinema, 103
Third World liberation movement, 3, 18
thirty-fifth parallel, 52–53
thirty-eighth parallel, 35
Three Mile Island, 111
three waves approach to immigration, 155n19, 159n72
"Thrilla in Manila" boxing match (1975), 61
Tiongson, Antonio, 154n12
Tolentino, Rolando, 46, 104–5, 109, 142, 174n73
Torres, Cristina Evangelista, 129
tourism, 60–61, 63, 69–70, 73, 75–76, 89, 172n50, 172n52, 185n25
transpacific, 22, 97, 138, 159n85, 167n110; collaborations, 8, 24, 28, 33–35, 40, 93, 112, 116, 120; governmentality, 127; movement, 54, 56, 98, 172n51; traffic, 4, 10
transparency thesis, 160n94
transportation policy, 24, 25, 73, 77, 107, 139, 170n40
Treaty of Amity (1973), 116
Trinidad, Recah, 66

tsismis, 105–6, 145
Tydings-McDuffie Act (1934), 10, 65

United Nations (UN), 11, 14, 16, 86, 94–95; Convention and Protocol on Refugees, 119, 181n20; Declaration of the United Nations (1942), 16; General Assembly, 71, 123; General Assembly Resolution 2658 (XXV), 173n55; High Commissioner for Refugees, 113; UNESCO, 99
University of the Philippines, 174n74
unmaking, 9, 26, 46, 51, 57, 108, 112
urban development, 3, 14, 25, 83, 106, 171n42
US Agency for International Development (USAID), 16, 101, 107
US Air Force, 173n59, 179n89
US Armed Forces, 115
US Army, 49, 129
US Border Patrol, 67
US Bureau of Indian Affairs, 130
US Census, 13
US Civil Aeronautics Board (USCAB), 69
US Department of Defense, 130
US Department of State, 30, 69, 131, 144, 161n3
US General Accounting Office (GAO), 127
US House of Representatives: Subcommittee on Asian and Pacific Affairs, 144
US Information Agency of Cultural Affairs, 41
US-Philippine War, 9
US Report of the Philippine Commission, 129

vaginal economy, 104, 179n83
Viernes, Gene, 1–7, 10

Vietnam, 33–35, 53, 126, 176n12; Saigon, 113; Tay Ninh Province, 28
Vietnam War, 12, 14, 32–33, 134, 138, 143; Philippines role in, 21, 28, 34–35, 42–44, 69, 115; refugees from, 113, 120
Vite, Doroteo V., 59

war crimes, 97
Washington, DC, 10–11, 28, 36, 59, 64, 168n5, 174n74, 184n7
Washington State, 168n5; Seattle, 1, 3–4, 10, 154n13
Westinghouse Corporation, 111
Williams, Randall, 95, 182n37
Williams, Raymond, 23, 43, 149, 156n31
Winant, Howard, 154n15
Wolfe, Thomas, 169n23
World Bank, 16, 60, 180n95; IMF–World Bank Conference (1976), 61
World War I, 117
World War II, 5, 11, 37, 42, 47, 50, 71, 97, 107; Battle of Manila, 44; Japan in Philippines during, 97, 115; Pacific Theater, 10; postwar period, 17–18, 71, 76, 95, 176n14
Wynter, Sylvia, 126, 160n94

Yoneyama, Lisa, 4, 22, 97, 156n26, 159n85, 178n50
Yoshimi, Shunya, 164n39, 167n110

Zambales, 100, 178n63
Zamboanga, 42
Zone One Tondo Organization (ZOTO), 108, 180n95

www.ingramcontent.com/pod-product-compliance
Lightning Source LLC
Chambersburg PA
CBHW020236170426
43202CB00008B/106